THE CHURCH AT PRAYER

THE CHURCH AT PRAYER
Introduction to the Liturgy
New Edition

THE CHURCH AT PRAYER

An Introduction to the Liturgy

New Edition

Edited by Aimé Georges Martimort
with the Collaboration of R. Cabié, I. H. Dalmais,
J. Evenou, P. M. Gy, P. Jounel, A. Nocent, and D. Sicard

Volume II

THE EUCHARIST

by

Robert Cabié

Translated by Matthew J. O'Connell

THE LITURGICAL PRESS
Collegeville, Minnesota

Cover design by Donald A. Molloy

THE CHURCH AT PRAYER—VOLUME II: THE EUCHARIST is the authorized English translation of *L'Eglise en Prière: L'Eucharistie,* published by Desclée, Paris-Tournai, 1983.
Nihil obstat: Rev. Robert C. Harren, J.C.L., *Censor deputatus.*
Imprimatur: ✝ George H. Speltz, D.D., Bishop of St. Cloud, July 28, 1986.

Excerpts from the English translation of *The Roman Missal* © 1973, 1985, International Committee on English in the Liturgy, Inc. (ICEL); excerpts from the English translation of *The Liturgy of the Hours* © 1974, ICEL; excerpts from the English translation of General Norms for the Liturgical Year and the Calendar (1969), the General Instruction of the Liturgy of the Hours (1974), and the General Instruction of the Roman Missal (1975) from *Documents on the Liturgy 1963–1979: Curial, Papal, and Conciliar Texts* © 1982, ICEL. All rights reserved.

Excerpts of prayers translated from the old Latin Roman Missal (Canon) are from *The Maryknoll Missal* edited by the Maryknoll Fathers (New York: Kenedy, 1964). All rights reserved.

Library of Congress Cataloging-in-Publication Data

Cabié, Robert.
    The Eucharist.

    (The Church at prayer ; v. 2)
    Translation of: L'Eucharistie.
    Bibliography: p.
    Includes index.
    1. Lord's Supper (Liturgy)—History.   2. Catholic Church—Liturgy—History.   3. Mass—History.   I. Title.
II. Series: Eglise en prière.   English ; v. 2.
BX1970.E313   1986   vol. 2   264'.02 s   86-20960
[BX2015.2]   [264'.02036'09]
ISBN 0-8146-1364-0

Contents

Preface

The third French edition of the present work was published in 1965, less than two years after the promulgation of the Constitution on the Liturgy of Vatican II. It was clear, of course, that this solemn document was but the starting point of a work of restoration and reform that could be carried out only gradually.

Now, twenty years after the Constitution *Sacrosanctum Concilium,* the reform of the liturgy is virtually complete. A task of immense scope, unparalleled in the history of the Church, brought bishops and liturgists together from all over the world, first in the Council for the Implementation of the Constitution on the Sacred Liturgy (1964–69) and then in the Congregation for Divine Worship (1969–75). The problems that the contemporary world and its culture (or, rather, its varied cultures) raise for the prayer of the Church were pointed out with great clarity by the Council, which also enunciated the principles to be followed in solving them. The application of these principles, however, led to a revision of perspectives and to decisions that we could not have clearly anticipated in 1965.

The new liturgical books, in fact, take a new approach to the act of celebrating: they always begin with instructions or introductions that are quite different in character from the rubrics of old, since they include doctrinal and spiritual guidelines, the pastoral aspect, and possible ways of adapting the rites in question.

This bold new approach would not have been possible without the work done, especially in the twentieth century, by the historians of liturgy and the theologians. The first French edition of *The Church at Prayer* was an attempt at a summary assessment of all that labor. But far from putting an end to research, the liturgical reform gave it a new stimulus because it raised new problems or called for a more profound and scholarly grasp of the tradition. Moreover, it was no longer isolated pioneers, as in the days of Duchesne and Batiffol, Baumstark and Andrieu, who ventured into this field. On the contrary: teams now meet periodically, as at the Semaines de Saint-Serge, and students are trained at liturgical institutes (the Liturgical Institutes of Paris and of San Anselmo in Rome have celebrated the twentieth anniversary of their foundation).

Scholars have been devoting their efforts especially to the prehistory of the Christian liturgy and to its beginnings and its relation to Jewish prayer. In addition, the comparative method initially developed by Baumstark has given a splendid impulse to the study of the Eastern and Western liturgies. It is no longer possible to reconstruct the history of the Roman liturgy without locating it in this broader framework. That same larger perspective is indispensable especially for answering doctrinal questions about the sacraments and for resolving the sensitive problem of adaptation to local Churches, as well as for inspiring the creative responses that adaptation calls for. The controversies to which the liturgical reform has given rise in various places are to be explained by an ignorance of the tradition and of the diversity it allows.

For all these reasons it has not been possible simply to correct and reprint *The Church at Prayer*. An entirely new edition is called for, one that will, on the one hand, highlight the spiritual and pastoral directions taken in the liturgical reform with which the name of Pope Paul VI will be permanently linked, and that will, on the other, set forth more fully than in earlier editions what we know of the varied expressions the Church has given to its prayer according to historical and geographical circumstances.

In keeping with the procedure adopted earlier for *L'Introduction à la Bible*, we shall publish separately each of the four parts of this new edition of *The Church at Prayer*. Practical considerations made us begin with Volume IV, *The Liturgy and Time*. Here, now, is Volume II.

* * *

The first edition of the new *Order of Mass* appeared in April 1969. At that time, although she was already suffering from the serious illness of which she was to die on December 18 of that year, Noële Maurice Denis Boulet still had strength enough for a thorough revision of the study of the Mass that she had contributed to the French editions of *The Church at Prayer*. To this end I visited her at Clermont and was impressed not only by her courage and serenity, but also by her undiminished contemplative enthusiasm for the sacred mysteries. Her new text appeared in 1973 in the English edition, *The Church at Prayer*, which was published by the Irish University Press. Since 1969, however, a number of factors—the successive revisions of the *General Instruction of the Roman Missal*; the two typical editions of the Sacramentary; more than a dozen years' experience of the revised Eucharistic celebration; the questions raised by ecumenism; and, not least, the many works published by exegetes, historians, and theologians—have made necessary a complete rewriting of this part of *The Church at Prayer*. In this new book, Robert Cabié, a priest of the diocese of Albi and my successor as professor of liturgy in the faculty of theology at Toulouse, gives us the fruits of his knowledge of liturgical history and his experience of both teaching and pastoral care.

Finally, let me remind the reader of the limits of this work; they are the same as those mentioned in 1961 in the very first French edition. Readers will not find here a complete exposition that includes the entire content of the instructions and introductions to the new liturgical books, any more than they would have found in earlier editions a complete course in rubrics. For that kind of information they must turn to the practical instruction that is given to students in institutions of priestly formation.

In addition, the contributors always suppose that their readers have at hand at least the main liturgical texts now in use. We urge them to be constantly rereading these texts and, even more, to discover the meaning of the rites by participating in them. It is by meditating on the texts, those now in use and those of the past, and by participating as fervently as possible in the liturgical celebration, that we will be able to enter with understanding into the mysteries of the praying Church, in which Christ himself is present and active.

Aimé Georges Martimort

Abbreviations

Gen	Genesis	Dan	Daniel
Exod	Exodus	Ezra	Ezra
Lev	Leviticus	Neh	Nehemiah
Num	Numbers	1-2 Chr	1-2 Chronicles
Deut	Deuteronomy	Bar	Baruch
Josh	Joshua	Jdt	Judith
Judg	Judges	1-2 Mac	1-2 Maccabees
1-2 Sam	1 and 2 Samuel	Sir	Sirach
1-2 Kgs	1 and 2 Kings	Tob	Tobit
Isa	Isaiah	Wis	Wisdom
Jer	Jeremiah	Matt	Matthew
Ezek	Ezekiel	Mark	Mark
Hos	Hosea	Luke	Luke
Joel	Joel	John	John
Amos	Amos	Acts	Acts of the Apostles
Obad	Obadiah	Rom	Romans
Jonah	Jonah	1-2 Cor	1-2 Corinthians
Mic	Micah	Gal	Galatians
Nah	Nahum	Eph	Ephesians
Hab	Habakkuk	Phil	Philippians
Zeph	Zephaniah	Col	Colossians
Hag	Haggai	1-2 Thess	1-2 Thessalonians
Zech	Zechariah	1-2 Tim	1-2 Timothy
Mal	Malachi	Titus	Titus
Ps (Pss)	Psalm(s)	Phlm	Philemon
Job	Job	Heb	Hebrews
Prov	Proverbs	Jas	James
Ruth	Ruth	1-2 Pet	1-2 Peter
Cant	Canticle of Canticles	1-3 John	1-3 John
Eccl	Ecclesiastes	Jude	Jude
Lam	Lamentations	Rev	Revelation
Esth	Esther		

WORKS MOST FREQUENTLY CITED

AAS	*Acta Apostolicae Sedis* (Rome, then Vatican City, 1909ff.).
Acta sanctorum	*Acta sanctorum collecta . . . a Sociis Bollandianis* (3rd ed.; Paris: Palmé, 1863ff., then Brussels: Bollandistes).
ALW	*Archiv für Liturgiewissenschaft* (Regensburg: F. Pustet, 1950ff.).
Andrieu, *OR*	M. Andrieu, *Les Ordines Romani du haut moyen âge* (5 vols. Spicilegium Sacrum Lovaniense 11, 23, 24, 28, 29; Louvain: Spicilegium, 1931ff.). A sixth volume is in preparation.
Andrieu, *PR*	M. Andrieu, *Le Pontifical Romain au moyen âge* (4 vols. ST 86, 87, 88, 99; Vatican City, 1938–41).
Brightman	F. E. Brightman, *Liturgies Eastern and Western* I. *Eastern Liturgies* (Oxford: Clarendon Press, 1896). Only Volume I was published.
CCL	Corpus Christianorum collectum a monachis O.S.B. abbatiae S. Petri in Steenbrugge, Series Latina (Turnhout: Brepols, 1954ff.).
CECSL	Consilium ad exsequendam Constitutionem de sacra liturgiae (Council for the Implementation of the Constitution on the Sacred Liturgy).
CSCO	Corpus Scriptorum Christianorum Orientalium editum consilio Universitatis Catholicae Americae et Universitatis Catholicae Lovaniensis (Louvain, 1930ff.).
DACL	*Dictionnaire d'archéologie chrétienne et de liturgie*, edited by F. Cabrol, H. Leclercq [and H. Marrou] (Paris: Letouzey et Ané, 1907–53).
Denz	H. Denzinger, *Ritus orientalium . . . in administrandis sacramentis . . .* (2 vols. Würzburg: Stahel, 1863; repr., Graz: Akademische Druck, 1961).
DOL	*Documents on the Liturgy 1963–1979. Conciliar, Papal, and Curial Texts.* Edited by the International Commission on English in the Liturgy (Collegeville: The Liturgical Press, 1982).
DS	*Enchiridion symbolorum, definitionum et declarationum de rebus fidei et morum*, edited by H. Denzinger. 32nd ed. by A. Schönmetzer (Barcelona: Herder, 1963).
EDIL	*Enchiridion documentorum instaurationis liturgicae* I. *1963–1973* (Turin: Marietti, 1976).
EL	*Ephemerides liturgicae* (Rome: Edizioni liturgiche, 1887ff.). For years with two series the references are to the series *Analecta ascetico-historicae*, without this being expressly stated.
Fabre-Duchesne	P. Fabre and L. Duchesne, *Le Liber censuum de l'Eglise romaine* (3 vols. Fontemoing: E. de Boccard, 1910–52).
GCS	Die griechischen christlichen Schriftsteller der ersten Jahrhunderte, edited by the German Academy of Sciences in Berlin (Berlin: Akademie Verlag, 1897ff.).

Ge — Old Gelasian Sacramentary = Ms. Reginen. Lat. 316 in the Vatican Library, ed. L. C. Mohlberg, P. Siffrin, and L. Eizenhöfer, *Liber sacramentorum Romanae aeclesiae ordinis anni circuli* (REDMF 4; Rome: Herder, 1960).

Gell — Sacramentaire de Gellone, Paris, Bibl. Nat., ms. lat. 12048, ed. A. Dumas (CCL 159; Turnhout: Brepols, 1981).

GILH — *General Instruction of the Liturgy of the Hours*, trans. in *DOL*.

GIRM — *General Instruction of the Roman Missal*, trans. in *DOL*.

GNLYC — *General Norms for the Liturgical Year and the Calendar*, trans. in *DOL*.

Gr — Gregorian Sacramentary, ed. J. Deshusses (Spicilegium Friburgense 12; Fribourg: Editions Universitaires, 1971).

Hänggi-Pahl — A. Hänggi and I. Pahl, *Prex eucharistica. Textus e variis liturgiis antiquioribus selecti* (Spicilegium Friburgense 12; Fribourg: Editions Universitaires, 1968).

HBS — Henry Bradshaw Society for Editing Rare Liturgical Texts. London, 1891ff.

JLW — *Jahrbuch für Liturgiewissenschaft*, ed. O. Casel (Münster: Aschendorff, 1921–41).

JTS — *Journal of Theological Studies* (London: Macmillan, and then Oxford: Clarendon Press, 1900ff.).

Le — The sacramentary formerly known as the Leonine Sacramentary. Manuscript of Verona, Bibl. Capitolare, LXXXV [80]. — Ed. L. C. Mohlberg, L. Eizenhöfer, and P. Siffrin, *Sacramentarium Veronense* (REDMF 1; Rome: Herder, 1955–56).

LP — L. Duchesne, *Le Liber pontificalis. Textes, introduction, et commentaire.* 2nd ed. by C. Vogel (Paris: E. de Boccard, 1955–57). 3 volumes.

LMD — *La Maison-Dieu. Revue de pastorale liturgique* (Paris: Cerf, 1945ff.).

LQF — Liturgiegeschichtliche (later: Liturgiewissenschaftliche) Quellen und Forschungen (Münster: Aschendorff, 1919ff.).

LXX — The Septuagint. — Ed. A. Rahlfs, *Septuaginta id est Vetus Testamentum graece iuxta LXX interpretes* (3rd ed.; Stuttgart: Württembergische Bibelanstalt, 1935).

Mansi — J. D. Mansi, *Sacrorum conciliorum nova et amplissima collectio* (31 vols.; Florence-Venice, 1757–98. Reprint and continuation, vols. 1–53; Paris, Leipzig, and Arnheim, 1901–27).

Martène — E. Martène, *De antiquis Ecclesiae ritibus.* (References to the various editions are given in A. G. Martimort, *La documentation liturgique de dom Edmond Martène* [ST 279; Vatican City, 1978].).

MGH — Monumenta Germaniae historica (Hannover: Hahn, and Berlin: Weidmann, 1826ff.).

MTZ — *Münchener theologische Zeitschrift* (Munich, 1950ff.).

OC   *Oriens christianus. Halbjahrshefte für die Kunde des christ-*
                lichen Orients (Wiesbaden, 1901ff.).

OCA   Orientalia christiana analecta (Rome: Pontificio Istituto Orien-
                tale, 1923ff.) (1923–34: Orientalia christiana; 1935ff.:
                Orientalia christiana analecta).

OCP   *Orientalia christiana periodica* (Rome: Pontificio Istituto
                Orientale, 1935ff.).

OR I, etc.   Ordo Romanus. Unless the contrary is indicated, the number
                accompanying this abbreviation is the one assigned in
                Andrieu, *OR.*

OR Mab   *Ordo Romanus* according to the numbering in J. Mabillon,
                Musaei Italici II (Paris, 1969) = PL 78:851–1372.

OS   *L'Orient syrien* (Paris, 1956–67).

PG   J. P. Migne, Patrologiae cursus completus, Series graeca
                (Paris-Montrouge, 1857–66). 161 volumes.

PL   J. P. Migne, Patrologiae cursus completus, Series latina
                (Paris-Montrouge, 1844–64). 221 volumes.

PLS   A. Hamann, *Supplementum Patrologiae Latinae* (Turnhout:
                Brepols, 1958–74). 5 volumes.

PO   Patrologia orientalis. First editors: R. Graffin and F. Nau
                (Paris: Firmin-Didot, then Turnhout: Brepols, 1903ff.).

POC   *Proche-Orient chrétien* (Jerusalem: Sainte-Anne, 1951–83).

PR   Pontificale Romanum (Roman Pontifical).

PRG   C. Vogel and R. Elze, *Le pontifical romano-germanique du*
                Xe siècle (ST 226, 227, 269; Vatican City, 1963–72). 3
                volumes.

QL   *Questions liturgiques et paroissiales*, then simply *Questions*
                liturgiques (Louvain: Abbaye du Mont César, 1910ff.).

RAC   *Reallexikon für Antike und Christentum*, ed. T. Klauser
                (Stuttgart: Hiersemann, 1950ff.).

RBén   *Revue bénédictine* (Abbaye de Maredsous, 1884ff.).

RechSR   *Recherches de science religieuse* (Paris, 1910ff.).

REDMF   Rerum ecclesiasticarum documenta, Series maior: Fontes
                (Rome: Herder, 1955ff.).

Renaudot   E. Renaudot, *Liturgiarum orientalium collectio* (Paris, 1716.
                More accurate 2nd ed.: Frankfurt: E. Baer, 1847, in 2
                volumes).

RevSR   *Revue des sciences religieuses* (Strasbourg: Palais Universitaire,
                1921ff.).

RHE   *Revue d'histoire ecclésiastique* (Louvain, 1900ff.).

ROC   *Revue de l'Orient chrétien* (Paris: Leroux, then Paris: Picard,
                1896ff.).

RR   Rituale Romanum (Roman Ritual).

RTAM   *Revue de théologie ancienne et médiévale* (Louvain: Abbaye
                du Mont César, 1929ff.).

Sacramentary   *The Sacramentary*, revised according to the second typical
                edition of the *Missale Romanum*, March 27, 1975 (Col-
                legeville: The Liturgical Press, 1985).

SC	Sources chrétiennes. Collection ed. by H. de Lubac and J. Daniélou (later: C. Mondésert) (Paris: Cerf, 1942ff.).
SCDW	Sacred Congregation for Divine Worship (May 8, 1969, to July 11, 1975).
SCR	Sacred Congregation of Rites. When this abbreviation is followed by a number, the reference is to *Decreta authentica Congregationis sacrorum rituum* (Rome, 1898–1927). 7 volumes or, more accurately, 5 volumes and 2 of appendixes.
SCSDW	Sacred Congregation for the Sacraments and Divine Worship (from July 11, 1975).
SE	*Sacris erudiri. Jaarboek voor Godsdienstwetenschappen* (Steenbrugge: St.-Pietersabdij, 1948ff.).
ST	Studi e testi (Rome, then Vatican City, 1900ff).
TA	Texte und Arbeiten, published by the Archabbey of Beuron, 1917ff. (Unless there is an indication to the contrary, the references are to the first section of this series.).
TS	Texts and Studies. Contributions to Biblical and Patristic Literature (Cambridge: Cambridge University Press, 1882ff.).
TU	Texte und Untersuchungen zur Geschichte der altchristlichen Literatur (Leipzig, then Berlin: Akademie Verlag, 1882ff.).
VSC	Vatican Council II, Constitution *Sacrosanctum Concilium* on the Sacred Liturgy. Latin text: *AAS* 56 (1964) 97–138. The translation of this document is that found in *DOL* (above).
ZKT	*Zeitschrift für katholische Theologie* (Innsbruck, 1877ff.).

GENERAL BIBLIOGRAPHY ON THE EUCHARIST

A. *Sources*

Missale Romanum, ed. typica, March 26, 1970; 2a ed. typica, March 27, 1975. English: *The Sacramentary,* trans. International Committee on English in the Liturgy (Collegeville: The Liturgical Press, 1973, 1985).

Ordo lectionum Missae, ed. typica, May 25, 1969; 2a ed. typica, January 21, 1981.

Lectionarium, ed. typica (3 vols.), September 30, 1970. English: *Lectionary for Mass* (Collegeville: The Liturgical Press, 1970).

De sacra communione et de cultu mysterii eucharistici extra Missam, ed. typica, June 21, 1973. English: *Holy Communion and Worship of the Eucharist Outside Mass,* in *The Rites of the Catholic Church* I New York: Pueblo, 1976), 449–512.

F. Cabrol and H. Leclercq, *Reliquiae liturgicae vetustissimae* (2 vols.; Monumenta ecclesiae liturgica 1; Paris: F. Didot, 1900–13).

J. Quasten, *Monumenta eucharistica et liturgica vetustissima* (Florilegium patristicum 7; Bonn: Hanstein, 1935).

B. Botte and C. Mohrmann, *L'ordinaire de la messe. Texte critique, traduction et études* (Etudes liturgiques 2; Paris: Cerf, and Louvain: Mont César, 1953).

F. E. Brightman, *Liturgies Eastern and Western* 1. *Eastern Liturgies* (Oxford: Clarendon, 1896).

E. Renaudot, *Liturgiarum orientalium collectio* (Paris, 1716; ed. 2a correctior in 2 vol., Frankfurt: J. Baer, 1847).

E. Mercenier and F. Paris, *La prière des églises de rite byzantin* 1 (Chevetogne, 1948²).

B. *Older Studies*

Amalarius of Metz, works ed. J. M. Hanssens, *Amalarii episcopi opera liturgica omnia* (ST 138–40; Vatican City, 1948–50). The *Expositiones missae* are in vol. 1; the *Liber officialis* is in vol. 2; and the *Eclogae* are in vol. 3. See PL 105:985-1242 and 1315-32.

Innocent III, *De sacro altaris mysterio libri sex* (PL 217:774-914).

St. Thomas Aquinas, *Summa theologiae* III, 83.

Nicholas Cabasilas, *A Commentary on the Divine Liturgy,* trans. J. M. Hussey and P. A. McNulty (London: SPCK, 1960).

Benedict XIV, *De sacrosancto sacrificio missae libri tres* (Rome, 1748, with many reprintings).

C. *Modern Studies*

P. Batiffol, *Leçons sur la messe* (Paris: Gabalda, 1941⁸).

A. Baumstark, *Liturgia romana e liturgia dell'esarcato* (Rome: Pustet, 1904).

_____, *Missale Romanum. Seine Entwicklung, ihre wichtigste Urkunden und Probleme* (Eindhoven: Uitgeverij Het Hooghuis, 1929).

_____, *Comparative Liturgy,* 3rd ed. by B. Botte, trans. F. L. Cross (Westminster, Md.: Newman, 1958).

C. Callewaert, *Sacris erudiri* (Steenbrugge: Abbatia S. Petri de Aldenbourg, 1940).

B. Capelle, *Travaux liturgiques* 2. *Histoire, La Messe* (Louvain: Mont César, 1962).

O. Casel, *La mémorial du Seigneur,* tr. H. Chirat (Lex orandi 2; Paris: Cerf, 1945).

N. M. Denis and E. Boulet, *Eucharistie ou la messe dans ses variétés, son histoire et ses origines* (Paris: Letouzey, 1953).

G. Dix (Anglican), *The Shape of the Liturgy* (Westminster: Dacre Press, 1945²).

J. B. Ferreres, *Historia del misal romano* (Barcelona: Subirana, 1929).

J. M. Hanssens, *Institutiones liturgicae de ritibus orientalibus* vols. 2–3 and Appendix (Rome: Gregorian University, 1930–32).

J. A. Jungmann, *The Mass of the Roman Rite: Its Origins and Development (Missarum Sollemnia),* trans. F. A. Brunner (2 vols.; New York: Benziger, 1951–55). 5th German ed., 1962.

H. Lietzmann (Protestant), *Messe und Herrenmahl* (Berlin: De Gruyter, 1955³. ET: *Mass and Lord's Supper,* trans. D. Reeve, with introduction and further inquiry by R. D. Richardson (Leiden: Brill, 1953–79).

A. Raes, *Introductio in liturgiam orientalem* (Rome: Pontificio Istituto Orientale, 1947), ch. 3: "De sacrificio eucharistico" (pp. 41–114).

M. Righetti, *La Messa. Commento storico-liturgico alla luce del Concilio Vaticano II, con un Excursus sulla Messa Ambrosiana di Mons. Pietro Borella* (Manuale di storia liturgica 3; Milan: Ancora, 1966³).

J. M. Sustaeta, *Misal y eucharistía. Estudio teológico, estructural y pastoral del nuevo Misal Romano* (Series Valentiana 2; Valencia: Fac. Teol. S. Vicente Ferrer, 1979).

F. Van de Paverd, *Zur Geschichte der Messliturgie in Antiocheia und Konstantinopel gegen Ende des vierten Jahrhunderts. Analyse der Quellen bei Johannes Chrysostomos* (OCA 187; Rome: Pontificio Istituto Orientale, 1970).

Introduction

Of all the recent liturgical reforms, the reform of the Mass is certainly the one that has most affected the people. It is here that liturgical changes, whether external or at a deeper level, have been brought home to both regular communicants and to those who attend Church only on major feasts or for marriages and funerals. The Eucharist is the celebration of which the people are most intensely aware because it is the most visible of all our liturgical celebrations, and it is the most visible because it is the high point of the sacramental system:

> The celebration of Mass, the action of Christ and the people of God arrayed hierarchically, is for the universal and the local Church as well as for each person the center of the whole Christian life. In the Mass we have the high point of the work that in Christ God accomplishes to sanctify us and the high point of the worship that in adoring God through Christ, his Son, we offer to the Father.[1]

This is why the Eucharist puts its seal on the beginning and the end of the believer's life: in the normal course of things, it comes after baptism and confirmation as the completion of Christian initiation, while in the form of Viaticum it becomes for the dying the seed of their future bodily resurrection. Moreover, since the liturgical year is the framework within which the Church lives its life, the Eucharist celebrated during the Easter Vigil takes on a special solemnity, for in a sense it once again steeps the disciples of Christ in the grace of their baptismal rebirth.

The Eucharist establishes the temporal rhythm of Christian life by means of the Sunday assembly every eighth day. This assembly is the place *par excellence* for the celebration of the Eucharist; even when the absence of a priest deprives communities of Sunday Mass, they retain their desire for it.

The Eucharist is the act that in a sense completes all the other sacraments and such major liturgical acts as religious professions, funerals, and the dedication of churches.

---

1. *GIRM* 1 (*DOL* 208 no. 1391).

In many Churches the Eucharist has also become the sacrament of everyday life for the more fervent among the people, who attend weekday Mass or a communion service. In the West, it has even become an expression of unceasing prayer in the form of adoration before the tabernacle, a practice supported by more solemn manifestations of Eucharistic devotion, such as processions and expositions of the Blessed Sacrament.

While the Mass, then, is always the Mass, no matter what the circumstances in which it is celebrated, the Church has nonetheless never put on the same level the Sunday assembly to which it summons all its members, assemblies held at the most important moments of human life, assemblies around the bishop,[2] and everyday assemblies.

The name commonly given to the Eucharistic celebration in the West tells us substantially little about it. The Latin word *missa* meant the "dismissal" of a group at the end of an assembly. How, then, from the end of the fourth century on, did it come to have the meaning we now give it? The reason may be that given by Isidore of Seville: because "at the moment when the sacrifice begins the catechumens are dismissed."[3] But the word *missa* covers the entire celebration, including the entrance rites and the Liturgy of the Word.[4] Nowadays people prefer to speak of the "Eucharist" rather than of "Mass," but the same difficulty of partial description makes itself felt again here. It is as though the reality of which we are speaking transcended all human words and could only be approached through symbolic terms, such as those used by the Fathers of the Church: "The Lord's Supper," "the breaking of bread," "sacred mysteries," "offering," "sacrifice," or "divine liturgy" (a name very widely used in the East).

Instituted as it was by Christ, the Mass has never ceased to be what it was in the beginning. And yet in the course of the centuries the addition of rites and prayers has caused its form to differ widely according to time and place, even while leaving its basic structure unaltered. In tackling this history I shall distinguish, somewhat arbitrarily, four main periods: the Mass prior to the liturgical books (to the end of the third century); the creative period in which the principal parts of the liturgy were enriched (to about the eighth century); the subsequent centuries in which the devotional imagination of the Christian peoples was given free rein, especially in connection with more secondary and external aspects;

---

2. VSC 41 (*DOL* 1 no. 41).

3. St. Isidore of Seville, *Etymologiae* VI, 19 (PL 82:252).

4. B. Botte, *"Ite Missa est,"* in B. Botte and C. Mohrmann, *L'ordinaire de la messe* (Etudes liturgiques 2; Paris: Cerf, 1953), 145–49; C. Mohrmann, *"Missa,"* *Vigiliae christianae* 12 (1958) 67–92; A. Coppo, *"Una nuova ipotesi sull'origine di 'Missa,' "* *EL* 71 (1957) 225–67; K. Gamber, *"Missa,"* *EL* 74 (1960) 48–52; *idem,* *"Nochmals zur Bedeutung 'Missa' als Opfer,"* *EL* 81 (1967) 70–73.

and, finally, the period of the liturgical movement and the reforms of Vatican Council II.

THE EUCHARIST PRIOR TO THE LITURGICAL

BOOKS

Chapter I

From Supper to Mass

BIBLIOGRAPHY

H. Schürmann, *Der Abendmahlsbericht Luk. 22, 7–38 als Gottesdienstordnung, Gemeindeordnung, Lebensordnung* (Die Botschaft Gottes, Neutestamentliche Reihe 1; Paderborn, Schöningh, 1957).

N. Koulomzine, "La sainte Cène dans le Nouveau Testament," in *Eucharisties d'Orient et d'Occident* I (Lex orandi 46; Paris: Cerf, 1970), 53–64.

J. Jeremias, *The Eucharistic Words of Jesus*, trans. N. Perrin from the 3rd German ed. (London: SCM, 1966).

V. Warnach, "Ein neuer Beitrag zur paulinischen Eucharistieauffassung," *ALW* 8 (1964) 457–67.

X. Léon-Dufour, *Le partage du pain eucharistique selon le Nouveau Testament* (Parole de Dieu; Paris: Le Seuil, 1982).

§1. The New Testament Accounts of the Institution of the Eucharist

In the spring of the year 55, Paul the Apostle wrote a letter to the Church of Corinth, which he himself had founded. Christians were a minority in this city and belonged to the poorest stratum of the population. This did not, however, prevent the existence among them of inequalities in wealth that could give rise to serious abuses at their assemblies.

> When you meet together, it is not the Lord's supper that you eat. For in eating, each one goes ahead with his own meal, and one is hungry and another is drunk. What! Do you not have houses to eat and drink in? Or do you despise the church of God and humiliate those who have nothing? What shall I say to you? Shall I commend you in this? No, I will not.
>
> For I received from the Lord what I also delivered to you, that the Lord Jesus on the night when he was betrayed. . . .[1]

---

1. 1 Cor 11:20-23, 23-26; see the table on pp. 10–12.

At this point comes the earliest account we have of the institution of the Eucharist. The occurrence of difficulties in the functioning of a rite already well established in the practice of the community forces Paul to clarify for this community the meaning of what it does. To this end he refers to the foundational event, that which has been "received from the Lord."

We naturally ask: What happened at the last meal that Jesus took with his disciples? The witnesses to it have not left us a description. It is true that the first three gospels[2] (John does not refer to what interests us here) are not occasional writings to the same extent that Paul's letters are; nonetheless they, too, have for their purpose to give an account of the life of the Churches in which they were composed. They received their final redaction some fifteen to twenty years after the letter to the Corinthians; thus they contain older elements (written notes already to some extent organized into a narrative), but also living tradition in the form of the gestures and words repeated at each celebration.

Of the three synoptic accounts Luke's is the closest to Paul's and seems to reflect most accurately the course of festive meals among the Jews.[3] First, the wine is made ready, and each of those present drinks in turn; this rite is accompanied by a prayer, the content of which is known from later testimonies: God was blessed for having given us the "fruit of the vine." In the Third Gospel this expression is found on the lips of Jesus as he first of all takes a cup. But the liturgy of the meal begins in the full sense when the father of the family breaks the loaf that will be distributed to the guests; as he does so he says a suitable prayer. Then, when the meal is over, he takes a further cup of wine and pronounces over it a longer prayer that is an important part of the ceremony. It is doubtless at these two moments—at the beginning and "after supper"—that we must locate the words of Jesus about his Body and his Blood; it is very likely for this reason that they are the only words Paul has kept.

The account of the Supper in Mark and Matthew is based on a different tradition; it is more fully developed and, in a sense, revised: there is no question of a first cup, and the words that the Lord spoke over that first cup, according to Luke, are now attached to the only remaining mention of wine. Above all, the two statements that gave rise to the description of the Eucharist as "the Body and Blood of Christ" are here presented as symmetrical and as having followed one upon the other, "as they were eating"; no reference is made to an intervening meal. The words spoken over the cup are different in form than in Luke, and there are other peculiarities as well.

---

2. Luke 22:14, 20; Mark 14:20-25; Matt 26:26-29; see table, pp. 10–12.
3. See table, pp. 10–12 and p. 21.

This new redaction is perhaps to be explained in part by the evolution of liturgical practice. At a very early date, it seems, Christians ceased to celebrate the Eucharist within the framework of a meal (even if they ate together before or after the Eucharist). If this was already the case (as is probable) at the period, and in the Churches in which Mark and Matthew wrote down their accounts, it is understandable that they should have passed over the details of Jewish table ritual and should have presented the Lord's actions with bread and wine as an uninterrupted sequence, since that was how they now occurred in Christian assemblies. Paul and Luke, on the other hand, remained faithful to the earlier testimonies; however, the new practice, which involved only a single thanksgiving spoken over the bread and the wine, would explain why they did not emphasize the formula for blessing the cup, although this was the most important part of the Jewish ceremonial.

Despite the duality of traditions, the same structure marks all the accounts; all show the same sequence of four verbs, the last of which, it is true, is not found in 1 Corinthians and Luke, although it is implicit in the context:

1. Jesus *took* bread, then a cup of wine,
2. he *gave thanks*, or pronounced the blessing,
3. he *broke* the bread,
4. he *gave* the bread and the cup to his disciples.

The words, "This is my body . . . my blood," are connected with the last of these actions, but it is important to situate them in the context provided by all four. Catechists and even theologians have too often indulged in deceptive abridgments in which only the words remained. To do so is to run the risk of turning them into quasi-magical formulas by omitting or telescoping the other actions, and especially the prayer that Jesus spoke.

The stereotyped character of the composition, in which the same key words recur in the various redactions, suggests that the writers were repeating a memorized text, namely, the one they were familiar with from the Eucharistic celebration. The same key words serve as clues in other New Testament passages, disclosing a reference to the Last Supper and evoking this in the reader's mind. This is the case, for example, with the multiplication of the loaves,[4] where the narrative follows the same pattern: "He took the bread . . . he gave thanks . . . he broke . . . he gave. . . ."

Furthermore, the same sequence of four verbs determined the course of the second part of the Mass:

---

4. Matt 14:18-21 and 15:32-38; Mark 6:31-44 and 8:1-10; Luke 9:12-17; John 8:1-10.

1. The presentation of the gifts, in which the offerings are "taken" and laid on the table.
2. The Eucharistic Prayer, into which the account of institution is set as a component part.
3. The breaking of the consecrated bread.
4. The communion rite.

In addition, some of the verbs have been used to give the entire rite its name. Thus the rite has been called "the Eucharist" ever since at least the end of the first century; yet thanksgiving (*eucharistia*) is only one element in the celebration. The same holds for "the breaking of bread" (*hē klasis tou artou*), which occurs in the Acts of the Apostles: a name was needed for this new institution, and Luke took his from one of Christ's actions at the Supper. Paul uses a more inclusive term, "the Lord's Supper," although he also says: "The bread which we break, is it not a participation [or: communion] in the body of Christ?"[5]

1 Corinthians 11:23-26	Luke 22:14-20
	[14]He sat at table, and the apostles with him. [15]And he said to them: "I have earnestly desired to eat this passover with you before I suffer; [16]for I tell you I shall not eat it until it is fulfilled in the kingdom of God." [17]And he took a cup, and when he had given thanks he said, "Take this and divide it among yourselves; [18]for I tell you that from now on I shall not drink of the fruit of the vine until the kingdom of God comes."
[23]The Lord Jesus on the night when he was betrayed took bread [24]and when he had given thanks, he broke it, and said: "This is my body which is for you.	[19]And he took bread, and when he had given thanks he broke it, and gave it to them, saying, "This is my body which is given for you.

_____

5. 1 Cor 10:16.

Do this in remembrance of me."	Do this in remembrance of me."
²⁵In the same way also the cup, after supper, saying, "This cup is the new covenant in my blood. Do this, as often as you drink it, in remembrance of me."	²⁰And likewise the cup, after supper, saying, "This cup which is poured out for you is the new covenant in my blood."
²⁶For as often as you eat this bread and drink the cup, you proclaim the Lord's death until he comes."	(¹⁸For I tell you that from now on I shall not drink of the fruit of the vine until the kingdom of God comes.")

Mark 14:22-25	Matthew 26:26-29
²²And as they were eating he took bread, and blessed, and broke it, and gave it to them, and said, "Take; this is my body." ²³And he took a cup, and when he had given thanks, he gave it to them, and they all drank of it. ²⁴And he said to them, "This is my blood of the covenant, which is poured out for many. ²⁵Truly, I say to you, I shall not drink again of the fruit of the vine	²⁶Now as they were eating Jesus took bread, and blessed, and broke it, and gave it to the disciples, and said, "Take, eat; this is my body." ²⁷And he took a cup, and when he had given thanks, he gave it to them, saying, "Drink it, all of you, ²⁸for this is my blood of the covenant, which is poured out for many for the forgiveness of sins. ²⁹I tell you I shall not drink again of this fruit of the vine

until that day	until that day
when I drink it	when I drink it
new	new
in the kingdom	in my Father's
of God."	kingdom."

§2. The Reading of the Scriptures and the Eucharist in the New Testament

St. Luke is the only evangelist to report the incident at Emmaus on Easter Sunday evening. After traveling with the Lord and failing to recognize him, two of his disciples persuaded him to remain with them for the evening meal. "When he was at table with them, he took the bread and blessed, and broke it, and gave it to them. And their eyes were opened and they recognized him."[6]

We have here a stereotyped formula for the Eucharist, but this sign of Christ's presence was itself supported by something else that introduced it and prepared the way for it while Jesus was still on the road with his companions: "Beginning with Moses and all the prophets, he interpreted to them in all the scriptures the things concerning him."[7]

The evangelist stresses the link between Scripture and the Eucharist when he has the disciples exclaim, after recognizing their guest: "Did not our hearts burn within us while he talked to us on the road, while he opened to us the scriptures?"[8] It is impossible to read these verses without thinking of the Jewish liturgy in the synagogue, where, every sabbath, the community listened to the reading of the Law and the Prophets. The passage here certainly reflects the meditation of a Christian community that is inspired by the manner in which it regularly celebrated the Eucharist. Every time it gathered in order to repeat in the Savior's memory what he himself had done on the eve of his passion, it recalled the sacred books and proclaimed the "today" in which the promises are fulfilled.

Initially, of course, the proclamation was not in writing, but in the words of witnesses who could personally attest that the death and resurrection of Christ fulfilled the Scriptures, as Peter had done when he emerged from the upper room on Pentecost. This is the situation we find in a passage of Acts: the faithful gather "to break bread," but first they listen to a sermon from Paul.[9] It is likely that changes came once the origi-

---

6. Luke 24:30.
7. Luke 24:27.
8. Luke 24:31.
9. Acts 20:7-11.

nal witnesses had written their memoirs, which were received with the same respect as the texts of the Old Testament. Thenceforth Christians, by and large, no longer took part in the Jewish assemblies; nonetheless, the synagogue service provided the model for their own assemblies. This must have been a gradual process.

§3. The First Mentions of the Eucharist Outside of the New Testament

In the year 112 Pliny the Younger, governor of the province of Pontus and Bithynia, sent a report to Emperor Trajan in which he asked what attitude was to be taken toward Christians. These people, he says, "habitually assemble on a set day, before sunrise, and sing a hymn to Christ as to a god. . . . They then go their ways and assemble again later on for their meal which, whatever may be said of it, is ordinary and harmless."[10] The description is rather puzzling, but could it be otherwise, coming from the pen of a pagan who sees the practice only as an external observer? In all likelihood, Pliny is speaking of Sunday ("a set day"), and one of the two gatherings must have been for the Eucharist (although the commentators disagree with one another as soon as further specification is attempted).

Does early Christian literature provide us with further information? The first document to be invoked must certainly be the *Didache*, a little book, probably of Syrian origin, that is in fact a compilation of several documents and may go back to the end of the first century or the beginning of the second. Further on I shall be looking at the prayers that the *Didache* proposes "for the eucharist";[11] for the moment I shall restrict myself to chapter 14, which belongs to the most recent part of the collection.

> On the dominical day of the Lord, come together to break bread and give thanks, after having, in addition, confessed your sins so that your sacrifice may be pure. But let anyone who is at odds with his fellow not join with you until he has first been reconciled, lest your sacrifice be profaned. For here is what the Lord says: "In every place and at all times let them offer me a pure sacrifice, for I am a great king, says the Lord, and my name is wonderful among the nations.[12]

What is said here confirms the indications gleaned from the New Testament: the passage deals with the Eucharist, which is described by the ac-

---

10. *C. Plinii Caecilii Secundi . . . epistolarum ad Traianum liber*, ed. M. Schuster (Bibliotheca Teubneriana; Leipzig: Teubner, 1933), 363–64. In French: Pline le Jeune, *Lettres* X, 96, trans. M. Durry (Paris: Les Belles Lettres, 1947), 74.

11. See p. 23.

12. *Didache* 14, ed. and French trans. W. Rordorf and A. Tuilier, *Doctrine des douze Apôtres* (SC 248; Paris: Cerf, 1978), 192.

tion of breaking bread in the midst of an assembly; the gathering is set for the first day of the week, designated here by a pleonastic phrase ("the dominical day of the Lord"). Also mentioned is the sacrificial nature of the rite. "Sacrifice" must doubtless be taken in a rather broad sense, and we must not read into it all the implications of a later theology. The emphasis is on a close analogy with the worship of the old covenant; the analogy justifies the application to this celebration of a gospel passage that deals with offerings in the temple. The confession of sins certainly presupposes a penitential prayer such as we find in contemporary writings.

At approximately the same period and in the same environment, Ignatius of Antioch provides the first explicit testimony to the role of the bishop who presides over the Eucharist as he does over the Church. His presiding shows the unity of the community to be signified by the Eucharist that is its source. "The only Eucharist to be considered legitimate is the one celebrated under the presidency of the bishop or of someone he has appointed."[13] "Be careful to take part in only one Eucharist; for there is but one flesh of our Lord Jesus Christ, one cup that unites us to his blood, and one altar, just as there is but one bishop with his presbytery and deacons."[14]

§4. The Celebration of the Eucharist at Rome in the Middle of the Second Century

All these indications show the importance and meaning of the Eucharistic assembly, but they hardly give us any idea of how the actual celebration proceeded. We are therefore fortunate to have the little treatise, known as the *First Apology*, which St. Justin addressed to Emperor Antoninus Pius (138–61) some decades later. Chapter 67 provides a description of the Sunday assembly, while chapter 65 has already described the Eucharistic liturgy proper (after a description of the baptismal rite). It will be helpful to read the two passages in parallel columns.[15]

> [67]On the day named after the sun, all who live in city or countryside assemble in the same place.

13. St. Ignatius of Antioch, *Ad Smyrn.* 8, in *Lettres,* ed. and French trans. P. T. Camelot (SC 10; Paris: Cerf, 1951), 162.

14. St. Ignatius of Antioch, *Ad Philad.* 4 (Camelot 142–43).

15. Justin, *Apologia I* 65 and 67, 3–5. The translation, with some modifications, is from L. Deiss, *Springtime of the Liturgy. Liturgical Texts of the First Four Centuries,* trans. M. J. O'Connell (Collegeville: The Liturgical Press, 1979), 92–94.

The memoirs of the apostles or the writings of the prophets are read for as long as time allows.

When the lector (*anaginōskōn*) has finished, the president (*ho proestōs*) addresses us and exhorts us to imitate the splendid things we have heard.

[65]After we have thus cleansed the person who believes and has joined our ranks, we lead him or her in to where those we call "brothers" are assembled.

We offer prayers in common for ourselves, for the one who has just been enlightened, and for all human beings everywhere. It is our desire, now that we have come to know the truth, to be found worthy of doing good deeds and obeying the commandments, and thus to obtain eternal salvation.

Then we all stand and pray.

When we finish praying, we greet one another with a kiss.

Then bread and a cup of water and mixed wine are brought to him who presides over the brethren.

As we said earlier, when we have finished praying, bread, wine, and water are brought up.

He takes them and offers prayers glorifying the Father of the universe through the name of the Son and of the Holy Spirit, and he utters a lengthy eucharist (*eucharistian . . . poietai*) because the Father has judged us worthy of these gifts.

The president then prays and gives thanks according to his ability (*hosē dynamis*).

When the prayers and eucharist are finished, all the people present give their assent with an "Amen!" "Amen" in Hebrew means "So be it!"

And the people give their assent with an "Amen!"

When the president has finished his eucharist and the people have all signified their assent, those whom we call "deacons" distribute the "eucharistified" (*eucharistē- thōtos*) bread and the wine and water over which the eucharist has been spoken, to each of those present; they also carry them to those who are absent.

Next, the gifts, which have been "eucharistified" (*eucharistēthen- tōn*) are distributed, and everyone shares in them, while they are also sent via the deacons to the absent brethren.

The Mass thus proceeds in accordance with a fundamental structure that has lasted to our own time: the assembly; the Liturgy of the Word, with readings, homily, and prayer of the faithful; the liturgy of the Eucharist, with the bringing up of bread and wine, a consecratory thanksgiving, and communion.

The first emphasis is on the assembly of the brethren: the Christians are not scattered, but gather in one place. Their assembly, moreover, is an organized one: at its head is a "president" who addresses the congregation after the readings, accepts the offerings, and says the Eucharistic Prayer. His function is not simply cultic, since, as we shall see further on, it is also his office to assist the poor in their needs. This president can only be the bishop, but others also play an active part in the celebration: the reader, those who bring up the bread, wine, and water (although the fact is stated in an impersonal way: the gifts "are brought up"), the deacons who distribute Communion, and the people themselves, whose "Amen" shows their participation.

The Liturgy of the Word includes passages from the New Testament; that is what is meant by "the memoirs of the apostles," an expression that Justin uses elsewhere for the gospels.[16] But the Old Testament is also read; this is probably what we are to understand by "the writings of the prophets." The only norm for the length of this part of the Mass is the time available; we may think, therefore, of a continuous reading of the books of Scripture, beginning each time at the point where the reading left off at the previous assembly. Next there is the homily, an exhortation to put into practice the Word that has been proclaimed.

Then come the intercessions, which are offered by all together and while standing. In his description of the baptismal liturgy Justin calls them "common prayers," in the sense that they concern the entire community; in them the community recommends to God the brethren, the newly baptized, and "all others, whoever they may be." It is not surprising that the faithful in their assemblies should address this kind of general petition to the Lord, for it was familiar to them. It goes back to St. Paul (1 Tim 2:1-2);

---

16. Justin, *Apologia I* 66, 3.

and when Polycarp, the elderly bishop of Smyrna, was arrested for martyrdom (probably in 177), he called to mind in his prayer "all those who had ever come in contact with him, both important and insignificant, famous and obscure, and the entire Catholic Church scattered throughout the world."[17]

At this point the kiss of peace is exchanged, at least when the sacraments of initiation are celebrated. The offerings are then brought up and given to the president. Christ's gesture of "taking bread . . . a cup" at the Supper is thus solemnized or highlighted as it were: the material for the Eucharist is not ready at hand for the bishop, but is brought to him in the sight of all. We are told repeatedly that the material is bread, wine, and water; we should not be surprised at the mention of water: the peoples of antiquity always diluted their drink, since it was too strong to be drunk neat unless one wanted to get intoxicated.

Next in order are "prayers and eucharists (or thanksgivings)," which are offered by the president. The description of the baptismal Mass brings out the Trinitarian character of the praise; the expression "according to his ability" points to the absence of any text to be read or recited from memory. The word "eucharistia" (thanksgiving) here refers to words that were undoubtedly regarded as consecratory, since the reason why the bread and wine are no longer ordinary food after the thanksgiving is that they have been "eucharistified," that is, a thanksgiving or eucharist has been said over them. The word "eucharist" even serves to designate the consecrated gifts:

> This food we call "eucharist," and no one may share it unless he believes that our teaching is true, and has been cleansed in the bath of forgiveness for sin and of rebirth, and lives as Christ taught. For we do not receive these things as if they were ordinary food and drink. But, just as Jesus Christ our Savior was made flesh through the word of God and took on flesh and blood for our salvation, so too (we have been taught) through the word of prayer that comes from him, the food over which the eucharist has been spoken becomes the flesh and blood of the incarnate Jesus, in order to nourish and transform our flesh and blood.[18]

The communion is surely preceded by a breaking of the bread, but this action is not mentioned. For that matter, the whole description of the communion is quite succinct: the deacons give the Eucharist to the faithful who are present and bring it to those who are absent.

---

17. *The Martyrdom of Polycarp* 8, in *The Acts of the Christian Martyrs*, ed. and trans. H. Musurillo (Oxford: Clarendon Press, 1972), 7–9.

18. Justin, *Apologia I* 66, 1–2 (Deiss 92).

§5. The Eucharistic Assembly, Sign of the Church

By the middle of the second century a first stage had been traversed in the development of the liturgy of the Mass; the essential elements were now in place, in the form in which they were to be found everywhere down to our own time. The Eucharist was no longer being celebrated within the framework of a meal; this change occurred at a very early point. The synagogal assembly on the sabbath inspired the formation of a first part of the ritual, once the New Testament had been put in writing and had been accepted in the various communities. The second part was organized by repeating in a broader and more detailed way what Jesus had done at the Supper. We know that at Rome the development had reached the stage attested by Justin, and it is likely that it was not limited to Rome. But what value would this information about Christian worship have for us if we did not also see the place it had in the life of the faithful as this was structured by the Sundays of the year?

It was "on the first day of the week" that the brethren "gathered together to break bread" when Paul visited Troas.[19] Justin, too, locates the assembly on "the day named after the sun," an expression intelligible to the pagans to whom his book is addressed, since the planetary week was now in use among the Romans.

> We gather together on the day of the sun because it is the first day, when God transformed darkness and matter and made the world; on this same day Jesus Christ, our Savior, rose from the dead. For he was crucified on the eve of the day of Saturn, and on the morrow of that day, that is, the day of the Sun, he appeared to his apostles and disciples and taught them the things which we have submitted for your examination.[20]

The day of assembly had the importance it did because the usual lot of Christians in the world was one of dispersion. They lived among pagans in a situation that Jews found difficult to understand, inasmuch as they themselves, by reason of ritual prescriptions and dietary prohibitions, were obliged to form groups in the Diaspora. Justin heard such reproaches quite often; that is why he puts them on the lips of a rabbi in his *Dialogue with Trypho, a Jew*: "The point that we find most difficult to grasp is that you call yourselves devout and regard yourselves as different from others, and yet you do not separate yourselves from their midst."[21] We are reminded of the remarks made by an anonymous author (end of the second century) in his *Letter to Diognetus*:

---

19. Acts 20:7.
20. Justin, *Apologia I* 67, 7 (Deiss 94).
21. Justin, *Dialogus cum Tryphone* 10, 3, ed. G. Archambault (Textes et documents 8; Paris: Picard, 1909), 48.

Christians are not distinguished from other human beings by country or language or clothing. . . . They live in the cities of Greeks or barbarians according to the lot that has befallen each; they conform to local usage in clothing, food, and manner of life, even while they also show forth the extraordinary and paradoxical laws that govern their spiritual republic.[22]

If Christians did not lose their own identity while living under these conditions, this was due largely to their assembly on Sundays. The Church to which they belonged became a visible reality for them there, and they renewed their strength by sharing the Word and the Bread.

More or less romanticized pictures of the life of the early communities have spread an image of assemblies in a cozy atmosphere in which all were happy to be together and rub elbows, sheltered from a society in which everyone's hand was against them. It is true, of course, that while Christ's followers were not being continually persecuted, they did live under threat of a condemnation that could mean death. It is very unlikely, however, that their attitude to their gatherings was of the kind we attribute to them. In order to attend, they often had to leave behind those to whom they felt most closely united by "flesh and blood": the still pagan members of their own family, workmates, people whose daily concerns they shared, but who had not accepted the gospel. This caused them suffering that undoubtedly was one source of their missionary zeal.

Moreover, while they did find brothers and sisters in the assembly, the bond was the joy which faith gives but which also has to bridge human distances in order to accept the gift of a love that is from the Lord. During the time of the celebration they had to do a certain violence to the social order that reigned in their everyday lives. The sharing that fraternal communion requires is mentioned by Justin immediately after his description of the Sunday assembly: "The wealthy who are willing make contributions, each as he pleases, and the collection is deposited with the president, who aids orphans and widows, those who are in want because of sickness or some other reason, those in prison, and visiting strangers—in short, he takes care of all in need."[23]

It is to be observed that the collection is not properly speaking a liturgical rite; the gifts are quite distinct from the bread and wine that are brought up before the thanksgiving. But the Eucharistic assembly also makes the Church visible as a community of love; in this way it once again challenges society with its inequities by becoming the place of a redistribution of goods.

---

22. *Ad Diognetum* 5, 1–2 and 4; ed. and French trans. H. Marrou (SC 33bis; Paris: Cerf, 1965²), 62.
23. Justin, *Apologia I* 67, 6 (Deiss 94).

Chapter II

From Jewish "Blessing" to Christian Eucharistic Prayer

BIBLIOGRAPHY

G. Dix, *The Shape of the Liturgy* (Westminster: Dacre Press, 1945²).

J. P. Audet, "Esquisse historique du genre littéraire de la 'bénédiction' et de l'"eucharistie' chrétienne," *Revue biblique* 65 (1958) 371–99.

L. Ligier, "Autour du sacrifice eucharistique. Anaphores orientales et anamnèse juive du Kippur," *Nouvelle revue théologique* 82 (1960) 40–55.

_____, "Anaphores orientales et prières juives," *POC* 13 (1963) 4–21, 99–113.

J. Godart, "Aux origines de la célébration eucharistique," *QL* 46 (1965) 8–25, 104–21.

L. Ligier, *Textus selecti de magna oratione eucharistica, addita Haggadah Paschae et nonnullis Judaeorum benedictionibus* (Rome: Gregorian University, 1965²).

_____, "De la Cène de Jésus à l'anaphore de l'Eglise," *LMD* no. 97 (1966) 7–51 (= *Rivista liturgica* 53 [1966] 480–522).

L. Bouyer, *Eucharist. Theology and Spirituality of the Eucharistic Prayer*, trans. C. U. Quinn (Notre Dame: University of Notre Dame Press, 1968).

L. Ligier, "La benedizione e il culto nell'Antico Testamento," in *Il Canone* (Liturgica, nuova ser. 5; Padua: Centro di Azione Liturgica, 1968).

_____, "La 'Benedizione' e la Cena pasquale di Gesù," in *ibid.*, 23–37.

_____, "Dalla Cena di Gesù all'anafora della Chiesa," in *ibid.*, 39–54.

A. Hänggi and I. Pahl (eds.), *Prex eucharistica. Textus e variis liturgiis antiquioribus selecti* (Spicilegium Friburgense 12; Fribourg: Editions universitaires, 1968), 5–60.

H. Cazelles, "L'Anaphore et l'Ancien Testament," in *Eucharisties d'Orient et d'Occident* I (Lex orandi 46; Paris: Cerf, 1970), 11–22.

K. Hruby, "L'action de grâce dans la liturgie juive," in *ibid.*, 23–31.

L. Ligier, "Les origines de la prière eucharistique," *QL* 53 (1972) 181–202.

K. Hruby, "La Birkat ha-Mazon," in *Mélanges B. Botte* (Louvain: Mont-César, 1972), 205–22.

T. J. Talley, "De la 'berakah' juive à l'eucharistie. Une question à réexaminer," *LMD* no. 125 (1976) 11–39.

G. Rouwihorst, "Bénédiction, action de grâce, supplication. Les oraisons de la table dans le Judaïsme et les célébrations eucharistiques des Chrétiens syriaques," *QL* 61 (1980) 211–40.

H. Wegman, "Généalogie hypothétique de la prière eucharistique," *QL* 61 (1980) 263–78.

G. Giraudo, *La struttura letteraria della preghiera eucaristica. Saggio sulla genesi di una forma* (Analecta biblica 92; Rome: Biblical Institute, 1981).

S. Légasse, *"Eucharistein et Eulogein,"* in *Mens concordet voci. Mélanges A. G. Martimort* 2 (Paris: Desclée, 1983).

"The president then prays and gives thanks according to his ability." These words of Justin do not tell us what the Eucharistic Prayer actually was in his time. The New Testament is equally silent about what Jesus said when he "gave thanks" or "blessed" the bread and cup. It would, however, be risky to accept our ignorance with resignation and to attend solely to the words explicitly cited in the accounts of the Supper, for example, "This is my body. . . . This is my blood." For unless we situate these words in the context of prayer in which they occurred, we may have an inadequate understanding of them. In the eyes of Justin, after all, the gifts were consecrated because they were "eucharistified," that is, because the thanksgiving was spoken over them.

§1. The Thanksgiving at the Supper

Is it legitimate to make use of Jewish traditions regulating festive meals?[1] These were committed to writing beginning only in the second century of the Christian era, but what the Mishnah reports from that period is certainly older. It seems permissible, therefore, to draw upon the chapter devoted to the *Berakoth* (singular: *Berakah*) or "blessings," especially those used at table.

At the first cup of wine and at the breaking of bread that began the meal, the following formulas were used: "Blessed are you, Lord our God, King of the universe, who create the fruit of the vine"; "Blessed are you . . . who bring forth bread from the earth."[2]

At the end of the entire service, there was a longer prayer, the *Birkat ha-mazon*, pronounced over a final cup of wine. The Mishnah does not give the complete text, but we can get an idea of it from later witnesses.[3] The prayer begins with a blessing in two parts: for the food and for the land:

> Blessed are you, Lord our God, King of the universe, who feed us and the whole world with goodness, grace, kindness and mercy. Blessed are you,

---

1. Whether the Supper was in fact a Passover meal, the important thing for us is that Luke intended to connect it with this "memorial" of the old covenant, of which it is the fulfillment. In any case, the Passover meal was distinguished from other festal meals only by the food served and a few words introduced into the usual formularies.

2. Mishnah, *Berakoth* VI, 1. (There is a Latin translation of the text in Hänggi-Pahl 6–7.)

3. See K. Hruby, *"La Birkat ha-Mazon,"* in *Mélanges B. Botte* (Louvain: Mont César, 1972), 205–22.

Lord, who sustain all things. We thank you, Lord our God, for giving us as our heritage a desirable, good and broad land, the covenant and the Torah, life and food. For all this we thank you and bless your name for ever and beyond. Blessed are you, Lord, for the land and our food.

The *Berakah* then turns into a *Tephillah*, or prayer of petition that the divine work thus far evoked may reach its completion: "Have mercy, Lord our God, on Israel your people, on Jerusalem your city, on your sanctuary and your dwelling, on Zion, the place where your glory dwells, and on the great and holy house upon which your name is invoked. . . . Blessed are you, Lord, who rebuild Jerusalem."[4]

There are other versions of these prayers that are more fully developed and that even diverge from one another on certain points. We must bear in mind, however, that we are dealing with an oral tradition: the formularies were handed down in the form of a detailed schema, along with some stereotyped expressions that everyone knew by heart; provided the schema and the expressions were used, a certain freedom was allowed in composing the prayer. Additions and variants did not detract from the consciousness of being in faithful conformity with what had been received and learned. Then, when the need was felt of fixing the prayer in writing, the schema and supporting expressions, and not the details of prayers once heard, were again the primary concern.

It is almost certain that at the Last Supper Jesus acted in the same way as other Jews of his day who presided at a festal meal. He must have used the formulas which custom dictated and which followed the lines of those cited above. At the same time, however, it is likely that he took advantage of the freedom that was his to introduce adaptations and perhaps even to give a new meaning to the ancient words.

The tradition distinguished two types of "blessing": short *berakoth* containing a single brief sentence, like the ones cited for the first cup and the bread, and lengthy *berakoth*, like the one at the end of the meal or those connected with the reading of the Torah in the synagogal service; this second type was more fully developed and ended with a petition. It is not beyond possibility that Mark and Matthew distinguished between the two types by using two different terms: "blessed" for the bread and "giving thanks" for the cup.

---

4. *Siddur Rav Saadja Gaon*, ed. I. Davidson, S. Assaf, and B. I. Joel (Jerusalem, 1941) 102–3. (Latin translation in Hänggi-Pahl 10–12.)

§2. The Prayer in the *Didache*

BIBLIOGRAPHY

> *Doctrine des Apôtres*, ed. H. Hemmer, G. Oger, and A. Laurent, in *Les Pères aposto-*
> *liques* (Textes et documents 10; Paris: Picard, 1926²).
> J. P. Audet, *La Didachè. Instruction des Apôtres* (Etudes bibliques; Paris: Gabalda,
> 1958).
> W. Rordorf, "Les prières eucharistiques de la *Didachè*," in *Eucharisties d'Orient et*
> *d'Occident* II (Lex orandi 46; Paris: Cerf, 1970), 1:64–82. A revised and completed
> version has been translated into English in *The Eucharist of the Early Christians*,
> trans. M. J. O'Connell (New York: Pueblo, 1978), 1–23.
> T. J. Talley, "De la 'Berakah' à l'eucharistie. Une question à réexaminer," *LMD*
> no. 125 (1976) 22–28: "La *Birkat ha-Mazon* et la *Didachè*."
> E. Mazza, "*Didachè* IX–X. Elementi per una interpretazione eucaristica," *EL* 92
> (1978) 393–419.
> W. Rordorf and A. Tuilier, *La Doctrine des douze Apôtres* (SC 248; Paris: Cerf,
> 1978).
> G. Giraudo, *La struttura letteraria*, 249–53.

In the collection of disparate texts known as the *Didache*, chapters 9 and 10 are generally assigned to an earlier author than the one who composed the passage cited above.[5] This earlier author in turn drew on already existing sources, since the prayers he sets before us have a very archaic character. It is thus likely that these prayers take us back close to the time of the first redaction of the Synoptic Gospels and into the communities of Palestine or Syria (where the mention of wheatfields on the hillsides would be quite in place).

[9]With regard to the eucharist, give thanks in this manner:
First, for the cup:
"We thank you, our Father,
for the holy vine of David your servant
which you have revealed to us through Jesus your servant.
    Glory be yours through all ages!"

Then for the bread broken:
"We thank you, our Father,
for the life and knowledge
which you have revealed to us through Jesus your servant.
    Glory be yours through all ages!

Just as the bread broken
was first scattered on the hills,
then was gathered and became one,
so let your Church be gathered

---

5. See p. 13.

from the ends of the earth into your kingdom,
for yours is glory and power
through Jesus Christ, for all ages!

Let no one eat or drink of your eucharist except those baptized in the name of the Lord. For it is of this that the Lord was speaking when he said, "Do not give what is holy to dogs."

[10]When your hunger has been satisfied, give thanks thus:
"We thank you, holy Father,
for your holy name
which you have made to dwell in our hearts,
and for the knowledge and faith and immortality
which you have revealed to us through Jesus your servant.
    Glory be yours through all ages!

All-powerful Master, you created all things
for your name's sake,
and you have given food and drink to the children of men
for their enjoyment
so that they may thank you.

On us, moreover, you have graciously bestowed
a spiritual food and drink
that lead to eternal life,
through Jesus your servant.
Above all, we thank you
because you are almighty.
    Glory be yours through all ages!

Lord, remember your Church
and deliver it from all evil;
make it perfect in your love
and gather it from the four winds,
this sanctified Church,
into the kingdom you have prepared for it,
    for power and glory are yours through all ages!

May grace come and this world pass away!
Hosanna to the God of David!
If anyone is holy, let him come!
If anyone is not, let him repent!
Marana tha! Amen!"

Let the prophets give thanks for as long as they wish.[6]

---

6. *Didache* 9–10; translation, with some modifications, from Deiss, *Springtime of the Liturgy*, 74–76.

The rubrical directions, which may be from the pen of the editor, specify: "for the cup," "for the bread broken," and "when your hunger has
been satisfied." They correspond to the three steps mentioned by Luke:
"He took a cup. . . . He took bread. . . . After supper." We should
therefore regard these two chapters as a single whole, a ritual similar to
that followed at Jewish festal meals. The celebration here is nonetheless
a Christian one, as is clear from the explicit references to Jesus, if from
nothing else. There is a short *berakah* for the first cup, another for the
bread broken, and a longer tripartite formula. In this last the first two
parts give the impression of being a transposition of the Jewish blessing
for food and land, covenant and Law, while in the *Tephillah* the completion of God's wonders takes the form of safeguarding the Church and
gathering it into the kingdom.

Some scholars interpret the ceremony in the *Didache* as simply a religious meal, perhaps one that preceded a sacramental celebration.[7] In the
view of others, however, this is itself the sacramental rite. If this second
interpretation is correct, the testimony here must go back to a very early
period, even if we regard it as coming from a community that kept the
primitive usage for a longer period than others did.

Such an interpretation is by no means untenable. The rubrics say: "with
regard to the eucharist," and, a little further on, "eucharist" means something that is eaten and drunk and that is, in addition, reserved to the baptized. True enough, there is no account of institution; on the other hand,
the text proposed is offered simply as a pattern for free composition; this
seems indicated by the remark at the end: "Let the prophets give thanks
for as long as they wish." The disciples were desirous of obeying the order
they had received: "Do this in memory of me." They had to put into words
the meaning of the rites they performed as they commemorated the Supper, the account of which (as we saw earlier) had very quickly taken on
a stereotyped form. Rather than introduce this evocation of meaning into
the text of the prayers they had inherited and that were simply the blessings spoken by Jesus, they may have decided to turn it into an introduction to the celebration, comparable to the commemoration of the Exodus
from Egypt in the celebration of the Passover. The formula "If anyone
is holy, let him come!" may indeed be taken as an invitation to celebrate
the sacrament, but may it not just as well be taken as an admonition before communion?—But we must bear in mind that any reconstruction is
hypothetical.

In any case, we may conclude that the Christian thanksgiving was seen
as heir of the Jewish "blessing." It consists above all in a meditation on

---

7. See J. P. Audet, *La Didachè. Instruction des Apôtres* (Etudes bibliques; Paris:
Gabalda, 1958), 415–17.

the Lord as author of all the wonderful things in both creation and in the history of salvation; it is a prayer of praise for the giver even more than of gratitude for the gifts received. This whole attitude is summed up in the word "eucharist." The term doubtless signified simply "gratitude" in the Greek spoken by the people; that is probably the reason why the Alexandrian translators of the Bible preferred other words. The usage of the Church, however, has given it a new meaning that derives from the Old Testament. In addition, the gospel gives the spirituality of Israel its most complete fulfillment, inasmuch as "to give thanks" becomes the equivalent of "celebrate the eucharist"; prayer becomes action.

§3. The Eucharistic Prayer in the *Apostolic Tradition*

BIBLIOGRAPHY

B. Botte, *La Tradition apostolique de saint Hippolyte* (LQF 39; Münster: Aschendorff, 1963), 30–33. Abridged edition in SC 11bis (Paris: Cerf, 1968).

R. H. Connolly, "The Eucharistic Prayer of Hippolytus," *JTS* 39 (1938) 350–69.

G. Dix, *The Treatise on the Apostolic Tradition of St. Hippolytus of Rome* (London: SPCK, 1939), 75–78.

J. M. Hanssens, *La Liturgie d'Hippolyte* (OCA 155; Rome: Oriental Institute, 1959), 431–41.

L. Bouyer, *Eucharist*, 158–82.

C. Giraudo, *La struttura letteraria*, 290–95.

The earliest dated Eucharistic Prayer that resembles ours goes back to about the year 225 and occurs in a document that scholars have identified with the *Apostolic Tradition* of Hippolytus. The prayer may therefore be regarded as originating in Rome, but it is not possible to determine the extent to which it represents the practice of the Roman Church. The author presents it as a composition based on tradition; he proposes it for the bishop's use, but he adds: "It is by no means necessary that he use the very words I have put down, as though he were anxious to recite them from memory."[8] Unfortunately, this Eucharistic Prayer, which must have been composed in Greek, has come down to us only in translations,[9] although these have made it possible to reconstruct the original text.

—The Lord be with you!
—And with your spirit!

---

8. *La Tradition apostolique de saint Hippolyte* 9, ed. B. Botte (LQF 39; Münster: Aschendorff, 1963), 28–29.

9. The document has come down to us in two Coptic dialects, in Arabic and Ethiopian, and, for parts of the text, in Latin. The Eucharistic Prayer, after the opening dialogue, is preserved only in Ethiopian and Latin.

—Lift up your hearts.
  —They are turned to the Lord.
—Let us give thanks to the Lord.
  —It is right and just.

We give you thanks, O God, through your beloved Child Jesus Christ, whom you have sent us in these last days as Savior, Redeemer, and Messenger of your will. He is your Word, inseparable from you, through whom you have created everything and whom, in your good pleasure, you sent from heaven into the womb of a virgin. He was conceived and became flesh, he manifested himself as your Son, born of the Holy Spirit and the Virgin.

He did your will and, to win for you a holy people, he stretched out his hands in suffering to rescue from suffering those who believe in you.

When he was about to surrender himself to voluntary suffering in order to destroy death, to break the devil's chains, to tread hell underfoot, to pour out his light upon the just, to establish the rule (of faith) and manifest his resurrection, he took bread, he gave you thanks and said: "Take, eat, this is my body which is broken for you."

In like manner for the cup, he said: "This is my blood which is poured out for you. When you do this, do it in memory of me."

Remembering therefore your death and your resurrection, we offer you the bread and the wine, we thank you for having judged us worthy to stand before you and serve you as priests.

And we pray you to send your Holy Spirit on the offering of your holy Church. Gather all those who share in your holy mysteries and grant that by this sharing they may be filled with the Holy Spirit who strengthens their faith in the truth.

May we be able thus to praise and glorify you through your Child Jesus Christ. Through him glory to you and honor, to the Father and the Son, with the Holy Spirit, in your holy Church, now and for ever and ever! Amen.[10]

Apart from the absence of the *Sanctus* and intercessions, the overall structure of this prayer is familiar to us and we may, without detracting from its basic unity, distinguish its component parts.

1. *Expression of thanksgiving.* After a dialogue between bishop and congregation, which is found almost everywhere with minor variations and which has antecedents in Jewish ritual, the prayer gives expression, as do the *berakoth*, to the reasons for blessing the Lord. The formulation here is clearly christological: the creative and redemptive work of the incarnate Word as he forms a people for himself through his death and resurrection. Every point that is mentioned is given as a motive for thanksgiving;

---

10. *La Tradition apostolique* 4 (Botte 11–17), trans. from Deiss 130–31.

the same theme reemerges in the anamnesis and is implicit in the final doxology. In other words, the entire prayer is "eucharistic."

2. *Account of institution.* The commemoration of the Supper is made part of the ongoing prayer, which at every point is addressed to the Father. The commemoration is very restrained, being limited to the essentials; it bears witness to an oral tradition that had remained independent of the redactions of the gospel.

3. *Commemoration (anamnesis) and offering.* In keeping with the command of Christ, "Do it in memory of me," the formulary continues: "Remembering therefore" and mentions the death and resurrection. In the biblical acceptance of the word, "to remember" is not simply to refer back to the past, as it is in our modern languages. The celebration takes us into the very memory of God himself, for whom "a thousand years are as a day,"[11] and makes us contemporary, after a fashion, with his wonderful deeds in the past.[12] If this is already true of the Israelite feasts, it is so in a much more real way for the Church, whose head is here and now alive and glorified. As a result, the Church can offer to God the sacrifice of its Lord as rendered present in the sacrament: "Remembering therefore . . . we offer. . . ." All this finds expression in a single sentence, as a single reality, and in close connection with the account of institution.

4. *Invocation of the fruits of the sacrifice upon the communicants.* "We pray you . . . ." After the thanksgiving comes the petition, in accordance with the structure specific to Jewish-Christian spirituality. Just as the thanksgiving acquired a sacramental dimension, so the petition asks that God's wonderful works may find their completion in the communion. The main object of the petition is, it seems, that the faithful should be "filled with the Holy Spirit," according to the expression used in the Acts of the Apostles in describing Pentecost,[13] and that their faith should be strengthened in the truth. They are to receive these graces, however, through participation in the sacred mysteries. That is, the bread and wine are, as it were, the vehicle that the Paraclete uses in order to produce his fruits in the lives of those who receive them. This very likely explains why this prayer begins with a petition for the coming of the Spirit on the offering.[14]

---

11. Ps 90:4.

12. See M. Thurian, *The Eucharistic Memorial*, trans. J. G. Davies (Ecumenical Studies in Worship 7–8; Richmond: Knox 1961).

13. Acts 2:2.

14. Whether these words, which may justify calling the passage an epiclesis, belong to the text as it came from Hippolytus, they carry only their obvious meaning: the divine life reaches the community through the Eucharistic species. See B. Botte, "L'épiclèse de l'anaphore d'Hippolyte," *RTAM* 14 (1947) 241–51, and L. Bouyer, *Eucharist* 170–77.

5. *Doxology*. The final words of the prayer revive the theme of thanksgiving to the Father through the mediation of Jesus Christ. To be noted is the original formula that recurs elsewhere in Hippolytus: "with the Holy Spirit in the holy Church."

6. *Amen*. This is certainly intended as the response of the congregation; see Justin's emphasis on it.

§4. An Early Syriac Anaphora

BIBLIOGRAPHY

E. C. Ratcliff, "The Original Form of the Anaphora of Addai and Mari," *JTS* 30 (1928–29) 23–32.

A. Raes, "Le récit de l'institution eucharistique dans l'anaphore chaldéenne et malabare des Apôtres," *OCP* 10 (1944) 216–26.

B. Botte, "L'anaphore chaldéenne des Apôtres," *OCP* 15 (1949) 259–76.

_____, "Problèmes de l'anaphore syrienne d'Addai et Mari," *OS* 10 (1965) 89–106.

L'anaphore maronite de saint Pierre III, ed. J. M. Sauget, in *Anaphorae syriacae* II/3 (Rome: Oriental Institute, 1973) 275–329 (Syriac text and Latin translation). French translation: M. Hayek, *Liturgie maronite. Histoire et textes eucharistiques* (Tours: Mame, 1964), 295–318.

W. Macomber, "The Oldest Known Text of the Anaphora of the Apostles Addai and Mari," *OCP* 32 (1966) 335–71.

D. Webb, "Variations dans les versions manuscrites de la liturgie nestorienne d'Addai et de Mari," *SE* 18 (1967–68) 478–523.

_____, "La liturgie nestorienne des apôtres Addai et Mari dans la tradition manuscrite," in *Eucharisties d'Orient et d'Occident* II (Lex orandi 47; Paris: Cerf, 1970), 25–49.

W. Macomber, "The Maronite and Chaldean Versions of the Anaphora of the Apostles," *OCP* 37 (1971) 54–84.

_____, "A Theory of the Origin of the Syrian, Maronite and Chaldean Rites," *OCP* 39 (1973) 235–42.

R. J. Galvin, "Addai and Mari Revisited. The State of the Question," *EL* 87 (1973) 383–414.

B. Spinks, "Addai and Mari and the Institution Narrative: the Tantalizing Evidence of Gabriel Garraya," *EL* 98 (1984) 60–67.

_____, "The Original Form of the Anaphora of the Apostles. A Suggestion in the Light of the Maronite Sharar," *EL* 91 (1977) 146–61.

Hippolytus is not the only ancient witness. The Syriac-speaking world has handed down a formulary that, judging by its archaic character, comes from about the same period. Unlike that of Hippolytus, however, it was not set down in writing in the third century, but remained a living part of the liturgy under two different forms: the Anaphora (the Eastern name for the Eucharistic Prayer) of Addai and Mari,[15] which is used by the Eastern Syrians, and the anaphora, preserved among the Maronites, known as the third anaphora of St. Peter or the *Sharar*.[16] Because it was not written down long ago it is difficult to date, and the original has to be reconstructed on the basis of later manuscripts.[17]

Here are the most important passages of the text as found in the two traditions[18]:

Addai and Mari	Sharar
1. It is right that every mouth should glorify and every tongue give thanks to the adorable and glorious name of the Father, the Son, and the Holy Spirit. He created the world in accordance with his graciousness and their inhabitants in accordance with his kindness. He saved mortals in accordance with his mercy and has shown great grace to us mortals.	Glory to you, adorable and glorious name of the Father and the Son and the Holy Spirit. You create the worlds in your graciousness and their inhabitants in your mercy, and out of graciousness you bring mortals to salvation.

(The *Sanctus* with its introduction)

2. With these heavenly armies we too give you thanks, O Lord, we your weak, frail, and lowly servants, for the great grace which you have given us and for which we can make no return. For you	We give you thanks, O Lord, we your sinful servants, to whom you have given your grace for which we can make no return. For you clothed yourself in our humanity that you might give us life through

---

15. W. F. Macomber, "The Oldest Known Text of the Anaphora of the Apostles Addai and Mari," *OCP* 32 (1966) 335-71 (Syriac text and Latin translation, 358-71). Macomber bases his edition on a tenth-century ms. discovered at Mossoul (the oldest mss. previously known dated from about 1500).

16. *Anaphora sancti Petri Apostoli tertia*, ed. with Latin trans. by J. M. Sauget, in *Anaphorae syriacae* II/3 (Rome: Oriental Institute, 1973) 275-329 (ms. of 1454).

17. See E. C. Ratcliff, "The Original Form of the Anaphora of Addai and Mari," *JTS* 30 (1929) 23-32; B. Botte, "L'Anaphore chaldéenne des Apôtres," *OCP* 15 (1949) 259-76; *idem*, "Problèmes de l'anaphore syrienne des apôtres Addai et Mari," *OS* 10 (1965) 98-106; H. Engberding, "Urgestalt, Eigenart und Entwicklung eines altantiochenischen eucharistischen Hochgebetes," *OC* (3rd series) 7 (1932) 32-48; *idem*, "Zum anaphorischen Fürbittgebet der ostsyrischen Liturgie des Apostel Addaj und Mar(j)," *ibid*. (4th series) 5 (1957) 102-24; T. J. Talley, "De la 'berakah' à l'eucharistie. Une question à réexaminer," *LMD* no. 125 (1976) 7-37 (30-34: "L'Anaphore d'Addai et Mari").

18. The translation of the Anaphora of Addai and Mari is taken, with modifications, from Deiss 160-63.

clothed yourself in our humanity that you might give us life through your divinity. You exalted our lowliness, you raised us up when we had fallen, you brought our mortal nature back to life, you forgave our sins. You justified us when we were sinners, you enlightened our minds. Our Lord and our God, you conquered our enemies, you gave victory to our frail, weak human nature, through the abundant mercies of your grace. For all your helps and graces to us, we offer you praise, honor, gratitude and adoration, now and always and for ever and ever. Amen.

3. O Lord, in accordance with your many mercies which are beyond numbering, remember with kindness all the devout and just fathers who were pleasing to you, as we now commemorate the body and blood of your Christ. We offer him to you upon the pure and holy altar as you taught us. Grant us your tranquillity and peace throughout all the days of this world.

(Intercessions)

4. And we too, Lord, your weak, frail, and lowly servants, who have gathered and are standing before you at this moment, we have received from tradition the rite that has its origin in you. We rejoice and give glory, we exalt and commemorate, we praise and celebrate this great and awesome mys-

your divinity. You exalted our lowliness, you raised us up when we had fallen, you brought our mortal nature back to life, you justified us when we were sinners, you forgave our sins, you enlightened our minds. You conquered our enemies, you gave victory to our frail, weak human nature. For all these graces we offer you praise and veneration in your holy Church, before your forgiving altar, now. . . .

O Lord, in your great mercy remember with kindness all the devout and just Fathers, as we now commemorate your body and blood, which we offer on your pure and holy altar, as you, our Master, taught us.

(Account of institution)

tery of the passion, the death, and
the resurrection of our Lord Jesus
Christ.

(Offering and intercession)

5. May your Holy Spirit come, Lord, may he rest upon this offering of your servants, may he bless and sanctify it, so that it may win for us, Lord, the forgiveness of offenses and the remission of sins, the great hope of resurrection from the dead and eternal life in the kingdom of heaven with all those who have been pleasing to you.

May your living and holy Spirit come, Lord, may he take his place and rest upon this offering of your servants, and may it bring, to those who receive it, the forgiveness of offenses and the remission of sins, the blessed hope of resurrection from the dead and eternal life in the kingdom of heaven for ever.

6. Because of your all-embracing, wonderful plan which you have carried out in our regard, we give you thanks and glorify you ceaselessly in your Church which you have redeemed through the precious blood of your Christ. With loud voices and faces unveiled we present you with praise and honor, gratitude and adoration to your living, holy, and life-giving name, now and always and for ever and ever. Amen.

Because of your glorious plan which you have carried out in our regard, we your sinful servants who have been saved by your victorious blood open our mouths thankfully in your holy Church, at your forgiving altar, and we give you thanks, now . . . .

1. *The Thanksgiving*

The opening dialogue, at least in the very full (and divergent) forms it takes in these two traditions, is certainly not part of the original redaction. The thanksgiving refers to creation and the redemptive work of Christ. The *Sanctus*, with the mention of the angels that introduces it, could be an addition that interrupts the flow of the earlier text. The original text has with some justification been compared to the Jewish formulas of blessing, the influence of which doubtless continued to be felt more strongly in this Semitic environment than elsewhere.

The prayer is initially directed to the divine Name. Probably at a later time, this was further explained by bringing in the Three Persons of the Trinity, but, in an as yet undeveloped theology, the "Name" may have been a way of referring to the Savior himself, especially since in section 2 he is the one addressed. The mention of "the abundant mercies of your grace" leads to a doxology and an Amen, as though to mark the end of a first part that perhaps corresponds to the element of praise in the *Berakoth*, where praise leads over to petition.

What follows is in fact a prayer of petition in which God is asked to remember with kindness the just of earlier times who were the beneficiaries of his marvelous deeds. This petition may have suggested the introduction of further intercessions, for while these intercessions date from very early times, they occur at this point only in the Chaldean anaphora. They probably serve as a transition to the sacramental perspective proper to the Eucharistic action as such.

It is to be noted that from this point (section 3) on the Addai and Mari formulary speaks of Jesus in the third person, whereas the *Sharar* continues to address him throughout, as may well have been the case in the original formulary.

2. *The Problem of the Account of Institution and the Anamnesis*

The point that has chiefly caught the attention of commentators on the Anaphora of Addai and Mari is the absence of the account of institution, although it may not have been missing in the earlier redactions.[19] Section 4, after all, does have the look of being an anamnesis. On the other hand, the connecting link with a mention of the Supper would, then, not be the idea of "remembering," but that of "assembly." As it happens, the Anaphora of Theodore, which is used in most of the Churches that also use the Anaphora of Addai and Mari, draws its inspiration in part from the latter and has an account of institution that ends with the words: "Do this in memory of me each time that you assemble."

The hypothesis that such a text may have existed here in Addai and Mari was established without reference to the *Sharar*. The *Sharar* does in fact have the missing text precisely at this point, but in a form different from the one just described. More importantly, the *Sharar* has no text that is parallel to the section of Addai and Mari that may be regarded as an anamnesis, although this section seems to be very old, since its lack of any sacrificial vocabulary suggests that it was composed prior to later, more developed forms of the anamnesis.

In view of the close connection that generally exists between the commemoration of the Supper and the anamnesis of the mysteries of Christ, it is at least surprising that each of these formularies has either an account of institution or an anamnesis but not both. In the face of these difficul-

---

19. See the argument of B. Botte in the two articles cited in n. 17. On this point, Botte departs from Ratcliff and has not won unanimous acceptance. I accept, however, most of his conclusions, which do not seem to be weakened either by Macomber's later discovery or by the comparison (which Botte does not make) with the *Sharar*.

ties we should bear in mind that the Syriac Eucharistic formulary was transmitted orally before being put in writing and may therefore have been altered. We may note, finally, that the Eucharistic Prayers of St. Peter and Theodore speak of a blessing over the bread and a thanksgiving over the cup, according to a distinction (rare in the liturgy) that is found in Mark and Matthew, although the prayers give no other sign of dependence on the gospels.

3. *The Invocation of the Fruits of the Sacrifice on the Communicants*

The prayer closes (section 5) with a petition in the form of an epiclesis. Some critics have had doubts of its authenticity,[20] but it seems to have indeed been part of the original text. In any case, it was written in Syriac and not translated from Greek, as can be inferred from the parallelism of its structure. Moreover, it is old, since it served as a model for later formularies of the Eastern Syrian tradition. Should we be surprised by the appearance here of the word "offering," which we would have expected to find in the anamnesis? Certainly it is not surprising to find mention of the fruits of the Eucharist, although there is no explicit statement that we receive them through communion. Only indirectly are these fruits presented as the work of the Spirit who is invoked upon the offering.

§5. Conclusion

The Syriac anaphora and the anaphora of Hippolytus, the two oldest that have come down to us, show an undeniable kinship, but also important differences. The latter are doubtless connected with the history of their composition, but they are due above all to the different environments in which these two formularies arose: Rome and the region of Edessa. If we compare the two with one another and with the information already gathered from Jewish tradition and the *Didache*, perhaps we may cautiously advance the following ideas on the origin and early development of the Eucharistic Prayer.

1. The earliest celebrations of the Eucharist must have followed the ritual which Jesus used at the Supper and which contained different "blessings" for the bread and the wine. At a very early date, however, this sche-

---

20. See Ratcliff and Botte. The problem arises from the fact that section 5 seems to be connected with the anamnesis in Addai and Mari. But this does not seem to be a sufficient reason for considering the epiclesis to be an interpolation, especially since the word "plan" is not preceded by a demonstrative pronoun, as was thought before Macomber's manuscript discovery. The end of the text (section 6) may be only preparing the way for the conclusion by summarizing what was said earlier.

ma was replaced by a single prayer based on the long *berakah* over the final cup; this change probably came when the Eucharist ceased to be celebrated within the framework of a meal.

2. By way of the Jewish liturgy for the table, the Eucharistic Prayer thus inherited the bipartite thanksgiving-petition structure that was characteristic of Israelite spirituality. In a second phase, the synagogal assembly and its practices also exercised an influence (this is the origin of the *Sanctus*); this probably happened at the time when Christians ceased to attend the synagogue and had to develop a complete ritual of their own.

3. The term "thanksgiving" became a technical term that incorporated the heritage of the "blessing": grateful praise of God's wonderful deeds; the joy of a creature whose needs are met by the Lord, and who begs him to continue his benefactions. But "eucharist" in turn enriched the ancient "blessing" by adding the christological dimension: it is through Jesus that God performs his wonderful deeds, and it is through him that our adoration rises to the Father.

4. In addition, the "eucharist" turned the "blessing" into an action, namely, the actualization of the Supper, that is, making it present and operative. The account of institution was given an easily memorized form so that it might be proclaimed at the "Lord's Supper." Originally the account may have preceded the thanksgiving; in any case, it soon acquired a place within it, where it is followed by the anamnesis, which expresses the "today" of the mystery being commemorated: the bread and wine become sacraments of the self-offering of the dead and risen Christ.[21]

5. The petition that constitutes the second part of the prayer likewise acquires a sacramental dimension, for the Spirit is asked to come upon the gifts and fill those who receive these in communion. The Church asks that the ritual act may find its completion in the lives of the faithful until the resurrection to which they look forward. The intercessions, like the *Sanctus*, certainly belong to a later stratum.[22]

---

21. See L. Ligier, "De la Cène à l'Anaphore de l'Eglise," *LMD* no. 87 (1966) 7–51, espec. 30–36, and "Les origines de la Prière eucharistique," *QL* 53 (1972) 181–82. According to Ligier, the thanksgiving originally ended with a formula that called for an Amen, not for an account. Then the block consisting of account and anamnesis was introduced at the point where the theme of thanksgiving reappeared. The account was not included for its own sake but in order to introduce the "Do this," that is, to urge the Church to perform the anamnetic action. Gradually, however, the account assumed increasing importance.

22. See p. 103.

' From House to Basilica

§1. Sunday Mass in a Home

Passing reference was made earlier to the liturgy celebrated in Troas in 58 A.D. that was the occasion for the restoration of a young man to life: "On the first day of the week, when we were gathered together to break bread, Paul talked with them, intending to depart on the morrow; and he prolonged his speech until midnight. There were many lights in the upper chamber where we were gathered. . . . And when Paul had gone [back] up [to the upper room] and had broken bread and eaten. . . ."[1]

The setting can be readily imagined: the celebration took place in a private home on the second floor, since it was there that the "living room" was to be found in houses that had one. Was the celebration, then, of a family kind, after the manner of, for example, the Jewish Passover? That is what is suggested by another passage in Acts: "And day by day, attending the temple together and breaking bread in their homes, they partook of food with glad and generous hearts."[2] But this verse comes from a different source that gives a somewhat idealized description of the first community in Jerusalem, and it is difficult to determine its precise historical value. In addition, what happens "in their homes" is here being opposed primarily to what happens "in the temple"; the point may be to highlight the customs specific to Christians who meanwhile continued to attend the temple.

At Troas, in any case, the gathering is of the whole Church: "we were gathered together"; "in the upper chamber where we were gathered," and

---

1. Acts 20:7-8, 11.
2. Acts 2:46.

the general atmosphere is of an assembly that includes more than a single family. The same kind of assembly was to be found in Corinth, according to what Paul says in his letter to the Christians of that city: "When you meet together, it is not the Lord's supper that you eat," or again, "Do you not have houses to eat and drink in?"[3] It is clear from this that those attending were in a place other than their own homes, and almost certainly in the home of one of their number who was able to place a room in his house at the disposal of all.

Was this custom followed for a long time? In 304 some of the faithful were being questioned before the imperial tribunal at Carthage; the proconsul asked one of them: "It was in your house that the gathering was held, contrary to the imperial edict?" "Yes, it was in my house that we celebrated the *Dominicum*"[4] (a term that undoubtedly signifies the Eucharist). But perhaps the situation reflected here may have been an exceptional one, caused by persecution, that "war waged by the demon" in order, among other things, "to destroy the basilicas of the Lord,"[5] as the redactor of the acts of these martyrs puts it. The word "basilica" is still rare at this period, but it seems nonetheless to show that buildings existed in which the faithful were accustomed to assemble. Such buildings are mentioned under other names[6] throughout the third century, but, except for the final years of the century, neither written documents nor archaeological finds allow us to say that the buildings were constructed specifically for this purpose and in accordance with a suitable plan.

We know, on the other hand, that communities sufficiently well off would acquire an ordinary house and adapt it to their needs. Thus in Rome Christians contracted with an innkeeper to buy a house that was in the public domain, and Emperor Alexander Severus (222–65) gave them preference on the grounds that a place of worship was preferable to a bar.[7] At Dura-Europos on the Euphrates archaeologists have discovered traces, prior to 256, of a dwelling that did not differ in structure from nearby houses, but in which a large room served for assembly and a small one had been made over into a baptistery[8]; frescoes show the liturgical use

---

3. 1 Cor 11:20-22.

4. T. Ruinart, *Acta sanctorum Saturnini, Dativi et aliorum plurimorum martyrum in Africa* (2nd ed.; Amsterdam, 1713), 387. These martyrs were from Abitina, a town near Membressa (the modern Madjez-el-Bab) in Tunisia.

5. *Ibid.* 482: "ut . . . basilicas dominicas subverteret."

6. "Houses of prayer" or "houses of God" (terms not specifically Christian), or "houses of the Church" or "churches."

7. Lampridus, *Vita Alexandri Severi* 6, in *Scriptores historiae Augustae* 49, ed. E. Hohl (Leipzig: Teubner, 1965), 290.

8. See M. J. Rostovtzeff *et al.*, *The Excavations at Dura-Europos, Conducted by Yale University and the French Academy of Inscriptions and Letters* VII–VIII (New Haven: Yale University Press, 1934).

made of these rooms. *The Teaching of the Apostles*, which dates probably from the first half of the third century, describes one such locale in full operation: the place for the bishop and priests in the eastern section; the seating for the laity, men and women; the role of the deacons; etc.[9]

Not all the local Churches, however, had the means to acquire such a building for themselves, and many were doubtless satisfied for a long time to meet in the home of one of their members, as they had done in olden days.

§2. Mass in Cemeteries

The popular mind is convinced that in time of persecution the faithful used to gather in the catacombs to celebrate secretly. But catacombs were ill-suited for such a purpose: they were known to everyone, and in most of them Christians were interred side by side with pagans. Moreover, in the middle of the third century the galleries dug by the Church for the burial of its members were narrow aisles leading off in rough fashion from a family area.

It is true that, according to a letter of St. Cyprian,[10] Pope Sixtus II was "put to death in a cemetery, on August 6" of 258, probably while he was presiding at the liturgy. But this must have occurred above ground. After all, the Christian community of the Eternal City had about twenty-five thousand members at that time and, even if all did not attend, it is impossible to conceive of the Eucharist, which was still the action of an assembly, being celebrated in a tiny underground room.[11] The pseudo-historical version of the catacombs that has been popularized by modern novels and films must therefore be regarded as a simple fiction.

This much is true: Christians sometimes celebrated in cemeteries, and the celebration was part of a cult of the dead. They had maintained the custom, widespread in Roman society, of coming to the tombs of their fellows on the anniversary of their deaths and celebrating a funeral banquet there. But for Christians this ritual had been expanded beyond the family group, and the sacrament had been substituted for a simple meal. *The Teaching of the Apostles* speaks of these gatherings in cemeteries, where Christians offered to God "an acceptable Eucharist."[12]

---

9. *Didascalia Apostolorum*, ed. F. X. Funk, *Didascalia et Constitutiones Apostolorum* I (Paderborn: Schöningh, 1905; repr., Turin: Bottega d'Erasmo, 1964), 158–66; trans. R. H. Connolly, *Didascalia Apostolorum* (Oxford: Clarendon Press, 1929), 119–24.

10. St. Cyprian, *Ep.* 39, 4; ed. L. Bayard (Paris: Les Belles Lettres, 1945), 1:99; *Ep.* 38, 2 (Bayard 1:96).

11. E. Josi, "Cimiteri cristiani antichi," *Enciclopedia cattolica* 3 (Vatican City, 1949) 1622.

12. *Didascalia Apostolorum* (Funk 276; Connolly 252).

It was probably in this way that Mass came to be offered on other days than Sunday, since the *dies natalis* ("birthday," i.e., into heaven) of the brethren who had fallen asleep in the Lord could, of course, fall on a weekday.

§3. The "House of the People of God"

BIBLIOGRAPHY

Atti del IX Congresso internazionale di archeologia cristiana, Roma 21–27 settembre 1975. I. *I monumenti cristiani precostantiniani* (Studi di antichità cristiana 32; Vatican City, 1978), especially 491–537 (papers of B. M. Apollonj Ghetti and N. Duval).

The Lord's Day continued, nonetheless, to be the principal day of assembly, and *The Teaching of the Apostles* orders the bishop to take great pains with the Sunday Eucharist, since it is a sign of the Church. The welcome shown to strangers at this Eucharist is no little part of the sign: once those who come from other parts have shown that they are truly believers, they must be made to feel at home, be they laity, priests, or bishops. A bishop is to be invited by his local colleague to preach to the people and to preside at the celebration or at least to pronounce the thanksgiving over the chalice. A special welcome is to be given to the poor, even if the bishop has to surrender his own chair and sit on the floor! The way of putting it may be exaggerated, but clearly one function of the assembly was to challenge the divisions that run through human society.[13]

This same outlook was operative in the choice of a model for Christian churches when, at the end of the third century, architects had to provide buildings constructed expressly as places of assembly. Temples, the dwellings of the gods, could not provide a model, since the main part, the room where the statue or symbols of the divinity were kept, was a small place, even though it might be surrounded by open spaces and colonnades. What was needed was "houses of the people," inasmuch as the people were the real dwelling of the Lord, a dwelling made of living stones.

Architects turned therefore to the basilicas, which were public buildings (therefore the adjective "imperial" that often accompanied "basilica") and served for the administration of justice, political meetings, and indeed all the other interactions of social life. Basilicas were rectangular in shape and divided into three or even five naves by two or four rows of columns; the framework of the roof was exposed. At one end, often at the bottom of an apse, was the seat of the judge or presiding officer. Such

---

13. *Ibid.* (Funk 170–72; Connolly 122–24).

a building could be easily adapted to liturgical use. The place of the bishop and his presbytery was, of course, already indicated; all that was needed further was an ambo for reading and a table, which could be movable, both of them facing the area in which the people were assembled. Once the Peace of Constantine was established, basilicas multiplied, their arrangement varying from country to country and especially from East to West.[14]

---

14. See J. Wagner, "Le lieu de la célébration eucharistique en Occident," *LMD* no. 70 (1962) 32–48; A. Raes, "La liturgie eucharistique en Orient: Son cadre architectural," *ibid.*, 49–66; P. Jounel, "L'assemblée chrétienne et les lieux du rassemblement humain au cours du premier millénaire," *LMD* no. 136 (1978) 13–37.

THE CREATION OF FORMULARIES AND THE ORGANIZATION OF RITES FROM THE FOURTH TO ABOUT THE EIGHTH CENTURY

Introduction

The liturgy of the Mass had to be adapted to the far larger buildings in which it was now being celebrated or, more accurately, to the ever larger assemblies that the end of persecution made possible. The essential gestures of the Eucharist were now orchestrated into a collection of rites that were intended to highlight them and bring out their meaning. The celebration became increasingly full, deriving its modes of expression from the customs of secular society, even as the bishops became officials of the Constantinian state and, like the priests of ancient paganism, received the same honors as magistrates.

These developments inevitably took different forms, however, depending on the culture peculiar to each region of the empire or to the Eastern countries that were not under Roman control. The great liturgical families thus came into existence, each accentuating a particular aspect of the ancient Eucharist, without, however, denying the heritage of the first centuries, which continued to ensure a basic unity among these families.

At the same time, the prayers handed down in oral tradition were put into writing and began to circulate from one community to another. As a result, local councils felt a legitimate need to be on guard. The Council of Hippo in 393, for example, ordained that "if any one copies for himself a model from some outside source, he is not to use it before submitting it to more learned brethren."[1] Bishops sometimes composed or revised formularies for use in their own Church; once written down, these began to circulate in booklets or *libelli*. The time came when these scattered notes were gathered into collections.

---

1. Council of Hippo, October 8, 393, canon 21b, in *Breviarium Hipponense*, ed. C. Munier in *Concilia Africae* (CCL 149; Turnhout: Brepols, 1974), 39. See E. J. Kilmartin, "Early African Legislation Concerning Liturgical Prayer" *EL* 99 (1985), 105–27.

§1. Sacramentaries and *Ordines*

BIBLIOGRAPHY

Principal documents

a) *Roman*

Sacramentarium Veronense (Cod. Bibl. Capit. Veron. LXXXV [80]), ed. L. C. Mohlberg, L. Eizenhöfer, and P. Siffrin (REDFM 1; Rome: Herder, 1956; repr. 1966, 1978).

Liber sacramentorum Romanae Aeclesiae ordinis anni circuli (Sacramentarium Gelasianum), ed. L. C. Mohlberg, L. Eizenhöfer, and P. Siffrin (REDFM 4; Rome: Herder, 1960).

Sacramentaire grégorien, ed. J. Deshusses (3 vols.; Spicilegium Friburgense 16, 24, 28; Fribourg: Editions Universitaires, 1971, 1978,² 1982).

Ordines Romani, Andrieu, *OR I.*

b) *Gallican*

Missale Gallicanum vetus (with Mone's seven Masses), ed. L. C. Mohlberg (REDFM 3; Rome: Herder, 1958).

Missale Gothicum, ed. L. C. Mohlberg (REDFM 5; Rome: Herder, 1961).

Missale Francorum, ed. L. C. Mohlberg (REDFM 2; Rome: Herder, 1957).

c) *Spanish*

Liber ordinum, ed. M. Férotin (Monumenta ecclesiae liturgica 5; Paris: Didot, 1904).

Liber mozarabicus sacramentorum, ed. M. Férotin (Monumenta ecclesiae liturgica 6; Paris: Didot, 1912).

Oracional visigótico, ed. J. Vives (Monumenta Hispaniae sacra, Series liturg. 1; Barcelona: Consejo superior de investigaciones cientificas, 1946).

Studies

E. Bourque, *Etude sur les sacramentaires romains* 1 (Studi di antichità cristiana 20; Vatican City, 1949); 2 (Quebec: Presses universitaires Laval, 1952); 3 (Studi di antichità cristiana 25; Vatican City, 1960).

A. Chavasse, *Le sacramentaire gélasien (Vat. Regin. 316)* (Bibliothèque de théologie IV/1; Tournai: Desclée, 1958).

J. Deshusses, "Les sacramentaires. Etat actuel de la recherche," *ALW* 24 (1982) 19–46.

The liturgical books containing the presidential prayers of the liturgy are known in the West as "sacramentaries," while in the East they are usually called "euchologies" *(euchologia).*² In the Latin tradition the formularies used are variable; the collections are therefore especially important.

2. *Euchologium Serapionis,* ed. F. X. Funk in his *Didascalia et Constitutiones Apostolorum* II (Paderborn: Schöningh, 1905), 158–95. See A. Strittmatter, "The 'Barberinum S. Marci' of Jacques Goar," *EL* 47 (1933) [329]–[367]; A. Jacob, "Les Euchologes du fonds Barberini de la Bibliothèque Vaticane," *Didaskalia* 4 (1974) 131–210.

The oldest Roman collection that has come down to us is the one erroneously called the "Leonine" Sacramentary. It is in fact a simple collection of booklets (*libelli*)[3] that someone gathered together in order to preserve and make use of them. No attempt was made, however, to organize them; thus there are several Masses for the same day, while nothing has been done to fill in gaps. The book represented a first and inevitably unsatisfactory stage. The passage of time brought books that followed the order of the liturgical year and aimed at providing a formulary for each celebration in the calendar. Two traditions became apparent: the "Gregorian" Sacramentary for functions at which the pope presided, and the "Gelasian" for use in churches in which the celebrant was a priest.[4]

The other Western Churches developed similar books. Those that have come down to us from Spain and Milan are of a later date, but they contain items that go back to an early period; the Gallican collections are known to us only in a form already contaminated by borrowings from the liturgy of the Eternal City. Such collections enable us, nonetheless, to see the riches peculiar to these venerable traditions in which Christian prayer found expression in the framework of a different culture and mentality.

The *Ordines* made their appearance at a later date. These are guides that describe the ceremonies in detail and were meant for the use of those not familiar with Roman customs when the latter were exported.[5] *Ordo* I, in the form we now have it, is a copy of an original that came from Rome, and was made (probably with some alterations) in the lands of Pepin the Short. *Ordo* III is a collection of notes or postscripts that were meant as a complement to *Ordo* I; the first two notes were certainly written at Rome, while the others are from a milieu in which people were familiar with Gallican usages.

At the end of the period that we are considering here, another type of work made its appearance and became extremely popular during the centuries that followed. I refer to the more or less allegorical explanations of the Mass rites; these also provide us with valuable information. In addition to the older writings of Pseudo-Dionysius, I may mention the *Ex-*

---

3. The "Leonine Sacramentary" or Sacramentary of Verona was discovered in an eighth-century ms. preserved in the city of Verona (Cod. Bibl. Cap. Veron. LXXXV [80]). The formularies date from the time of Gelasius (492–96) down to that of Vigilius (537–55); some may be even older.

4. See *The Church at Prayer* I.

5. The collection of *Ordines Romani* was published by J. Mabillon, *Musei Italici tomus II, complectens antiquos libros rituales sanctae Romanae ecclesiae, cum commentario praevio in Ordinem Romanum* (Paris: Apud viduam E. Martin, 1689 = PL 78:851ff.). M. Andrieu has provided a modern critical edition. A few of the oldest *Ordines* are authentically Roman. For the Mass: *OR* 1 and 3 = Andrieu, *OR* 2:65–108 and 129–33.

planation of the Ancient Gallican Liturgy, wrongly attributed to Bishop
Germanus of Paris, and, for the Byzantine East, the commentary of St.
Germanus of Constantinople.[6]

The liturgical books were organized only in stages, and it was not until the seventh and eighth centuries that the work begun in the fourth was
completed. This is the period we shall now study in order to see how the
liturgy of the Mass developed. We must bear in mind, however, that the
celebration of the liturgy is the action of a living people and that written
formularies and notes by rubricists can never convey a complete picture
of it.

§2. The Participation of the People

BIBLIOGRAPHY

R. Hierzegger, "Collecta und Statio: Stationsprozessionen im frühen Mittelalter,"
ZKT 60 (1936) 511–54.

The active participation of the Christian people in their assemblies or
"synaxes" had a profound influence on the life of the Church in the age
of Constantine, and it continued to be important in the centuries that followed, even though certain functions were gradually taken over by more
experienced groups, such as choirs (scholae cantorum). Popular participation sometimes took exuberant forms, so much so that in their homilies the Fathers, notably St. John Chrysostom, had to recall their
congregations to order and discipline in the course of the celebration.

The testimonies to this liturgical vitality are so numerous that it is impossible to give a satisfactory overview of them. I shall simply mention
here the prayer of the Jerusalem community, which Egeria so admiringly
describes in the travel diary she wrote at the end of the fourth or beginning of the fifth century.[7]

Here we see the people hastening to churches brightly lit each morning and evening by numerous lamps and candles. Monks and consecrated
virgins have already come to sing hymns, antiphons, and psalms. We see
the ministers and all the clergy from the basilicas escorting the bishop as
he enters to celebrate the sacred mysteries. We hear the children loudly
repeating the Kyrie eleison and the readers proclaiming Scripture passages

---

6. Pseudo-Dionysius, Hierarchia ecclesiastica 3 (PG 3:424–45); Ps-Germanus, see n.
16, p. 56; St. Germanus of Constantinople, ed. N. Borgia, Il commentario liturgico di
S. Germano patriarca costantinopolitano e la versione latina di Anastasio Bibliotecario
(Grottaferrata, 1912).

7. Itinerarium Egeriae 24–49, ed. A. Franceschini and R. Weber (CCL 175; Turnhout:
Brepols, 1965). 67–90; trans. J. Wilkinson, Egeria's Travels (London: SPCK, 1971), 123–47.

that are always adapted to the day and place. We hear the cries, groans, and weeping of the participants as the story of the Lord's passion and resurrection is read. We hear the bishop preaching his homily in Greek while, as he goes along, a priest translates it into Syriac, and brothers and sisters in the congregation explain it in Latin to those who speak only this language. We see the people pressing forward for Communion. We listen to the exhortations of the deacons as they direct the prayer of the people or bid them bow for the president's blessing or dismiss them while reminding them to come to the next assembly. With men and women of every age and condition we take part in the procession that moves from one of the holy places to the church where the Eucharist will be celebrated; if the way is long, it advances at an easy pace so that the crowd will not become fatigued. Egeria doubtless shows us a privileged instance, since Jerusalem is a pilgrimage city; nonetheless, we find a similar participation, with minor differences, at Antioch, Hippo, or Arles.

Comparable participation at Rome is seen in the "stational" Mass of the bishop. In this context the word *statio*[8] signifies an assembly convoked in advance for a specified day and in a specified building. The entire clergy of the city accompanies their bishop, and the faithful from the various parts of the city are represented in greater or lesser degree. The oldest and most important stations were at the Lateran, but many urban or cemetery basilicas took turns in welcoming this pilgrimage of the local Church, a phenomenon that was henceforth linked to the course of the liturgical year.[9]

This is the assembly for which the simple yet imposing ceremonial of *Ordo* I was intended. The pope presides over his people who have gathered for the Eucharist; he has his presbytery around him and is assisted by deacons and many ministers; dignitaries of the papal court are present. The "stational" Mass is, as it were, the model of all liturgies; after many centuries it has been restored to its rightful place by the Second Vatican Council: ". . . the preeminent manifestation of the Church is present in the full, active participation of all God's holy people in these liturgical celebrations, especially in the same Eucharist, in a single prayer, at one altar at

---

8. The word *statio* was used by Christians from the second century on to signify a public fast. But St. Cyprian already uses it for community assemblies that are not necessarily liturgical (see *Ep.* 44, 2, Bayard 2:111, see 113. See also the *libellus*, or pamphlet, published by the enemies of Pope Damasus, PL 13:81 and 83). This use of *statio* is close to the meaning of the word in secular classical Latin.

9. The Lectionary of Würzburg (seventh century) contains the oldest known list of stations; see G. Morin, "Liturgie et basiliques de Rome au milieu du VIIe siècle," *RBén* 28 (1911) 296–330. On some days, especially in Lent, the clergy and people went in procession to the stational basilica from another church where they had gathered; the gathering was called the *collecta*.

which the bishop presides, surrounded by his college of priests and by his ministers."[10]

---

10. *VSC* 41 (*DOL* 1 no. 41).

Chapter I

The Entrance Rites

BIBLIOGRAPHY

J. A. Jungmann, *The Mass of the Roman Rite* 1:261–390.
P. E. Gemayel, *Avant-messe maronite. Histoire et structure* (OCA 174; Rome: Oriental Institute, 1965).

St. Justin's description of Sunday Mass in the mid-second century begins with the readings. There is no entrance rite apart from the assembling of the faithful, the importance of which is emphasized.[1]

§1. The Entrance of the President and His Greeting of the Congregation

BIBLIOGRAPHY

W. C. Van Unnik, *"Dominus vobiscum*. The Background of a Liturgical Formula," in *Studies in Memory of T. W. Manson* (Manchester: Manchester University Press, 1959), 270–305.
B. Eager, "The Lord Is With You," *Scripture* 12 (1960) 48–54.
H. Ashworth, *"Et cum spiritu tuo.* An Inquiry into Its Origin and Meaning," *Clergy Review* 51 (1966) 122–30.
M. Theurer, *"Et cum spiritu tuo.* Zur biblischen und liturgischen Bedeutung des Ausdrucks," *Theologie der Gegenwart* 8–9 (1965–66) 104–5.
J. Lécuyer, " 'Et avec ton esprit,' " in *Mens concordet voci. Mélanges liturgiques offerts à Mgr Martimort* 2 (Paris: Desclée, 1983).

I. THE CELEBRANT'S ENTRANCE AND VENERATION OF THE ALTAR

The first entrance rite to make its appearance (probably during the fourth century) was the actual entrance of the celebrant into the basilica.

---

1. See p. 14.

At a very early date this took the form of a solemn procession. Later developments in the Roman liturgy had ministers carrying a thurible and the lights to be placed around the table of sacrifice.

The oldest documents do not expressly mention a veneration of the altar, even though, from the time of St. Ambrose on, the altar was regarded as a symbol of Christ. According to *Ordo* I the bishop venerates the altar by kissing it, after having first knelt at a prie-dieu (*oratorium*) and recollected himself for a few moments.

In the Roman liturgy of the seventh and eighth centuries, the entrance of the president was preceded by the entrance and enthronement of the gospel; the pope greeted not only the altar, but the book that had been placed upon it. But this double entrance was not kept; eventually the gospel was carried in by a deacon in the procession of ministers. In most of the Eastern rites, and especially among the Byzantines, the homage paid to the Word of God has overshadowed the entrance of the priest into the sanctuary; in the "Little Entrance," the "Wisdom" of God, who comes to instruct his people, is carried in and presented to the congregation.

II. THE PRESIDENT'S GREETING
AND THE CONGREGATION'S RESPONSE

The first words of the presiding celebrant are the greeting he gives to the congregation on turning around to face it.

Writing in 426 about a miraculous cure that had been effected just before the beginning of Mass one Easter day, St. Augustine has this to say: "I advanced toward the people. The church was full, and cries of joy echoed through it: 'Glory to God!' 'God be praised!' No one was silent, the shouts were coming from everywhere. I greeted the people and they began to cry out again in their enthusiasm. Finally, when silence was restored, the readings from sacred scripture were proclaimed."[2]

It is clear that there was no entrance song and that the Liturgy of the Word began immediately after the greeting. Elsewhere Chrysostom complains of the noise that fills the church when "the president prays for peace, like a man entering his paternal home."[3]

"Peace to you" (or "to all") was the formula used in Antioch and Constantinople. In the West and in Egypt "The Lord be with you" was also used. The response everywhere was "And to (or: with) your spirit." The

---

2. St. Augustine, *De civ. Dei* XXII, 8, 22, ed. B. Dombart and A. Kalb (CCL 48; Turnhout: Brepols, 1955), 826. See St. John Chrysostom, *In Mat. Hom.* 12, 6 (PG 50:384-85): "The church is a house belonging to all. Once you have entered in before us, we too enter . . . and when I say, 'Peace to all,' you answer, 'And with your spirit.' "

3. St. John Chrysostom, *In Ep. I ad Cor. hom.* 36, 5 (PG 61:313).

response, like the celebrant's greeting, was of Semitic origin, and we would expect it to have been translated into Latin and Greek with a simple "And to (with) you." That is not what happened, and the reason is to be found in the commentaries of the Fathers: "He gives the name 'spirit' not to the soul of the priest but to the Spirit he has received through the laying on of hands."[4]

The assembly, then, has a celebrant who presides in the name of the Lord; it comes into being in response to a call from God; it is the image of a Church of which Christ, here symbolized by his minister, is the head.

§2. Development of the Entrance Rites in the Roman Liturgy

I. THE ENTRANCE SONG

BIBLIOGRAPHY

P. Wagner, *Origines et développement du chant liturgique* (Paris: Desclée, 1904), 68–78.

R. J. Hesbert, *Antiphonale missarum sextuplex* (Brussels: Vromant, 1935).

C. Callewaert, *"Introitus,"* EL 52 (1938) 484–89.

J. Froger, *"Le chant de l'introit,"* EL 62 (1948) 248–55.

According to *Ordo* I,[5] which dates from the eighth century or perhaps the end of the seventh, the entrance antiphon (*antiphona ad introitum*) was functional; that is, it began when the ministers began their entrance, and it ended when the procession was complete. The antiphon was accompanied by a psalm with as many verses as were required; later on the material of the song was reduced, probably because the more solemn melodies used for the antiphon itself became longer, while at the same time the clergy reached the altar more quickly. Singing was in use before the middle of the sixth century, since it was then that the notice (lacking in any historical value), which the *Liber Pontificalis* attributes to Pope Celestine I († 432), was composed.[6]

In the Roman chant books the texts chosen for the Introit set the tone for the celebration by conveying the spirit of the feast or liturgical season. The custom of naming a Mass from its first words had more than merely practical value. Thus the very first text in these books, the *Ad te levavi* ("To you I lift up . . .") of the first Sunday of Advent, immedi-

---

4. Narsai of Nisibis, *Hom.* 17, ed. R. H. Connolly, *The Liturgical Homilies of Narsai* (TS 8/1; Cambridge: Cambridge University Press, 1909), 8.

5. *OR* I, 44–49 (Andrieu, *OR* 2:81–83).

6. *LP* 1:89.

ately established the atmosphere of serene confidence that characterizes the preparation for Christmas; by means of words that the melody caused to become imbedded in the memory, the prayer of the congregation was brought into harmony with that of the Church as it awaits the Lord's return. "No one who waits for you shall be put to shame" (Ps 25:3). On days that did not have so marked a tone of their own, as, for example, the ordinary Sundays of the year, the chants took advantage of the various moods of the psalter in order that Christians might steep themselves in the praise and supplication of God's people.

II. THE ORATION OR COLLECT

BIBLIOGRAPHY

M. Cappuyns, "La portée religieuse des collectes," *SL* 6 (1928) 93–103.
B. Capelle, *"Collecta,"* RBen 42 (1930) 197–204 (= *Travaux liturgiques* 2:192–99).
P. Bruylants, *Les oraisons du missel romain. Texte et histoire* (2 vols.; Etudes liturgiques 1; Louvain: Mont César, 1952).
K. Gamber, *"Oratio ad collectam.* Ein Beitrag zur römischen Stationsliturgie," *EL* 82 (1968) 45–47.
A. Dumas, "Les sources du nouveau missel romain," *Notitiae* 7 (1971) 37–42, 74–77, 94–95, 134–36, 276–80, 409–10.

The prayer known as the oration or collect was the second essential component of the entrance rites; it came after the *Kyrie* and *Gloria* and marked the end of this section. In it the president drew the people after him as he turned to God and addressed him; if the president is the sign of Christ's presence in the assembly, it is in order that through him Christ may lead them to the Father.

The Roman orations, the formularies of which are both compact and concise, perhaps first made their appearance in the type known as *Orationes solemnes* ("solemn prayers"),[7] but they are also found at numerous points in the liturgy, as seen in the embryonic sacramentaries that go back to the end of the fifth century.

Like the comparable prayers in the General Intercessions or prayer of the faithful, the orations display a four-phase movement:

1. *Oremus* ("Let us pray"): the president urges the congregation to pray.

2. A period of silence for the private prayer of the participants.

3. The priest, acting in the name of the people, addresses the Father by recalling his attributes or great deeds (*Deus qui*, "God, who . . .") and presents a specific request (*praesta quaesumus*, "grant, we beseech

---

7. See p. 72.

you") that gathers up, as it were, all the petitions that the faithful have expressed privately. This accounts for the name "collect," which, however, was not yet used at Rome in this sense.[8] The prayer ends with a Trinitarian formula that expresses, in a remarkably balanced way, both the equality of the Persons and the way in which each of them is approached in Christian experience.

4. *Amen.* By this response the members of the congregation unite their private prayers to those of everyone else, to that of the Church as it finds expression through the minister, and to that of Christ himself who is invoked as mediator (*per Jesum Christum,* "through Jesus Christ . . .").

III. THE *KYRIE ELEISON*

BIBLIOGRAPHY

E. Bishop, "*Kyrie eleison,*" in his *Liturgica Historica* (Oxford: Clarendon Press, 1918), 116–36.

B. Capelle, "Le Kyrie de la messe et le pape Gélase," *RBén* 46 (1934) 126–44 (= *Travaux liturgiques* 2:116–34).

_____, "Le pape Gélase et la messe romaine," *RHE* 35 (1939) 22–34 (= *Travaux liturgiques* 2:135–45).

C. Callewaert, "Les étapes de l'histoire du Kyrie," *RHE* 38 (1942) 20–45.

B. Capelle, "L'oeuvre liturgique de saint Gélase," *JTS* 52 (new ser., 2) (1951) 129–44 (= *Travaux liturgiques* 2:146–60).

P. Borella, "Kyrie eleison e prece litanica nel rito ambrosiano," *Jucunda laudatio* 2 (1964) 66–79.

There is disagreement on the origin of the *Kyrie* in the Roman Mass; I shall come back to the point in discussing the General Intercessions.[9] *Christe eleison*(s) were sung as well as *Kyrie eleison*(s). Their number was not yet fixed in *Ordo* I but was left to the discretion of the celebrant (*annuat quando vult mutare numerum laetaniae,* "let him nod when he wants to change the number of the litanic invocations"). Shortly after, however, before the end of the eighth century, the number was fixed at three *Kyrie*(s)

---

8. See n. 9, p. 47. — The term *collectio* is of Gallican origin. In the Verona Sacramentary some Masses have but a single prayer (oration) before the prayer over the gifts, while others have two; the Masses attributed to Gelasius are of both kinds. Two orations are also found in most of the formularies in the Gelasian Sacramentary. Scholars have asked whether the second oration may not represent a conclusion for the General Intercessions. See B. Capelle, "Messes du pape S. Gélase dans le Sacramentaire de Vérone," in his *Travaux liturgiques* 2:70–105, and "L'oeuvre liturgique de saint Gélase," *ibid.* 146–60; A. Chavasse, "L'oratio 'super sindonem' dans la liturgie romaine," *RBén* 70 (1960) 313–23.

9. See p. 73.

and three *Christe*(s).[10] This number then gave rise to the Trinitarian interpretation, which is evidently not primitive.

In Eastern usage, since ancient times, the words are repeated over and over, and the plea is addressed to Christ, a practice justified by New Testament theology. In the Septuagint *Kyrios* was chosen as the Greek translation for the ineffable name of God. Christian faith then applied the name to Jesus (see Rom 10:9), because after his obedience unto death on the cross he was proclaimed "Lord to the glory of God the Father" (Phil 2:9-11).

IV. THE *GLORIA IN EXCELSIS DEO*

BIBLIOGRAPHY

    P. Maranget, "Le Gloria in excelsis," *SL* 6 (1927) 81-91.
    B. Capelle, "Le texte du Gloria in excelsis Deo," *RHE* 44 (1949) 439-57 (= *Travaux liturgiques* 2:176-91).

This is one of those nonbiblical "psalms" (*psalmoi idiotikoi*) that can be traced back to the primitive Church and that were composed on the model of the New Testament hymns. After being used initially as a morning prayer,[11] it was introduced into the Roman Mass for Christmas at the beginning of the sixth century,[12] then into Masses for Sundays and the feasts of martyrs if a bishop was presiding,[13] and finally into these Masses no matter who the celebrant was (in accordance with a tendency that manifested itself in Frankish territory from the eighth century on[14]).

The singing of the *Gloria* remained the mark of a more solemn celebration. It is a hymn of praise to the Father, in which he is thanked for his glory, and his peace is proclaimed to human beings, who are the object of his good will. The hymn also contemplates the Son as he sits at the Father's right hand. The Spirit is simply mentioned at the end, but his presence is manifest in the scriptural inspiration of the hymn as a whole.

---

    10. *OR* I, 52 and *OR* IV, 40 (Andrieu, *OR* 2:84 and 159).
    11. See *The Church at Prayer* IV, pp. 212, 235, and 241.
    12. *LP* 1:253 (and see 99, n. 36).
    13. But priests were allowed to use it at the Easter Vigil and at their installation after ordination: *OR* XXXIX, 27 (Andrieu, *OR* 4:285), and *Gr*, no. 2.
    14. *OR* XV, 124 (Andrieu, *OR* 3:121).

§3. Development of the Entrance Rites in the Other Western Liturgies

I. THE AMBROSIAN LITURGY

BIBLIOGRAPHY

P. Borella, "L'ingressa della messa ambrosiana," *Ambrosius* 24 (1948) 83–90.

_____, *Il rito ambrosiano* (Biblioteca di scienze religiose III/10; Brescia: Morcelliana, 1964), 141–54.

The rites in use at Milan during this period have had to be reconstructed from later documents. The entrance song was called *Ingressa* and was in the form of an antiphon unaccompanied by a psalm. The *Gloria* preceded a triple *Kyrie* (without any *Christe*), the two chants forming a single whole from the standpoint of melody; on the Sundays of Lent the combination was replaced by a diaconal litany for which two formularies were employed alternately.[15] An *Oratio super populum* ("prayer over the people") concluded the rites; the name suggests that it was a kind of blessing of the congregation. It was not preceded by an *Oremus*. The *Dominus vobiscum* that comes immediately before it had originally the same function as the president's greeting to the congregation in the Roman liturgy; it was pushed back to this point as the introduction to the celebration became more extensive.

II. THE LITURGIES OF GAUL AND SPAIN

BIBLIOGRAPHY

A. Wilmart, "Germain de Paris (Lettres attribuées à)," *DACL* 6/2 (1924) 1049–1102.

E. Griffe, "Aux origines de la liturgie gallicane," *Bulletin de littérature ecclésiastique* 52 (1951) 17–43.

A. M. Franquesa, "Die mozarabische Messe," *Liturgie und Mönchtum* 26 (1960) 58–70.

L. Brou, "Etudes sur la liturgie mozarabe. Le Trisagion de la messe d'après les sources manuscrits," *EL* 61 (1947) 305–33.

E. Griffe, *La Gaule chrétienne à l'époque romaine* 3 (Paris: Letouzey et Ané, 1965), 165–68.

The beginning of the Mass was for a long time characterized by great restraint; only at the end of the sixth century did the entrance rites begin to expand. According to the *Explanation of the Ancient Gallican Liturgy* (*Expositio antiquae liturgiae gallicanae*), which was wrongly attributed to St. Germain of Paris († 576), and which in all probability did not pre-

---

15. *Divinae pacis* and *Dicamus omnes*. See p. 73.

date the seventh century,[16] the Mass began with an *Antiphona ad prae-legendum* ("antiphon to be said at the beginning"), an entrance song that was still unknown to Gregory of Tours and Caesarius of Arles; we do not know what structure it had in Gaul. In tenth-century Spain it included a wordy biblical antiphon, a psalmic verse, and the repetition of part of the biblical antiphon.[17]

Then, after the deacon had called for silence, the president greeted the assembly: *"Dominus sit semper vobiscum"* ("The Lord be with you always"). Then the *Aius* ("Holy"), which is attested for feast days in the Spanish liturgy, rang out; this was the *Trisagion* of the Eastern Church, sung here in Greek and Latin and followed by an *Amen*.[18] Next, three young children sang the *Kyrie* three times in unison.

In Gaul, the "prophecy," that is, the Canticle of Zechariah (Luke 1:68-79), was then intoned; it was sung by two alternating choirs. It is perhaps the oldest element in this set of rites, being already mentioned by Gregory of Tours.[19] It was followed by a *Collectio post prophetiam* ("Collect after the prophecy"); the formularies for this prayer have been preserved in the liturgical books; it seems to have had a baptismal signification. In Spain the *Benedictus* was sung only on June 24; on Sundays and feast days (except in Advent and Lent) the *Gloria in excelsis* was sung at this point and was likewise followed by a prayer; we have, however, only late witnesses to this practice.

§4. Development of the Entrance Rites in the Eastern Liturgies

BIBLIOGRAPHY

J. M. Hanssens, *Institutiones liturgicae de ritibus orientalibus* 3 (Rome: Gregorian University, 1930), 1–156.

A. Raes, *Introductio in liturgiam orientalem* (Rome: Oriental Institute, 1947), 62–75.

---

16. Pseudo-Germanus, *Expositio antiquae liturgiae gallicanae* I, 1, ed. E. C. Ratcliff (HBS 98; London: Henry Bradshaw Society, 1971), 3–5. See A. Wilmart, "Germain de Paris (Lettres attribuées à)," *DACL* 6/2 (1924) 1049–1102, and R. Cabié, "Les lettres attribuées à saint Germain de Paris et les origines de la liturgie gallicane," *Bulletin de littérature ecclésiastique* 73 (1972) 183–92 (= *Mélanges . . . offerts à Mgr Griffe*).

17. See the Antiphonary of León. The sixteenth-century Mozarabic liturgy changed the name to *Officium*.

18. The *Aius* did not yet exist at the beginning of the sixth century. Otherwise, Avitus of Vienne, who speaks of it being Eastern, would have mentioned it; see his *Ep. 3 ad Gondebaldum regem* (PL 59:210–12).

19. Gregory of Tours, *Historia Francorum* VIII, 7, ed. H. Omont and G. Collon (Paris: Picard, 1913), 305.

The introductory rites of the Mass underwent their first development in the sixth and seventh centuries. I must restrict myself here to essentials.

I. THE TRISAGION AND THE TROPARION *HO MONOGENĒS*

This is doubtless the oldest element in the opening part of the liturgy: *Hagios ho Theos, hagios ischyros, hagios athanatos, eleison hēmas* ("Holy God, holy strong One, holy immortal One, have mercy on us"). In the first years of the sixth century Avitus of Vienne mentions this Eastern custom *inter missarum initia* ("among the opening rites of the Mass").[20] He even cites the expanded text with the phrase *ho staurōtheis di'hēmas* ("who were crucified for us"), which caused such an uproar among the Greeks, because it seemed unorthodox to them. They gave the Trisagion a Trinitarian interpretation; consequently, the addition seemed monophysitic. Whether or not this criticism was justified, the phrase thus attacked was retained only among the Jacobites and Armenians.

In any event, the hymn became very popular in all the Eastern Churches, which connected it with the Book of the Gospels. It was sung as the book was brought in at the beginning of the Liturgy of the Word and placed on the altar. This rite was given an especially solemn form among the Byzantines.[21] In eastern Syria the procession went to the center of the nave, where the Book of the Gospels was placed on the *bêma*,[22] likewise to the accompaniment of the Trisagion. Among the Copts and Ethiopians the hymn was sung before the reading of the gospel, since it was then that the procession took place; but this does not seem to have been the original practice. In the beginning, the book must have been carried in the procession in which the ministers entered the church; in time, however, the entrance of the book became the sole focus of attention, overshadowing the entrance of the celebrant, of which the hymn was the accompaniment.

A further entrance rite made its appearance among the Byzantines, seemingly about 535,[23] perhaps initially on days when the procession took

---

20. See n. 18 above. The Trisagion was supposedly taught by angels to a child at Constantinople when Proclus was patriarch (434–46). In telling the legend, John Damascene adds that the hymn was sung at the Council of Chalcedon in 451, but he does not say it was sung at Mass: *De fide orth.* 3 (PG 94:1021).

21. The rite of the "Little Entrance" (see p. 60).

22. Among the Eastern Syrians the *bêma* is a kind of podium located in the middle of the church, on which the ministers have their place during the first part of the Mass. Among the Byzantines the same word denotes the sanctuary. See J. Dauvillier, "L'ambon ou bêma dans les textes de l'Eglise chaldéenne et de l'Eglise syrienne au moyen âge," *Cahiers archéologiques* 6 (1952) 11–30.

23. Emperor Justinian is said to have introduced it. See *Theophanis chronologia* (Leip-

on greater importance. This rite—a second entrance song—was the singing of Psalm 95 along with the troparion *Ho Monogenēs*. The text reads:

> Only Son and Word of God, immortal One, for our salvation you deigned to take flesh of the holy Mother of God, Mary ever virgin. Abiding unchanged, Christ our God, you became man and, having been nailed to the cross, you destroyed death by your death. You are one of the holy Trinity and equally glorified with the Father and the Holy Spirit. Save us!

II. THE PRAYER

Between these two songs was inserted a presidential prayer that differed in form and spirit from the Roman collect.[24] It was preceded by a short litany. This may originally have been simply a diaconal exhortation: *Tou Kyriou deēthōmen* ("Let us pray to the Lord"), to which the congregation may have answered with a *Kyrie eleison*; the celebrant then prayed.

These various components, with the opening greeting coming after them, were in place by the end of the seventh century. This part of the celebration would continue to develop later on through a complex and confused accumulation of contributions from various sources.

---

zig, 1885), 92; V. Grumel, "L'auteur et la date de composition du tropaire *Ho Monogenēs*," *Echos d'Orient* 22 (1923) 398–418.

24. The prayer in question is the "Trisagion prayer." For Egypt see the *Euchologion of Serapion* 1 (first prayer of Sunday), ed. F. X. Funk, *Didascalia et Constitutiones Apostolorum* 2:158.

Chapter II

The Liturgy of the Word

BIBLIOGRAPHY

M. Righetti, *Manuale di storia liturgica* 3 (Milan: Ancora, 1956²), 200–60.
J. A. Jungmann, *The Mass of the Roman Rite* 1:391–494.

The Bible was the first and, for almost three centuries, the only liturgical book. The readings began at the point reached at the previous liturgy, and they continued until the president gave the signal to stop. This was what is known as *lectio continua* ("continuous reading").

The framework or pattern for this part of the celebration was derived from the synagogue. Just as the synagogal liturgy included successive readings from the Torah and the Prophets, so the Christian liturgy includes several readings taken from various parts of the Bible. It became a binding custom throughout the Church that the final and climactic reading should be from the gospel, which sheds its light on the other New Testament writings that preceded it. These other New Testament readings in turn come after "the law of Moses and the prophets and the psalms,"[1] since they are the "fulfillment" of these. The homily, for its part, says in effect: "Today this scripture has been fulfilled in your hearing."[2] It is a repetition of what Jesus did in the synagogue at Nazareth, for "he is present in his word, since it is he himself who speaks when the holy Scriptures are read in the Church."[3]

---

1. Luke 24:44.
2. Luke 4:21.
3. *VSC* 7 (*DOL* 1 no. 7).

§1. The Book and the Ambo

BIBLIOGRAPHY

M. Righetti, *Manuale di storia liturgica* 1 (Milan: Ancora, 1964³), 299–306 and 469–73.

Once the liturgical year began to take shape, the *lectio continua* was interrupted on certain days and made way for passages more adapted to the feast being celebrated. A "reading list" or *comes* ("companion") was introduced in order to keep a record of the pericopes or extracts from Scripture that were appropriate for various circumstances. Concretely, the list took the form either of marginal notes in the copy of the Bible used in a particular church or of a list placed at the beginning or end of the volume; in either case the first and last words of the passage were indicated. Such a list came to be known in Latin-speaking countries as a *Capitulare*. Only later on did lectionaries appear that contained, in the order required by the calendar, the passages to be read in the liturgy.

Lectionaries generally were broken down into several volumes, and the one containing the gospels was given special homage and veneration. In the Roman Mass of the seventh century it was carried to the altar before the entrance of the bishop, and in Constantinople at the same period "the entrance of the gospel signified the coming of the Son of God." This is the first attestation of the "Little Entrance."[4]

But however important the book is in itself, it acquires its full meaning only when it is opened in the sight of all the people, so that they may receive the word of life from it. Christian practice again shows its Old Testament roots[5] when the reader takes his position in an elevated place in order that he may be seen by all, and his reading may be understood as a sign of the Lord speaking to his people.[6] Thus the ambo (or pulpit), which is located either in front of the congregation or, as in the Syrian churches, at the center of the nave, is one of the focal points of liturgical action; it is distinct from the altar and, as such, manifests the importance proper to the Liturgy of the Word as a special part of the sacred action.

---

4. St. Germanus of Constantinople, *Exegesis* 24, in N. Borgia, *Il commentario liturgico di S. Germano patriarca costantinopolitano e la versione latina di Anastasio Bibliotecario* (Grottaferrata, 1912), 21.

5. See Neh 8:4.

6. St. Cyprian, *Ep.* 39, 4, ed. L. Bayard 1 (Paris: Les Belles Lettres, 1925), 99, says with regard to a confessor whom he has appointed lector: "What more was needed except to have him mount the ambo . . . in order that in accordance with his merits he might read the teachings and gospel of the Lord from this elevated place where he was visible to the entire congregation?" See *Ep.* 38, 2 (Bayard 1:96).

§2. The Proclamation of the Scriptures

BIBLIOGRAPHY

Würzburg Comes, ed. G. Morin, "Le plus ancien Comes ou lectionnaire de l'Eglise romaine," *RBén* 27 (1910) 40–74.

F. C. Burkitt, "The Early Syriac Lectionary System," *Proceedings of the British Academy* 10 (1923) 301–38.

B. Capelle, "Notes sur le lectionnaire romain de la messe avant saint Grégoire," *RHE* 34 (1938) 556–59 (= *Travaux liturgiques* 2:200–3).

Liber commicus, ed. J. Pérez de Urbel and A. Gonzáles (Monumenta Hispaniae sacra, ser. liturg. 2–3; Madrid: Consejo superior de investigaciones cientificas, 1946–55).

P. Salmon, *Lectionnaire de Luxeuil* (Collectanea biblica latina 7; Vatican City, 1944).

G. Kunze, *Die gottesdienstliche Schriftlesung I. Stand und Aufgaben der Perikopenforschung* (Göttingen: Vandenhoeck und Reprecht, 1947).

A. Chavasse, "Les plus anciens types du lectionnaire et de l'antiphonaire romains de la messe," *RBén* 62 (1952) 3–94.

M. Hayek, *Liturgie maronite. Histoire et textes* (Paris: Mame, 1964).

P. M. Gy, "La question du système de lectures de la liturgie byzantine," in *Miscellanea liturgica . . . Lercaro* 2 (Rome: Desclée, 1967), 251–61.

A. Renoux, *Le Codex arménien Jérusalem 121* (PO 35–36; Turnhout: Brepols, 1969–71).

J. Mateos, *La célébration de la Parole dans la liturgie byzantine* (OCA 191; Rome: Oriental Institute, 1971), 27–126.

The readings were taken from the canonical books; the Council of Hippo in 393 decreed that "apart from the canonical books nothing is to be read in the Church under the name of 'divine scriptures.'"[7] The final phrase is important, because the passions of the martyrs were proclaimed during the assembly, at least in Africa[8] and Gaul (where the lives of the confessors were also read)[9]; this practice resulted in the preservation of valuable writings that elsewhere were forgotten and lost.

---

7. *Breviarium Hipponense* 36, ed. C. Munier, *Concilia Africae* (CCL 149; Turnhout: Brepols, 1974), 43.

8. St. Augustine, *Serm. Denis* 14, 3 (St. Cyprian) and 16, 7 (Scillitan martyrs), ed. G. Morin, *S. Augustini sermones post Maurinos reperti* (= *Miscellanea Agostiniana* 1; Rome: Vatican Press, 1930), 67 and 80.

9. Gregory of Tours, *De virtutibus sancti Martini* II, 49 (St. Martin); *Miraculorum liber* II, 16 (St. Julian); *In gloria martyrum* 85 (St. Polycarp), ed. W. Arndt and B. Krusch, MGH *Script. rer. Merov.* I, 2 (1884), 626, 571, 545–46. See H. Urner, *Die ausserbiblische Lesung im christlichen Gottesdienst* (Göttingen: Vandenhoeck und Ruprecht, 1952); B. de Gaiffier, "La lecture des Actes des martyrs dans la prière liturgique en Occident," *Analecta Bollandiana* 72 (1954) 134–66.

I. THE NONEVANGELICAL READINGS

BIBLIOGRAPHY

> A. Baumstark, *Nichtevangelische syrische Perikopenordnung des ersten Jahrtausends* (LQF 15; Münster: Aschendorff, 1921).
> W. H. Frere, *Studies in Early Roman Liturgy* III. *The Roman Epistle-Lectionary* (Alcuin Club Collection 32; Oxford: Oxford University Press, 1935).
> A. Chavasse, "Le calendrier dominical romain au VIᵉ siècle. L'épistolier et l'homéliaire prégrégoriens," *RechSR* 38 (1952) 234–46; 41 (1953) 96–122.
> O. Rousseau, "Lecture et présence de l'Apôtre à la liturgie de la messe," *LMD* no. 62 (1960) 69–78.

a) *More than two readings.* Books II and VIII of the *Apostolic Constitutions*—which despite their different origins are in agreement on this point—mention four readings before the gospel: Law, Prophets, Epistles, and Acts.[10] The division of the Old Testament into two sections, in accordance with Jewish usage, has continued down to our day among the Eastern Syrians; the Western Syrians added a third division, the sapiential books, which are read between the Law and the Prophets, and they also have two pericopes from the New Testament.

b) *Two readings.* Other Churches[11] were satisfied with two readings, one from each of the Testaments. This usage is attested for Spain by the *Liber commicus*, the main lines of which were set at the end of the seventh century; for Gaul by Gregory of Tours and the Lectionary of Luxeuil;[12] and for Antioch and Constantinople by St. John Chrysostom.[13]

c) *One reading.* The Byzantine liturgy, however, ended up having only one reading before the gospel.[14] Many of Augustine's homilies presuppose the same organization of the readings, even if on certain days there may have been a reading from the prophets and another reading.[15] There are indications that the Roman Church, too, followed this practice, but if so, it changed before the seventh century.[16]

---

10. *Constitutiones Apostolicae* II, 57, 5–9, and VIII, 5, 11–12 (Funk 1:161–63 and 476).

11. Today the Copts and Ethiopians have three readings before the gospel, all of them from the New Testament: Paul, Catholic Letters, and Acts, but this practice is doubtless not primitive.

12. Gregory of Tours, *Historia Francorum* IV, 16, ed. R. Poupardin (Paris: Picard, 1913), 120; *Lectionnaire de Luxeuil*, ed. P. Salmon (Collectanea Biblica Latina 7 and 9; Rome: Abbaye Saint-Jérôme, 1944–53).

13. F. Van de Paverd, *Zur Geschichte des Messliturgie in Antiocheia und Konstantinopel gegen Ende des vierten Jahrhunderts. Analyse der Quellen bei Johannes Chrysostomos* (OCA 187; Rome: Oriental Institute, 1970), 94–129.

14. St. Germanus of Constantinople, *Exegesis* 28 (Borgia 25).

15. St. Augustine, *Serm.* 176, 1; 112; 165; 170 (PL 38:950, 643, 902, 927–32). Augustine speaks of three readings because he counts the psalm as a reading.

16. A. Chavasse, *Le sacramentaire gélasien* (Tournai: Desclée, 1958), 190–97.

d) *The reader.* The nonevangelical readings were entrusted to one of the faithful, who in the beginning needed only to be able to read, speak clearly, and lead a decent life. By the third century, however, the office had become a stable function for which there was an appropriate blessing.[17] It was not considered unsuitable for children to exercise the function, since their pure voices enabled them to be heard distinctly in the large naves of the basilicas.

II. THE RESPONSORIAL PSALM

BIBLIOGRAPHY

R. J. Hesbert, *Antiphonale missarum sextuplex* (Brussels: Vromant, 1935).

J. Froger, *Les chants de la messe aux VIIIe et IXe siècles* (Tournai: Desclée, 1950), 17–24.

B. Stäblein, "Graduale," in *Die Musik in Geschichte und Gegenwart* 4 (Kassel–Basel: Bärenreiter, 1956).

R. J. Hesbert, "Le graduel, chant responsorial," *EL* 95 (1981) 316–50.

A. G. Martimort, "Fonction de la psalmodie dans la liturgie de la Parole," in *Liturgie und Dichtung (Festschrift W. Dürig)*, to be published.

Beginning with the very first witnesses to the organization of a Liturgy of the Word, all the Churches had a psalm, sung in responsorial form, in this part of the Mass. St. Augustine, for example, speaks of "the psalm which we have just heard sung and to which we have responded in song."[18] Unlike the alleluia, there was generally only one psalm, no matter how many other readings there might be; this meant that it was not a simple response during which one might meditate on the reading from Scripture that had just been proclaimed. Augustine often made the psalm the subject of his homily, thus putting it on the same level as the reading from Paul and the gospel.[19]

When the celebration included Old Testament readings, the psalm followed these, as in Book II of the *Apostolic Constitutions*. This is the case with the *šurraya* of the Eastern Syrians, the Spanish *psallendum* (there can be doubt about the Gallican *responsorium*), and, it seems, the Ambrosian *psalmellus*. When there was but a single nonevangelical reading, practices differed: the Byzantine *prokimenon* came before this reading, while at Rome and in Africa the responsorial psalm came after it. This

---

17. See *Traditio apostolica* 11 (Botte 30–31). See n. 6, p. 60.

18. St. Augustine, *Enarr. in ps.* 119, ed. E. Dekkers and J. Fraipont (CCL 40; Turnhout: Brepols, 1956), 1776.

19. For example, St. Augustine, *Enarr. in ps.* 138 (CCL 40:1990): the reader has read the wrong psalm, and the preacher, seeing in this mistake a sign from God, decides to give his homily on the psalm that has actually been read.

variation in cases where there was no Old Testament reading may be a sign that the psalm served originally as the final reading from the Old Testament.

This chant was usually executed by a reader from the ambo[20]; at times, however, it was done by a deacon, as in Gaul in the time of Gregory of Tours[21] and at Rome before Gregory the Great.[22]

At a later stage there was a universal tendency to reduce this psalmody to a few verses and even to replace it with ornate melodies sung by cantors who thus deprived the people of their participation.[23]

III. THE PROCLAMATION OF THE GOSPEL

BIBLIOGRAPHY

S. Beissel, *Entstehung der Perikopen des römischen Messbuches* (Freiburg: Herder, 1907).

G. Godu, "Evangiles," *DACL* 5 (1922) 852–923.

A. Eizenhöfer, "Der Allelujagesang vor dem Evangelium," *EL* 45 (1931) 374–82.

T. Klauser, *Das römische Capitulare evangeliorum* (LQF 28; Münster: Aschendorff, 1935).

J. Froger, "La correspondance apocryphe du pape saint Damase et de saint Jérôme sur le psautier et le chant de l'alleluia," *EL* 62 (1948) 6–48.

B. Stäblein, "Alleluia," in *Die Musik in Geschichte und Gegenwart* 1 (Kassel: Bärenreiter, 1951), 331–50.

C. Thodberg, *Der byzantinische Alleluiarionzyklus* (Monumenta musicae byzantinae, Subsidia 8; Copenhagen: Munksgaard, 1966).

A. G. Martimort, "Origine et signification de l'alleluia de la messe romaine," in *Kyriakon (Festschrift J. Quasten)* (Münster: Aschendorff, 1970), 2:811–34 (= *Mens concordet voci* 1 [Paris: Desclée, 1983]).

a) *The alleluia.* Another bit of singing, before the gospel, includes the repetition of alleluia, thus bringing out the paschal character of the proclamation of the Good News.[24] The presence of the alleluia in all the Eastern liturgies [25] is a sign of its antiquity: it is found in the old Jerusalem lec-

---

20. Later on at Rome the reader only climbs onto the steps (*gradus*) of the ambo; this doubtless explains the name "gradual" for the antiphon sung at this point.

21. Gregory of Tours, *Historia Francorum* VIII, 3 (Poupardin 302).

22. St. Gregory the Great, Roman Synod of 595, ed. P. Ewald, *Registrum epistolarum* I (MGH *Epist.* 1; 1887), 363. The pope here abolished a practice that was open to abuse, that is, the practice of choosing deacons solely for their fine voices.

23. There was no alternative at this point but to urge the people to meditate on the reading they had heard, while the singers were chanting the gradual; this explains the modern term "meditation song," which was unknown in the older tradition.

24. See Rev 9:1-7.

25. The only exception is the Ethiopian rite, although the alleluia has there been introduced into the deacon's exhortation urging the congregation to listen to the gospel.

tionary; it is a constitutive element in the *Zummārā* of the Eastern Syrians, the *Hûlôlo* of the Western Syrians, and the *Hallel of David* of the Maronites; it follows the Trisagion among the Copts; and, after having lost its verses, remains in the *Allēlouia* of the Byzantines. The connection between this chant and the reading that follows is attested by an apocryphal writing of the fourth or fifth century: "Sing Alleluia, and read the gospel."[26]

The same was not true of the West. We have no early witness to the alleluia for Milan and Spain, and the Gallican tradition likewise seems not to have known it.[27] At Rome Gregory the Great said he had heard the alleluia in Masses outside of the Easter season,[28] but was this an alleluia sung before the gospel? If the pope was speaking simply of the general use of this acclamation in the Eucharistic liturgy, then we may think that the chant of which we are speaking here was introduced under Eastern influence (the earliest liturgical books included verses in Greek) and that the borrowing occurred at a period when several Byzantine elements were being taken over for use at Rome; this would take us to the second half of the seventh century.[29]

b) *The gospel.* All the liturgies had the reading of the gospel preceded by a procession in which lights[30] and incense[31] were used to honor the book as a sign of Christ's presence.

The call for silence and attention, which also preceded the first reading in some Churches, was now issued in a more emphatic way: *Proschō-*

---

26. *Martyrium Matthaei*, ed. R. A. Lipsius and M. Bonnet, *Acta apostolorum apocrypha* 2 (Leipzig: Mendelssohn, 1898), 252–53, trans. M. R. James, *The Apocryphal New Testament* (Oxford: Clarendon Press, 1924), 460–62. According to this legend a voice from heaven addresses the cited words to a bishop when asking him to organize a Eucharistic assembly.

27. Pseudo-Germanus, *Expositio antiquae liturgiae gallicanae* 8–10 (Ratcliff 6–7) has the gospel preceded by the *Benedictio* (canticle of the three young men), the response *Osanna fili David*, and a repetition of the *Aius* from the beginning of the celebration.

28. St. Gregory the Great, *Ep. ad Joannem Syracus.*, ed. P. Ewald and L. M. Hartmann, *Registrum epistolarum* II (MGH *Epist.* 2; 1899), 59. The pope cites a supposed letter of St. Jerome that was forged in the sixth century. The dossier also includes: Sozomen, *Historia ecclesiastica* 13 (PG 67:1475) and John the Deacon, *Ep. ad Senarium* 13, ed. A. Wilmart, *Analecta Reginensia* (ST 133; 1933), 178.

29. A. G. Martimort, "Origine et signification de l'alleluia de la messe romaine," in *Kyriakon (Festschrift J. Quasten)* (Münster: Aschendorff, 1970), 2:826–34.

30. St. Jerome, *Contra Vigilantium* 7 (PL 23:346), says, in the year 378, that in all the churches of the East lamps were lighted at the gospel as a sign of joy, but it seems that the same was not true at Rome at that period. The custom was finally introduced at Rome: *Ordo* I mentions the two candlesticks carried by acolytes; seven were used in Gaul in the time of Pseudo-Germanus.

31. Germanus of Constantinople, *Exegesis* 30 (Borgia 25), speaks of the incensations performed at this point. In Rome at the same period a lighted censer was carried before the Book of the Gospels (*Ordo* I).

men ("Let us be attentive!"), *Silentium facite!* ("Silence!"). Sometimes the congregation was also told to remain standing: *Orthoi . . . .* This posture for listening to the gospel denotes watchfulness and symbolizes our state of being risen with Christ; it was observed everywhere.

In the beginning, it was undoubtedly a reader who proclaimed this Word of the Lord, as he did the other passages from the Bible. Very soon, however, it became customary to reserve the reading of the gospel either to a deacon (the Byzantine and Armenian rites, and all the Western rites) or even, as elsewhere, to the president or another priest. The minister announced the name of the evangelist from whom the passage was taken. The Roman liturgy alluded at this point to the *lectio continua*: "Continuation of the holy gospel according to . . .," but, in the time of *Ordo* I, it did not yet have any of the other formulas which it subsequently took over from Gallican usage and which are also attested for the East: *Eirēnē pasin* ("Peace to all"), *Dominus vobiscum* with its response, and the acclamation of the congregation: *Doxa soi, Kyrie, doxa soi, Gloria tibi, Domine* ("Glory to you, O Lord"). After the reading, except at Rome, there was an exultant choral chant that echoed the Word of God. The kissing of the book by the reader as an act of homage was extended in the seventh century to all the clergy present and even, in some Churches, to the entire congregation, as is still the case among the Copts and Ethiopians.

Some Churches compiled a *Diatessaron*, that is, a text in which the Four Gospels were conflated to form a single narrative. But such a text did not remain long in use anywhere because it gave rise to serious criticisms.[32]

Everything thus conspired to make the proclamation of the gospel a high point of the celebration. The proclamation was not simply a reading of a text, however beautiful; it was a living Word that was received in an attitude of prayer.

§3. The "Today" of God's Word

BIBLIOGRAPHY

I. Herwegen, "L'Ecriture sainte dans la liturgie," *LMD* no. 5 (1946) 7–20.

A. Bea, "Valeur pastorale de la Parole de Dieu dans la liturgie," *LMD* nos. 47–48 (1956) 129–48.

---

32. P. Salmon, *Le Lectionnaire de Luxeuil* (Collectanea Biblica Latina 7; Rome: Abbey of St. Jerome, 1944), lxx–lxxiii; A. S. Marmadji, *Diatessaron de Tatien*, Arabic text with French translation (Beirut, 1935); C. Peters, *Das Diatessaron Tatians* (OCA 123; Rome: Oriental Institute, 1939); J. Leloir, "Le Diatessaron de Tatien," *OS* 1 (1956) 208–31, 313–34.

P. Jounel, "The Bible in the Liturgy," in *The Liturgy and the Word of God* (Papers of the Third National Congress of the Centre Pastorale Liturgique, Strasbourg, 1958; Collegeville: The Liturgical Press, 1959), 1–20.

A. G. Martimort, "Praesens adest in verbo suo . . .," in *Acta Congressus de Theologia Concilii Vaticani II* (Vatican City, 1968), 300–15 (= *Mens concordet voci* 1 [Paris: Desclée, 1983]).

I. THE DISTRIBUTION OF THE BIBLE IN THE LITURGY

The very fact of proposing a specific passage of Scripture for a given day and even the division into verses represent a kind of rereading of the Bible by the Church and a way of actualizing its message. I cannot here compare the various systems of readings that have been followed in the various traditions, and I note simply that there are some more or less universal constants, such as the proclamation of Acts and the Gospel of John during the Easter season, certain passages of John during Lent in preparation for baptism, the story of the Tower of Babel on Pentecost, the episode of Martha and Mary on feasts of the Blessed Virgin, and so on.

II. THE HOMILY

The homily was certainly the most important way of bringing out the "today" of God's word. Biblical exegesis, historical commentary, doctrinal and moral instruction—all of which were aspects of the preaching of the Fathers—played their part in the intention of actualizing the Scriptures in the life of the Christians who had gathered for ecclesial prayer and were soon to scatter again and return to the world. The homily was thus an integral part of the liturgical action and was normally delivered by the president and, in particular, by the bishop. The bishop, however, often assigned this function to a priest, sometimes even when he himself was present, more rarely to a deacon, and only in exceptional circumstances to a layperson. For the period under consideration here, there are hardly any examples of a deacon or a layman preaching except in the East.[33] In meeting a comparable need the Latin Church resorted instead to collections of patristic homilies that a minister would read in the absence of a priest.[34]

---

33. We may think of Ephraem the Deacon and of Origen, who was a layman when he preached in Jerusalem and Antioch; when his own bishop protested, he was told that this was not an isolated case; see Eusebius of Caesarea, *Historia ecclesiastica* VI, 19, 17–18, ed. G. Bardy (SC 41; Paris: Cerf, 1955), 2:117–18.

34. Council of Vaison, can. 2, ed. C. De Clercq, *Concilia Galliae* II (CCL 148A; Turnhout: Brepols, 1963), 79. See Pseudo-Germanus, *Expositio* 13 (Ratcliff 8).

A homily had two essential characteristics. First, its theme was taken from components of the celebration; these were generally the readings from Scripture, but they might also be the sacramental signs or formularies like the Creed and the Our Father. Second, it was an informal talk in which being understood by the audience was more important than literary pretensions; St. Augustine, for example, did not hesitate to use Berber words (*punici*) and to elicit reactions from the people he was addressing.[35]

As the Carolingian Age approached, however, this part of the liturgy fell into disuse; the *Ordines Romani* say nothing of it. The same phenomenon was observable in the East.

III. FROM WORD TO SACRAMENT

The Liturgy of the Word was always directed toward the celebration of the sacrament, even when, as the ancient discipline of the catechumenate makes clear, it was geared to hearers who would not immediately share in the sacrament. Moreover, even though the words pronounced at the heart of the "mysteries" were not themselves always taken from Scripture, they were intelligible only against the background of biblical revelation. It was natural, then, that the actions which make the actions of Christ live again for human beings—and this is especially true of the Eucharist—should be preceded by the reading of the sacred books.

The readings certainly prepare the hearers for the subsequent actions, but they also share in advance in the efficacy of these actions. The justification for this doctrine is the incarnation of the Savior: the Word became flesh. What God promised he has fulfilled through his Son. Once the Son was glorified, the Church continued to make him visible; the Church is the "sacrament" of the Lord whereby he proclaims and effects salvation. There is thus a kind of analogy between the "two tables," but one that is dynamic, not static. That is to say, because the Word leads on to the efficacious signs of grace, it produces the first fruits of these salutary actions. We may even say that this movement begins with the very existence of Christians. God speaks in their lives to the extent that these lives are oriented toward the reception of the Word as a freely given gift that flows from the offering of the Body and Blood of Christ in the celebration of his paschal mystery. "The gospel," says Augustine, "is Christ's mouth. He sits in heaven but does not cease to speak on earth."[36]

---

35. St. Augustine, *Enarr. in ps.* 123, 8 (CCL 40:1831). See A. Olivar, *Els auditoris cristians antics* (Barcelona: Reial Acadèmia de Bones Lletres, 1983).
36. St. Augustine, *Serm.* 85, 1 (PL 38:520).

The General Intercessions
or Prayer of the Faithful

BIBLIOGRAPHY

P. Borella, "L'oratio fidelium ripristinata," Ambrosius 40 (1964) 435–61.
_____, "L'oratio fidelium nelle sue varie forme strutturali," Ambrosius 41 (1965) 9–23.
P. De Clerck, La "prière universelle" dans les liturgies latines anciennes. Témoignages patristiques et textes liturgiques (LQF 62; Münster: Aschendorff, 1977).

As we saw earlier, St. Justin provides the first witness to the General Intercessions or prayer of the faithful, a practice that is found in all the Churches (at least in the period for which we have descriptions of the Mass). According to Hippolytus of Rome, this prayer was a prerogative of the faithful; only after the newly baptized had left the baptistery did they participate in it for the first time.[1] Catechumens had to leave the assembly before this prayer began.

§1. The Dismissal of the Catechumens

BIBLIOGRAPHY

P. Borella, "La missa o dimissio catechumenorum," EL 53 (1939) 60–110.

The dismissal of the catechumens after the Liturgy of the Word is everywhere attested, though the formulas used differed. The practice made its appearance once preparation for baptism took an organized form. We find

---

1. Traditio apostolica 21 (Botte 54–55): "Henceforth they will pray with the rest of the people, for they do not pray with the faithful before obtaining all this."

Tertullian already finding fault with the heretics on this score: "Who is a catechumen? Who a baptized believer? No one can tell. All listen [to the Word] in the same way, all pray in the same way."[2]

In the Eastern Churches the rite of dismissal included a prayer for those about to be dismissed; they were given a blessing and then the deacon bade them to leave the church. The same ceremony was then repeated for those who had only been inscribed as candidates for baptism, for those already engaged in an immediate preparation for the sacrament, and for other categories of people excluded from the Eucharist (penitents, for example). The General Intercessions formed the concluding part of this rite, once the faithful alone remained.[3]

In the West the dismissal was often mentioned but scarcely described.[4] Roman *Ordo* XI preserves the formula used: *"Caticumeni recedant! Si quis caticumenus est, recedat! Omnes caticumeni exeant foras"* ("Let catechumens depart! Any who are still catechumens must leave! All catechumens outside!"),[5] but this *Ordo* dates from a period when for practical purposes only infants were being baptized. In some Churches the dismissal came before the gospel, a practice rejected by the Council of Orange in 441.[6] Pseudo-Germanus speaks of the prayer of the priest and the exhortation of the deacon, but as survivals from the past.[7]

§2. The General Intercessions in the East

BIBLIOGRAPHY

> J. M. Hanssens, *Institutiones liturgicae de ritibus orientalibus* 3 (Rome: Gregorian University, 1930), 234–60.

In the East the prayer of the faithful took the form of a diaconal litany of intentions that seems by the end of the fourth century to be already made up of fixed formulas, each followed by a response that the people

---

2. Tertullian, *De praescript. haer.* 41, 2, ed. P. Refoulé and P. de Labriolle (SC 46; Paris: Cerf, 1954), 221.

3. See *Constitutiones Apostolorum* VIII, 6, 1–11, 6 (Funk 1:478–94).

4. See St. Augustine, *Serm.* 49, 8 (PL 38:324): "After the sermon the catechumens are dismissed and the faithful remain"; St. Ambrose, *Ep.* 20, 4 (PL 16:995): "After the readings . . . when the catechumens have been dismissed . . . ."

5. *OR* XI, 29 (Andrieu, *OR* 2:425).

6. Council of Orange, can. 17, ed. C. Munier, *Concilia Galliae* I (CCL 148; Turnhout: Brepols, 1963), 83: "It is decreed that the gospels are to be read to the catechumens in all the churches of our provinces." In other regions the old custom was retained, since Amalarius of Metz, *Liber officiorum* III, 68, 3 (Hanssens 2:371), could say in the ninth century: "It is our custom to dismiss the catechumens before the gospel."

7. Pseudo-Germanus, *Expositio* 15 (Ratcliff 9).

addressed to Christ: *Kyrie eleēson,* "Lord, have mercy." The response was a very popular one and passed into liturgies in other languages; it was sometimes translated into those tongues, sometimes kept in its Greek form.

There may have been a different form of this prayer, at least in Egypt. The Euchologion of Serapion has three prayers, apparently to be said by the president, for fertility (of the soil), for the Church, and for the bishop and community.[8]

§3. The General Intercessions in Africa

The prayer of the faithful, to which Tertullian perhaps alludes around the year 200,[9] is clearly attested by St. Augustine. Not infrequently the bishop of Hippo ended his homilies by asking his hearers to turn to the Lord: *Conversi ad Dominum,* that is, in all probability, to the East. "Turning to the Lord, let us pray to him for ourselves and all of his people who are here with us in his house, that he may deign to guard and protect them through Jesus Christ. . . ."[10]

It seems that the president proposed intentions, each with a specific object: "For [so and so], in order that . . .," and that the faithful probably made the intention their own with an "Amen."[11] The formulation of the intentions had doubtless not yet become fixed, although a fairly precise vocabulary had already been developed that would allow this kind of fixation.

§4. The General Intercessions at Rome

BIBLIOGRAPHY

M. Cappuyns, "Les *orationes sollemnes* du vendredi saint," *QL* 23 (1938) 18–31.
P. Borella, "L'*oratio super sindonem,*" *Ambrosius* 34 (1958) 173–76.
A. Chavasse "L'oraison *super sindonem* dans la liturgie romaine," *RBén* 70 (1960) 313–23.
See also above, on the *Kyrie,* pp. 53–54.

---

8. *Euchologion of Serapion* (Funk 2:160–71).

9. Tertullian, *De oratione* 18, 1, ed. G. F. Diercks (CCL 1; Turnhout: Brepols, 1954), 267.

10. St. Augustine, *Serm.* 100 and 362 (PL 38:605; 39:1634); also *Serm.* 34; 182; 272; etc. See W. Rötzer, *Des heiligen Augustinus Schriften als liturgiegeschichtliche Quelle* (Munich: Max Hüber, 1930), 113–15.

11. St. Augustine, *Ep.* 127, 2; 217, 26, ed. A. Goldbacher (CSEL 57; Vienna, 1911), 404 and 421–22.

I. THE SOLEMN PRAYERS (*ORATIONES SOLLEMNES*)

In the beginning we find a solemn form of intercession that has survived in the Roman Missal in the Good Friday office. Each intercession has an invitatory; this is followed by a period of silence (the congregation kneels for this on days of penance) and a prayer that repeats the petition and leads to the congregation's "Amen."[12] This practice seems to have been well established by the middle of the fifth century. The invitatories, however, seem to be older than the prayers and may, at an earlier stage, have been followed only by the silent prayer of the congregation.[13] The Roman Church doubtless had formularies other than the one that has survived,[14] although these would probably have followed the same model.

II. THE "INTERCESSION OF GELASIUS" (*DEPRECATIO GELASII*)

It was perhaps in the time of Pope Gelasius (492–96) that things changed. To him, at any rate, is attributed not only the composition, but also the introduction into the Roman liturgy, of a litanic prayer that was probably inspired not directly by Eastern practice, but by Latin texts used in northern Italy or other regions of the West.[15] According to what seems to be the best manuscript, the intercessions of Gelasius called for the response *"Domine, exaudi et miserere"* ("Lord, hear and have mercy"); at Milan, however, the response used was *Kyrie eleison.* But since no manuscript is older than the ninth century, and since the manuscripts reflect formularies actually used in the liturgy, it is not impossible that the two expressions, the first of which is simply a translation of the second, were interchangeable.

---

12. Critical ed. and commentary by P. De Clerck in his *La "prière universelle" dans les liturgies latines anciennes. Témoignages patristiques et textes liturgiques* (LQF 62; Münster; Aschendorff, 1977), 125–43.

13. According to P. De Clerck, the invitatories date from the period 250–320, although they show some subsequent alterations.

14. See Ambrosiaster, *In I Tim.* 2, ed. H. J. Vogels (CSEL 81, 3; Vienna, 1969), 259–60. This author, who lived in Rome in the second half of the fourth century, seems to know not only the invitatories of the *Orationes Sollemnes* but others as well. Prosper of Aquitaine, *Capitula* 8 (PL 51:209–10), refers to the entire formulary, but he has other sources for it, perhaps the Gallican tradition.

15. See the title given in many mss.: "Deprecatio quam papa Gelasius . . . constituit esse canendam" ("Intercession which Pope Gelasius . . . decreed should be sung"). Critical ed. and commentary in P. De Clerck, 166–67. Among Western models are formularies that draw heavily on Eastern prayers: *Dicamus omnes* (Stowe Missal) and *Divinae pacis* (Milan), still used in the Milanese Liturgy. See n. 15, p. 55.

III. THE GENERAL INTERCESSIONS AND THE *KYRIE*

In any case, we can hardly avoid connecting this innovation with two further changes in Roman practice: the appearance of the *Kyrie* at the beginning of Mass (before 529[16]) and the suppression of the General Intercessions (in the course of the sixth century[17]). A hypothesis immediately suggests itself: the Gelasian intercessions, with their undeniably more popular style, replaced the older *Orationes sollemnes* and were then shifted to the entrance rites. The facts were doubtless not quite that simple, and the new location of the intercessions would have to be explained.

One might also think that the *Kyrie* has a different origin, unconnected with any series of intentions. However, even in the Milanese *Divinae pacis*, which is a replica of Greek models and perhaps older than Gelasius, the *Kyrie*, though not used as a response,[18] is nonetheless connected with the litany that it concludes. And when St. Gregory says later on that in "daily Masses" the "things customarily said" are omitted,[19] he has always been understood as referring to rites that are proper to the deacon in the Eastern tradition.

Thus, even when used alone, the *Kyrie* remained, by reason of its origins, a response to a litany. We can only form conjectures to explain its introduction into the Roman Mass.[20] One thing is well-nigh certain: that before they disappeared, the General Intercessions had acquired a different form than the one they still have on Good Friday. We may think, moreover, that this different form was due to the pope whose name remains attached to a well known "Intercession," since we have no evidence that the new form, which was certainly known in the other Churches of the West, was used in Rome before the time of Gelasius.

§5. The General Intercessions in Gaul and in Spain

BIBLIOGRAPHY

E. Griffe, "Aux origines de la liturgie gallicane," *Bulletin de littérature ecclésiastique* 52 (1951) 17–43.

---

16. See the Council of Vaison (529), can. 3; ed. C. De Clercq, *Concilia Galliae* 2 (CCL 148A), 79.

17. There is no trace of the General Intercessions in the collection of *libelli missae* (booklets of Masses) known as the Leonine Sacramentary; the latest texts in this collection are from the middle of the sixth century.

18. Critical ed. and commentary in P. De Clerck, 155–66.

19. St. Gregory the Great, *Ep.* 9, 26, ed. L. M. Hartmann (MGH *Epist.* 2; Berlin, 1899), 59: "In cotidianis autem missis alia quae dici solent tacemus, tantummodo kyrieleison et Christe-eleison dicimus, ut in his deprecationis vocibus diutius occupemur."

20. See the hypotheses of Capelle and Chavasse; see also the bibliography and state of the question in P. De Clerck, 282–84.

M. Ramos, *Oratio admonitionis. Contribución al estudio de la antigua Misa Española* (Granada, 1964).

_____, "Rasgos de la *Oratio communis* según la *Oratio admonitionis* hispánica," *Hispania sacra* 17 (1964) 31–45.

I. IN GAUL

The General Intercessions are attested for Gaul in the sixth century. A Council of Lyons, which dates somewhere between 518 and 523, says with regard to individuals doing penance: "We grant them permission to pray in the holy places until the prayer of the people that is read after the gospel."[21] Gregory of Tours makes no reference to the intercessions, but this does not mean he did not know of them, since nowhere does he give us a complete description of the Eucharistic celebration.

The reference by the Council of Lyons does not tell us how the intercessions were performed. One of the earliest Latin formularies is found in an Irish missal under the name of *Deprecatio sancti Martini pro populo* ("Intercession of St. Martin for the people"),[22] but the title is from the ninth century, while the text itself, evidently imported from the East, tells us nothing about the early tradition of the Churches of Gaul, which is unknown to us.[23] Yet this text may have actually been used in Gaul, because, even if the practice represents an adoption of foreign custom, Pseudo-Germanus does seem to be speaking of General Intercessions that took the form of a diaconal litany: *De prece. Levitas psallere pro populo* ("The prayer [of the faithful]. The deacons sing in behalf of the people"). In any case, the rite ended with a presidential prayer or *Collectio post precem* ("Collect after the prayer [of the faithful]").

II. IN SPAIN

In his list of the formularies that make up the proper of each Mass, Isidore of Seville († 633) specifies two interventions of the priest (*admonitio* and *invocatio*, "exhortation" and "invocation") that must have framed the intentions.[24] But we do not know either the tenor of these intentions or the minister who proposed them. The books that have come down to

21. Council of Lyons, Appendix, in C. de Clercq, *Concilia Galliae*, 41.

22. Critical ed. and commentary in P. De Clerck, 145–54; *The Stowe Missal*, ed. G. F. Warner 2 (HBS 32; London: Henry Bradshaw Society, 1906), 6–7.

23. According to P. De Clerck, the fact that Prosper of Aquitaine refers to the *Orationes Sollemnes* in his controversy with the semi-Pelagian monks of southeastern Gaul presupposes that the monks used this formulary. But the argument needs careful handling.

24. Isidore of Seville, *De ecclesiasticis officiis* I, 15 (PL 83:752).

us show usages that have undergone a good many changes; in the *Missale Mixtum*, however, there are a few traces whose archaic character betrays their great age.[25]

III. THE "EASTER PRAYERS" (*ORATIONES PASCHALES*)

The Easter Vigil in the Spanish and Gallican sacramentaries contains formularies similar to the Roman *Orationes sollemnes*.[26] But, as P. de Clerck observes, this similarity seems "to have resulted from a restructuring of one or more litanies into the liturgical form peculiar to the *Orationes sollemnes*." The usages of the Apostolic See had made their way into Gaul, and the same influence was felt in Spain; at that point a redactor "adapted to the taste of the day" elements present in local practices. Scholars have noted that in witnesses from the Peninsula each sequence within a series has a tripartite plan: between invitatory and prayer there is a repetition of an intention that is assigned to a deacon; this intention is found by itself, with its music, in the *Antiphonary of León*. This may point to a traditional prerogative of this minister, since his interventions were added to the model that the redactors were imitating.

§6. Conclusion

The General Intercessions can be seen to mark the end of the entire Liturgy of the Word and at the same time to be, as it were, the threshold of the Eucharist proper. Coming as they do after the dismissal of the catechumens, they are a privilege of the faithful, and they underscore the latter's priestly character. To present to God the appeals and hopes of the entire human race is to share in the care and concern of the Priest of the New Covenant who gave his life for the salvation of the world; it is to share in his mission. We may say that the intercessions represent the other side of evangelization, since speaking of human beings to God is inseparable from speaking of God to human beings.

---

25. *Missale mixtum* (PL 85:114 or 540).

26. Critical ed. and commentary in P. De Clerck, 231–65. For Spain see J. Bernal, "Los sistemas de lecturas y oraciones en la vigilia pascual hispana," *Hispania sacra* 17 (1964) 283–347.

Chapter IV

The Preparation of the Gifts

BIBLIOGRAPHY

E. Bishop, "The Diptychs," an appendix in R. H. Connolly, *The Liturgical Homilies of Narsai* (TS 8; Cambridge: Cambridge University Press, 1909), 97-117.

F. Cabrol, "Diptyques," *DACL* 4 (1920) 1045-94.

J. Coppens, "L'offrande des fidèles dans la liturgie eucharistique ancienne," *SL* 5 (1926) 99-123.

B. Capelle, "Pour une meilleure intelligence de la messe: l'Offertoire," *QL* 17 (1932) 58-67.

F. Cabrol, "Offertoire," *DACL* 12 (1936) 1946-62.

V. Kennedy, "The Offertory Rite," *Orate Fratres* 12 (1938) 193-98, 244-49, 295-98.

C. Callewaert, "De offerenda et oblatione in missa," *Periodica de re morali, canonica, liturgica* 33 (1944) 61-94.

A. Clark, "The Function of the Offertory Rite in the Mass," *EL* 64 (1950) 309-44; see *EL* 67 (1953) 242-47.

B. Capelle, "Innocent Ier et le canon de la messe," *RTAM* 19 (1952) 6-16 (= *Travaux liturgiques* 2:236-47).

—————, "L'intercession dans la messe romaine," *RBén* 65 (1955) 181-91 (= *Travaux liturgiques* 2:248-57).

K. Pursch, "Die Probleme des Offertoriums und Versuche ihrer Lösung," *Internationale kirchliche Zeitschrift* 46 (1956) 1-27, 105-30.

P. Borella, "Oratio fidelium et dittici nelle segrete dell'offertorio," *Ambrosius* 36 (1960), Supplemento, [1]-[21].

R. Berger, *Die Wendung offerre pro in der römischen Liturgie* (LQF 41; Münster: Aschendorff, 1964).

R. F. Taft, *The Great Entrance. A History of the Transfer of Gifts and Other Preanaphoral Rites of the Liturgy of St. John Chrysostom* (OCA 200; Rome: Oriental Institute, 1975, 1978²).

The Eucharistic liturgy proper begins with a set of rites that has different names in different traditions and is generally known in the West as the "Offertory." In order to avoid the ambiguities in this name (which has a historical explanation), this part of the Mass became known, once the

Missal of Paul VI was introduced, as the "Preparation of the gifts." And in fact the original and essential nucleus of this part of the liturgy was the deposition on the altar of the bread and wine that would become the Body and Blood of Christ.

In the course of the centuries, other rites were added to this nucleus. At times these may have somewhat obscured the meaning of the action, but more often, especially during the period we are examining here, they enriched the introduction to the Eucharist proper. Thus the table of sacrifice was covered with a cloth; the paten and cup were brought forward, and their contents were displayed as very simple foods (yet foods prepared by human hands) that the Lord had chosen for the feeding of his people. Moreover, lest the attention of the congregation be narrowly focused on the bread and wine as material objects, emphasis was placed on an action of the faithful as the first step in the process that would eventually lead the congregation into the very heart of the mystery.

§1. The Donation of Bread and Wine by the Faithful

Jesus took bread and then the cup. As early as the second century these actions of the Lord were to some extent given solemn form[1]: the paten and cup were carried to the altar after the Liturgy of the Word. A little later, Hippolytus tells us that this service was a diaconal function.[2] In time a new element was added to this originally simple rite: the faithful brought to the church the foods they had on their own tables at home.

This custom is explicitly attested in the West. St. Cyprian, for example, inveighs against a matron who dared come with empty hands: "You are rich and well-to-do; yet you think you celebrate 'the Lord's Supper' (*Dominicum*) even though you . . . come to it without an offering (*sacrificium*) and receive a part of the offering brought by a poor person. Consider the widow in the gospel. . . ."[3]

St. Augustine says that his mother let no day pass without bringing her offering to the altar.[4] As for Rome, the life of St. Gregory tells of a woman who when receiving Communion recognized a piece of the bread she had baked herself and, because her faith was unenlightened, had trouble accepting it as the Body of Christ.[5] For Gaul, in addition to the

---

1. See pp. 16–17.
2. *Traditio apostolica* 4 and 21 (Botte 11 and 55).
3. St. Cyprian, *Liber de opere et eleemosinis* 15, ed. G. Hartel (CSEL 3; Vienna, 1868), 384; PL 4:612–13.
4. St. Augustine, *Conf.* V, 9 (CCL 27:66).
5. Paul the Deacon, *S. Gregorii Magni vita* 23 (PL 75:52–53).

recommendations of Caesarius of Arles,[6] there is the testimony of Gregory of Tours: a widow of Lyons daily offered about a gallon of Gaza wine.[7] The same practice seems to have been followed in the East, since each of the great liturgical families has Eucharistic prayers in which those who have contributed the oblation for the Eucharist are mentioned in the intercessions.[8]

§2. The Procession with the Offerings

This participation of the faithful gave rise to a liturgical act, at least in some regions.

In Africa and at Rome, the beginning of the Eucharistic liturgy was marked by a procession of offerers, parallel to the communion procession. St. Augustine sees in this double procession an expression of the "marvelous exchange" represented by the incarnation: Christ takes our humanity in order to bestow on us his divinity.[9] The offerers approached the bishop and his ministers and gave them the gifts while a psalm was sung.[10] According to the detailed description of this rite that is given in *Ordo Romanus* I (eighth century),[11] the choir, which because of its activity could not take part in the procession, showed their participation by giving a subdeacon the water, which he poured into the chalice.[12]

In Gaul, on the other hand, the faithful deposited the bread and wine in the sacristy before the celebration; these gifts were then carried to the altar in solemn procession by the deacons and other ministers at the beginning of the Eucharistic liturgy proper.[13] The gifts were carried in a receptacle that was known as the "tower," from its shape, which was inspired by the structure that covered the burial place of Christ in the basilica of the Anastasis in Jerusalem. Because the gifts were thus hidden, it was pos-

---

6. St. Caesarius of Arles, *Serm.* 13 (Appendix to a sermon of St. Augustine); ed. G. Morin, *S. Caesarii opera omnia* (CCL 103; Turnhout: Brepols, 1953²), 65. See also *Serm.* 1 (Morin 9); 14 (Morin 71); 16 (Morin 77); 19 (Morin 89); 229 (Morin, CCL 104:908).

7. Gregory of Tours, *Liber miraculorum in gloria confessorum* 64, ed. B. Krusch (MGH, *Script. aev. Merov.*) 1 (1885) 785–86.

8. See pp. 81–82 and n. 26.

9. St. Augustine, *Enarr. in ps.* 129, 7 (CCL 40:1894–95; PL 37:1700–1).

10. The singing of the psalm is described as an innovation, which St. Augustine had to defend against conservative critics. See *Retractationes* II, 11 (PL 32:634).

11. *OR* I, 66–85 (Andrieu, *OR* 2:90–95).

12. The water was poured into the chalice in the form of a cross, probably so that it might better mix with the wine, but the gesture was subsequently interpreted as a blessing. See p. 162.

13. Gregory of Tours describes this rite in passing in connection with an unworthy deacon who let the offerings (*mysterium dominici corporis*) fall to the ground as he was carrying them to the altar: *Liber miraculorum in gloria martyrum* 85 (ed. B. Krusch, 545–46). See also *OR* XV (Andrieu, *OR* 3:122–23).

sible, Gregory of Tours relates, for a "good-for-nothing deacon" to substitute "a very rough local wine" for the Gaza wine "which he kept for
his own gullet."[14] The marks of veneration given to the gifts suggest a
procession of the Blessed Sacrament, down to the words used in desig-
nating them, such as *mysterium dominici corporis* ("mystery of the Lord's
body").[15] The *Explanation of the Old Gallican Liturgy* even says that the
Body of Christ is carried and his Blood offered.[16] The gifts were already
being looked upon, by anticipation, as what they would become through
the consecration.

The East provides no comparably explicit testimonies. The deacons
deposited the gifts on the Eucharistic table, but how did these gifts get
from the hands of the laity to those of the ministers? It is probable that
the ministers received the bread and wine at the beginning of the celebration, since, if this transfer occurred when the time came to put the gifts
on the altar, it would be difficult to explain how this whole part of the
Mass could be passed over in silence by John Chrysostom, the Jerusalem
Catecheses, and the Egyptian and Chaldean documents. The fact that these
say nothing of it suggests that even the transfer of the gifts to the altar
took place without solemnity.

A lack of solemnity, however, did not exclude a certain spaciousness
in the action, if we may trust the scattered allusions to it in this period.
Addressing the newly baptized, Athanasius of Alexandria says: "You will
see the deacons bringing the loaves and chalice and placing them on the
altar."[17] Theodore of Mopsuestia, in the Antioch region, is reminded of
Christ "going forth" to his passion "when the offering to be presented goes
forth on the patens and in the chalices . . . when the deacons bring in
from outside the 'parcel' for the oblation."[18]

This description, including the symbolism attached to the rite, reminds
us of Gallican usages and foretells the developments that would give rise
in the Byzantine rite to the "Great Entrance." The latter is attested beginning in the eighth century, but it may be earlier. Some scholars see in a
sermon of Patriarch Eutychius (552-65)[19] allusions to the Cherubic Hymn,
which accompanied the processions with the offerings and gave it an allegorical meaning: "We who symbolize the Cherubim and sing the Thrice

---

14. See n. 7 on preceding page.

15. See n. 13 on preceding page.

16. Pseudo-Germanus, *Expositio* 18 (Ratcliff 10–11).

17. St. Athanasius in a lost work that is cited in Eutychius of Constantinople, *De Paschate
et S. Eucharistia* 8 (PG 86:2401).

18. Theodore of Mopsuestia, *Homiliae catecheticae* 15 (first catechesis on the Mass),
ed. R. Tonneau and R. Devreesse (ST 145; Vatican City, Bibliotheca Apostolica Vaticana,
1949), 503 and 505.

19. See n. 17 above.

Holy to the life-giving Trinity lay aside all worldly cares that we may welcome the King of heaven and earth, who is invisibly accompanied by legions of angels."

To the accompaniment of this majestic hymn and clouds of incense, the priest and deacon carried the bread and chalice to the sanctuary, passing among the people who bowed or prostrated themselves in devotion. Sinners were here uniting themselves to the angelic liturgy, just before the offering of the sacrifice that the King of heaven would not disdain to receive.

The other Eastern Churches continued to observe a greater simplicity. In many cases, nonetheless, they assigned a certain importance to the place, usually located elsewhere in the church or close to it, where the gifts were accepted and prepared.

§3. The Meaning of the Offering

I. THE INTENTIONS OF THE OFFERERS AND THE "READING OF NAMES"

By contributing the bread and wine, Christians intended to claim a share in the fruits of the Eucharist. In about 458 Victor of Vita (North Africa) speaks of a blind man who had been miraculously cured and who approached the altar in order to present there "the offering which the bishop receives for his salvation."[20] A Council of Mâcon, in 585, bids the faithful make their contribution "in order that they may be freed of the burden of their sins."[21] A widow of Lyons believed firmly that her deceased husband "found rest on the day when she presented the offering to the Lord for his soul."

The contribution of bread and wine was thus made in the same spirit with which in our time the faithful offer a stipend for a Mass, with this difference: that the contributors had to participate in the celebration, and that they were not the only ones engaged in the offering. The people of that day could not imagine that they were paying a priest to pray in their place or that they were buying a Mass to which they acquired an exclusive right. Rather, the sacrifice was being offered for the salvation of the world, but individuals could, by their contributions, gather its fruits and apply these to their own intentions.

---

20. Victor of Vita, *De persecutione vandalica* 2, 17 (PL 58:217).
21. *Concilium Matisconense* (548), can. 4, ed. C. De Clercq, *Concilia Galliae* (CCL 148A), 240–41.

St. Jerome, however, did call attention to a different kind of ambiguity that arose from the practice of reading the names of those who contributed the bread and wine, in order to recommend them to the Lord. Here is how he expresses his dissatisfaction:

> Nowadays they read out the names of those who make an offering. Thus the Eucharist that is the ransom of sinners turns into praise of these people; they forget the widow of the gospel whose gift of two small coins to the treasury outweighed the offerings of the rich.
>
> In the churches the deacons read aloud the names of the offerers . . . and they present themselves with a thrill of delight for the plaudits of the congregation, while their conscience torments them.[22]

The Letter of Innocent I to Bishop Decentius of Gubbio, in 416, shows us a different practice on this point. In the Roman tradition the pope placed this rite within the Eucharistic Prayer: "First of all, it is necessary to recommend the offerings [an allusion to the formula that follows the *Sanctus*], and it is then [in the *Memento*] that the names of the offerers are read so that they may be mentioned during the holy mysteries."[23] The same practice was already being followed in Africa in the time of St. Cyprian; the latter speaks of a Christian who "does not deserve to be mentioned at the altar during the prayer of priests."[24]

Innocent goes on to specify: "during the holy mysteries and not during what precedes them." The allusion is to a custom on which the pope's correspondent, whose letter has not come down to us, must have insisted. We know in fact that in Gaul and Spain the rite in question did take place "before the mysteries," since it followed directly upon the bringing of the gifts to the altar. The rite ended with the prayer called *Post nomina* ("after the names"), the formularies for which have been preserved in the liturgical books.[25] In these Churches the Eucharistic Prayer did not include intercessions.

In the East we find several mentions of "those who are named in the holy churches." Were the names read at the mention of the offerers during the anaphora? "Deign to be mindful, Lord, of those who contributed the offerings today to your holy altar, those for whom each one makes offering, those whom each has in mind, and those whom we now recom-

---

22. St. Jerome, *In Hieremiam prophetam* II, 108, ed. S. Reiter (CCL 74; Turnhout: Brepols, 1960), 116; idem, *In Hezechielem prophetam* VI, 16, ed. F. Glorie (CCL 75; Turnhout: Brepols, 1964), 238.

23. Innocent I, *Ep. ad Decentium*, ed. R. Cabié (Bibliothèque de la RHE 58; Louvain: Publications Universitaires, 1973), 22 and 40–44.

24. St. Cyprian, *Ep.* 1, 2, (Bayard 3).

25. See the Gallican and Visigothic books, especially the *Liber ordinum* from Silos (seventh century), ed. M. Férotin (Monumenta Ecclesiae liturgica 5; Paris: Firmin-Didot, 1904), 235–36.

mend to you" [the celebrant makes remembrance of those whom he wishes among the living].[26]

But it is just before the opening dialogue of the Eucharistic Prayer that we find Theodore of Mopsuestia saying in his catecheses: "The names of the living and the dead are read from the church's tablets," and he explains that the prayer for those named extends, through them, to the multitude of the faithful.[27] A century later, Pseudo-Dionysius locates at this same point the "mystical proclamation of the diptychs," but his commentary on this is concerned with "those who have lived holy lives" and not any longer with those who presented the gifts.[28]

This development was fairly universal: attention was turned increasingly to those for whom the sacrifice was offered, and especially to the deceased.[29]

II. THE PARTICIPATION OF A PRIESTLY PEOPLE

The contribution of bread and wine as a way of gaining a participation in the fruits of the Eucharist was an expression of the priesthood of the faithful. The non-baptized were excluded from it, and Hippolytus called attention to the first time that the newly baptized performed this act, on the day of their initiation. "Those to be baptized will bring nothing with them except what each one brings for the Eucharist. For it is fitting that those who become worthy of doing so should provide the gifts on that same occasion."[30]

The Council of Elvira in Spain (*ca.* 300) reminded the faithful that the bishop should not receive the offering of a person who was not going to communicate[31]; this recommendation reappeared frequently from then on. Penitents, like catechumens, had already been dismissed from the assembly before the moment came for presenting the gifts. But, while those preparing for baptism were not given this honor, the faithful, and espe-

---

26. Anaphora of St. James (Jerusalem) (Hänggi-Pahl 254). See also the Syrian Anaphora of the Twelve Apostles (*ibid.*, 268): ". . . for those who have offered these gifts, for those who are regularly named in your holy churches . . . ."

27. Theodore of Mopsuestia, *Homiliae catecheticae* (Tonneau-Devreesse 527).

28. Pseudo-Dionysius, *Hierarchia ecclesiastica* 3, 2, and 3, 3, 9 (PG 3:425 and 437).

29. See Pseudo-Germanus, *Expositio* 21 (Ratcliff 13).

30. Hippolytus, *Traditio apostolica* 20 (Botte 45). Note the detail added in some witnesses: "except a single loaf for the Eucharist" ("nisi unum panem ad eucharistiam").

31. Council of Elvira, can. 28, ed. J. Vives, *Concilios visigóticos e hispano-romanos* Barcelona–Madrid: Consejo superior de investigaciones cientificas, 1963), 6: "Episcopum placuit ab eo qui non communicat munus accipere non debere."

cially the sponsors of the catechumens, could and should offer for them, that is, not in their place but for their intention.[32]

§4. A Fraternal Sharing

BIBLIOGRAPHY

B. Capelle, "Quête et offertoire," *LMD* no. 24 (1950) 121–38 (= *Travaux liturgiques* 2:222–35).

St. Justin described the Sunday assembly as the place where Christians shared with one another.[33] This was not simply because the Sunday liturgy provided an occasion for gathering and so for dealing with questions concerning the life of the Church. It was also because the "breaking of bread" together laid upon Christians the obligation of "fraternal communion" (see Acts 2:44-45). This fraternal communion was not, however, a liturgical rite, and it was therefore mentioned outside the description of the celebration proper.

The contribution of bread and wine by the faithful had its own special meaning, but it also had for its larger context the duties of fraternal charity. Thus Cyprian blushed for shame at the rich who at communion time received a portion contributed by the poor. At Rome, and doubtless elsewhere as well, only a portion of what was contributed for the Eucharist was used for this purpose, inasmuch as there was always more than required. The remainder found its way to the tables of the clergy (since the community had to support them) and of the needy.

In its practice, however, the Church carefully distinguished between offerings intended for consecration and all others. The Council of Carthage in 397 laid down this rule: "In the celebration of the Mass (*in sacramentis corporis et sanguinis Domini*) nothing is to be offered except what is in accord with the tradition that originates in the Lord himself, namely, bread and wine mixed with water."[34] But this same assembly also adverted to the matter of first fruits (only those of wheat and the vine were allowed) and of milk and honey at a Christian initiation: "Although these are offered on the altar, they receive a separate blessing, in order to show that they are clearly distinct from the sacrament of the Lord's body and blood."

---

32. Provision is made for this in the old Roman liturgy of the scrutinies. See *OR* XI, 32 (Andrieu, *OR* 2:425): "Et offeruntur oblationes a parentibus vel ab his qui ipsos suscepturi sunt," See also p. 134.

33. See pp. 14–19.

34. Council of Carthage, can. 23 (according to the *Breviarium Hipponense*), ed. C. Munier, *Concilia Africae* (CCL 149), 39–40.

Apart from bread and wine, then, everything else, even if contributed at Mass, had to be set aside away from the altar; this was a way of underscoring the different status of these other gifts. But these prescriptions had to be often repeated, because there seems to have been frequent confusion on the subject. The distinction was even further blurred by variation in customs and especially by the substitution of money for gifts in kind.

The contribution of bread and wine was not only an effective sign of fraternal sharing; it expressed another attitude as well, inasmuch as the followers of every religion spontaneously perform a cultic act by giving something that belongs to them. In the Eucharist, however, this simple act has a further context, inasmuch as the sacrifice is constituted not by the presentation of gifts but by the memorial of the Supper together with the consecration. When Christians associate themselves with the action of the Lord who, before giving thanks, took bread and a cup, it is the fruits of this mystery that they prepare to receive for themselves and for those to whom they wish to apply them.

§5. The Prayer over the Gifts

BIBLIOGRAPHY

V. Raffa, *Commento alle "orazioni sulle offerte"* (Sussidi liturgico-pastorali 10; Milan: Opera della Regalità, 1966).

Such are the ideas expressed in the only presidential prayer that is part of the preparation of the gifts in the early Roman tradition. This prayer, known as the *Super oblata* ("over the gifts") in the Gregorian Sacramentary, forms the conclusion of this part of the Mass.

The formularies are short and even simpler in style than the collect, but they are also filled with the words used in the Eucharistic Prayer for the sacrificial offering. In the prayers over the gifts, however, the sacrificial offering is related to the symbolism in the concrete gesture of depositing the gifts on the altar. Thus: the loaves piled up on the table (*muneribus altaria cumulata*) express the poverty of those who are incapable of gratifying the Lord either by their merits or by their gifts (*nihil in nobis quod placare te possit*). But these loaves also express the fidelity of the givers in doing what the Lord himself has prescribed (*quae tuis sunt instituta praeceptis*); thus the fruits of the sacrifice are bestowed in advance (*ut divinis rebus et corpore famulemur et mente*).[35]

---

35. *Le* no. 238 (p. 31); no. 165 (p. 21); no. 80 (p. 11); no. 624 (p. 81).

Chapter V

The Eucharistic Prayer

BIBLIOGRAPHY

a) *Collections of texts and translations*

A. Hänggi and I. Pahl, *Prex eucharistica. Textus e variis liturgiis antiquioribus selecti* (Spicilegium Friburgense 12; Fribourg: Editions universitaires, 1968).

A. Hamann, *Prières eucharistiques des premiers siècles à nos jours* (Foi vivante 113; Paris: Desclée De Brouwer, 1969).

Anaphorae syriacae (Rome: Oriental Institute, 1939ff.).

See also Renaudot and Brightman in the General Bibliography.

b) *Comprehensive studies*

P. Cagin, *L'eucharistia. Canon primitif de la messe, ou formulaire essentiel et premier de toutes les liturgies* (Scriptorium Solesmense II. L'Euchologie latine 2; Tournai: Desclée, 1912).

I. Rahmani, *Les liturgies orientales et occidentales etudiées séparément et comparées entre elles* (Beirut, 1929).

J. M. Hanssens, *Institutiones liturgicae de ritibus orientalibus* 2 and 3: *De missa* . . . . Also: *Indices et versiones* (= Appendix ad t. 2 et 3) (Rome: Gregorian University, 1930–32).

L. Bouyer, *Eucharist. Theology and Spirituality of the Eucharistic Prayer*, trans. C. U. Quinn (Notre Dame: University of Notre Dame Press, 1968).

J. Godart, "Traditions anciennes de la grande prière eucharistique," *QL* 47 (1966) 248–78; 48 (1967) 9–36, 198–218.

L. Maldonado, *La plegaria eucarística. Estudio de teología bíblica y litúrgica sobre la misa* (Biblioteca de autores cristianos 273; Madrid: Editorial católica, 1967).

Eucharisties d'Orient et d'Occident. Semaine liturgique de Saint-Serge, 1965 (2 vols., Lex orandi 46–47; Paris: Cerf, 1970).

A. Bouley, *From Freedom to Formula. The Evolution of the Eucharistic Prayer* (Studies in Christian Antiquity 21; Washington, D.C.: The Catholic University of America Press, 1981).

The Sacrifice of Praise. Studies on the Themes of Thanksgiving and Redemption in the Central Prayers of the Eucharistic and Baptismal Liturgies, in Honor of A. Couratin (Bibliotheca EL, Subsidia 19; Rome: Edizioni liturgiche, 1981).

The fourth and fifth centuries were a period of intense creativity in the area of Eucharistic Prayers. The period of oral tradition was now past; the formularies were put in writing and began to circulate among the communities. The Armenians and Georgians were especially skillful in assimilating for their own use texts from other places; they were not, however, the only ones.

§1. A Period of Intense Creativity

I. THE EASTERN CHURCHES

In the fourth century the eastern part of the Roman Empire saw a revival of Greek studies, of which Antioch became a famous center. Redactors of the Christian prayer of thanksgiving adopted the norms of Greek clarity. The masterpiece of the new approach was the Anaphora of St. Basil, which actually came from the pen of this Cappadocian Doctor. The prior material that he improved was a prayer—which perhaps already owed something to him—called the "Alexandrian Anaphora of St. Basil."[1] It acquired this name from the role it subsequently played in Egypt, but it was in fact a Syrian composition and reflected the outlook of the area in which it was composed.

So, for that matter, did numerous other anaphoras, such as the Anaphora of the Apostles (also Syrian), which is the source of the one we know under the name of St. John Chrysostom[2]; at Jerusalem, the Anaphora of St. James[3]; at Alexandria, the Anaphora of St. Mark (or the Anaphora of St. Cyril as it is known in its later Coptic adaptation).[4]

---

1. Byzantine Anaphora of St. Basil (Hänggi-Pahl 230–43); Alexandrian Anaphora of St. Basil (*ibid.* 348–57). — See H. Engberding, *Das eucharistische Hochgebet der Basiliosliturgie. Textgeschichtliche Untersuchungen und kritische Ausgabe* (Theologie des christlichen Ostens 1; Münster, 1931); B. Capelle, "Les liturgies 'basiliennes,' " Appendix in J. Doresse and E. Lanne, *Un témoin de la liturgie copte de S. Basile* (Bibliothèque du Muséon 47; Louvain, 1960); A. Raes, "L'authenticité de la liturgie byzantine de S. Basile," *Revue des études byzantines* 16 (1958) 158–61; *idem,* "Un nouveau document sur la liturgie de S. Basile," *OCP* 26(1960) 401–11.

2. Anaphora of the Twelve Apostles (Hänggi-Pahl 265–68); Anaphora of St. John Chrysostom (*ibid.*, 223–29). See G. Khouri-Sarkis, "L'origine syrienne de l'anaphore byzantine de S. Jean Chrysostome," *OS* 7 (1962) 3–68.

3. Anaphora of St. James (Hänggi-Pahl 244–61). See A. Tarby, *La prière eucharistique de l'Eglise de Jérusalem* (Théologie historique 17; Paris: Beauchesne, 1972).

4. Anaphora of St. Mark (Hänggi-Pahl 101–15); Coptic Anaphora of St. Cyril (*ibid.*, 135–39); oldest fragments (Strasbourg Papyrus, Manchester Papyrus, Der-Balyzeh Fragment: *ibid.* 116–27). See R. G. Coquin, "L'anaphore alexandrine de S. Marc," in *Liturgies d'Orient et d'Occident* 2 (Lex orandi 47; Paris: Cerf, 1970), 51–82.

While all these formularies, as well as others, bear the mark of the localities in which they were composed, and though each has its own special form, they also have common characteristics that reveal something of the overall plan we saw in Hippolytus.

On the other hand, a different tradition seems to have been operative in the Edessa region and in Mesopotamia, both of which were at this time on the edge of the Empire or outside its borders; the dominant culture was Semitic, the language Syriac. In addition to the Anaphora of Addai and Mari, there were two other Eucharistic Prayers from these areas— those of Nestorius and Theodore of Mopsuestia; the originals of these were doubtless composed in Greek, but in any case they differ in character from those mentioned in the preceding two paragraphs.[5] Egypt had a "prayer of offering" that went under the name of Serapion, a mid-fourth-century bishop of Thmuis, though he was probably not its author; this prayer shows certain archaic traits.[6]

The *Apostolic Constitutions* is a compilation from various sources that the author has not tried to harmonize. The "mystical Eucharist" of Book VII is a modified version of the prayer in the *Didache* and is so dependent on its original that its use in a Church of the fourth century is hardly probable. The anaphora of the "Clementine Liturgy" in Book VIII is inspired by Hippolytus.[7] Only in the extensive expansions of Hippolytus' prayer is it possible to glimpse fourth-century practice; but for a valid judgment in this area we would have to have some idea—which we do not—of the intermediate stages between the *Apostolic Tradition* and the "Clementine Liturgy."[8] The same kind of caution is required in evaluating the "Eucharist or thanksgiving over the offering" in *The Testament of Our Lord*,[9] an apocryphal document composed probably in eastern Syria in the second half of the fifth century.

In addition to directly euchological texts, there are the more or less explicit citations of such prayers in the mystagogical catecheses. The desire of the bishops of antiquity that the newly baptized should understand the sacramental rites led them to cite the formularies themselves and ex-

---

5. Anaphora of Theodore of Mopsuestia (Hänggi-Pahl 381–86); Anaphora of Nestorius (*ibid.*, 387–96). For the Anaphora of Addai and Mari see pp. 29–34.

6. Anaphora of Serapion (Funk 2:172–76; Hänggi-Pahl 128–33). See B. Botte, "L'euchologe de Sérapion est-il authentique?" *OC* 48 (1964) 50–56.

7. *Constitutiones Apostolorum* VII, 25–26 and VIIII, 4–51 (Funk 1:410–14 and 496–514).

8. See R. Cabié, "Les prières eucharistiques des 'Constitutions apostoliques' sont-elles des témoins de la liturgie du IVe siècle?" *Bulletin de littérature ecclésiastique* 84 (1983) 83–99.

9. *Testamentum Domini*, ed. I. E. Rahmani (Mainz, 1899), 38–45; trans. F. Nau, re-edited P. Ciprotti, *L'Octateuque de Clément* (Paris: Lethielleux, 1967), 36–38. See L. Ligier, "L'anaphore de la *Tradition apostolique* dans le *Testamentum Domini*," in *The Sacrifice of Praise. Studies . . . in Honor of A. Couratin* (Rome: Edizioni liturgiche, 1981), 91–106.

plain their meaning. The result is information of great value, especially when we are in a position to compare these testimonies with the anaphoras that have come down to us. I am thinking here especially of the catecheses of Theodore of Mopsuestia for the Antioch area and those of Jerusalem, that go under the name of St. Cyril but perhaps are really from his successor, John.[10]

II. THE WESTERN CHURCHES

BIBLIOGRAPHY

B. Botte, *Le canon de la messe romaine. Edition critique, introduction et notes* (Textes et études liturgiques 2; Louvain: Mont César, 1935).

L. Eizenhöfer, *Canon missae Romanae*. Pars I, *Traditio textus* (Rerum ecclesiasticarum documenta, Series minor 1; Rome: Orbis Catholicus, 1954).

P. Borella, "Il 'Canon missae' ambrosiano," *Ambrosius* 30 (1954) 225–57.

E. Bishop, "On the Early Texts of the Roman Canon," in his *Liturgica Historica* (Oxford: Clarendon Press, 1918), 77–115.

Le canon de la messe = Cours et conférences des Semaines liturgiques 7 (1928) (Louvain: Mont César, 1929).

A. Baumstark, "Das Problem des römischen Messkanons," *EL* 53 (1939) 204–44.

G. Ellard, "Interpolated Amens in the Canon of the Mass," *Theological Studies* 6 (1945) 380–91.

C. Callewaert, "Histoire positive du canon romain," *SE* 2 (1949) 95–110.

H. Frank, "Beobachtungen zur Geschichte des Messkanons," *ALW* 1 (1950) 107–19.

B. Capelle, "Innocent Ier et le canon de la messe," *RTAM* 19 (1952) 5–16 (= *Travaux liturgiques* 2:236–47).

B. Botte and C. Mohrmann, *L'Ordinaire de la messe. Texte critique, traduction et études* (Etudes liturgiques 2; Paris: Cerf, and Louvain: Mont César, 1953).

B. Opfermann, "Die Erforschung des römischen Messkanons," *Theologie und Glaube* 44 (1954) 263–79.

J. A. Jungmann, *The Eucharistic Prayer. A Study of the Canon Missae*, trans. R. T. Batley (Notre Dame: Fides, 1956).

E. Griffe, "Trois textes importants pour l'histoire du canon de la messe," *Bulletin de littérature ecclésiastique* 59 (1958) 65–72.

P. Borella, "Il canone della messa romana nella sua evoluzione storica," *Ambrosius* 35 (1959), *Supplemento*, [26]–[50].

K. Gamber, "Canonica prex. Eine Studie über den altrömischen Messkanon," *Heiliger Dienst* 17 (1963) 1–16.

P. Borella, "Unità e continuità del Canone nei testi ambrosiani del Giovedì santo e della veglia pasquale," *Ambrosius* 41 (1965) 79–100.

La Maison-Dieu no. 87 (1966): *Le canon de la messe*.

10. Theodore of Mopsuestia, *Homiliae catecheticae* 15 and 16 (1st and 2nd on the Mass) (Tonneau-Devreesse 461–601). —Cyril of Jerusalem, *Catecheses mystagogicae* 5, 4–10, ed. A. Piédagnel and trans. P. Paris (SC 126; Paris: Cerf, 1966), 150–61. See A. Tarby (n. 3, above).

P. Borella, "Evoluzione storica e struttura letteraria del Canone della messa romana,"
in *Il canone. Studio biblico, teologico, storico, liturgico* (Liturgica, nuov. ser. 5;
Padua, 1968), 95–113.

M. Ramos, *La gran oración eucarística en la antigua misa española* (Granada:
Facultad de Teología, 1963).

M. S. Gros, "El *ordo missae* de la tradición hispánica A," in *Liturgia y música
mozárabes* (I. Congreso internacional de estudios mozárabes, Toledo, 1975;
Toledo: Instituto de San Eugenio, 1978), 45–64.

Complete formularies for the Eucharistic Prayer appear in the West
only at a later period, although there is sure evidence that at least a number of component parts go back to the fourth century.

No text has survived from the Church of Africa, which was the first
to use Latin in its liturgy. We know only that "the prayer (*oratio*) at the
altar should always be addressed to the Father" and that a Mauretanian
bishop compiled a collection of liturgical formularies.[11] While Augustine
can hardly be said to have cited the words of the anaphora, he was
nonetheless concerned with the participation of the congregation and especially its interior attitude at this point in the celebration. It is from this
point of view that he comments on the opening dialogue and the concluding Amen.

The earliest witnesses to the practice of the Roman Church do not come
from the Eternal City but from Milan, where St. Ambrose cites a lengthy
passage that is very close in its tenor to the central part of the Roman
Canon.[12] Elsewhere, the Visgothic liturgical books preserve fragments that
are adaptations of a version of the Roman prayer that is earlier than the
one known to us.[13] There are allusions in St. Leo (440–61) and Gelasius
(492–96) to expressions in this later formulary, but the formulary cannot
be regarded as having reached its definitive state until after St. Gregory
(590–604).[14]

In any event, one thing is certain: the Roman Canon was not a simple
development of the prayer in the *Apostolic Tradition*. Note must also be
taken of the fact that Rome had only one formulary for the Eucharistic
Prayer, although this allowed for variable "prefaces" and a few variable
inserts. Pope Vigilius, writing to Profuturus of Braga in 538, says that

---

11. Council of Hippo (393), can. 21, in *Breviarium Hipponense*, ed. C. Munier, *Concilia Africae* (CCL 149), 39. — Gennadius, *Liber de scriptoribus ecclesiasticis* 78 (PL 58:1103).

12. St. Ambrose, *De sacramentis* IV, 21–22, 26–27, ed. B. Botte (SC 25bis; Paris: Cerf,
1961), 114–16; Hänggi-Pahl 421–22.

13. *Liber ordinum*, ed. M. Férotin (Monumenta Ecclesiae liturgica 5; Paris: Firmin-Didot,
1904), 321–22, 239–41, 265; *Liber mozarabicus sacramentorum*, ed. M. Férotin (Monumenta
Ecclesiae liturgica 6; Paris: Firmin-Didot, 1912), nos. 1440 and 627.

14. The *Liber Pontificalis* tells of two additions made to the earlier text: "sanctum sacrificium, etc." in the *Supra quae*, and "diesque nostros in tua pace disponas" in the *Hanc igitur*.
The changes are attributed respectively to St. Leo I and St. Gregory I (*LP* 1:239 and 312).

we do not have a different set of Mass prayers (*ordinem precum in celebra- tione missarum*) for particular seasons or feasts, but always use the same text in consecrating the gifts offered to God (*eodem tenore oblata Deo munera consecrare*). When we celebrate the feasts of Easter, the Lord's Ascension, Epiphany, or the saints of God, we add special paragraphs proper to the day.[15]

In the Churches of Gaul and Spain the Eucharistic Prayer was made up of three formulas that varied from Mass to Mass; two of them came before and one after the account of institution (this was the only unvary- ing prayer; it began with the word *Pridie*, "on the day before . . ."). In Gaul the three were called the *Immolatio* or *Contestatio*, the *Collectio post Sanctus*, and the *Post mysteria* or *Post secreta*; in Spain they were known as the *Illatio*, *Post Sanctus*, and *Post pridie*. The texts we have of these prayers do not go back before the sixth century; moreover, they have come down to us, especially those for the area north of the Pyrenees, in forms modified by external influences or by eventual confusions among the various prayers.

III. THE VARIOUS NAMES FOR THE EUCHARISTIC PRAYER

Various designations were used for the Eucharistic Prayer, depending on time and place; none of them, however, expressed in a fully adequate way the reality being named. All of them were words that had another meaning as well; for this reason, while the technical meaning they had acquired made them useful, they themselves seemed to say that there is no fully satisfactory name for this action that is unparalleled in human experience.

The Greeks used the word *anaphora*, which by its etymology meant "elevation, lifting up," but was also currently used in speaking of an offer- ing; it was for this reason that it was used of the Eucharistic Prayer. It had its equivalent in the Syriac *qorbana*; the Latin term *oratio oblationis* ("prayer of offering") was also found. It should not be concluded, how- ever, that the Eucharist was being reduced to a simple offering; the vocabu- lary used was evocative rather than descriptive; it formally expressed one aspect of the Eucharistic Prayer, while pointing to a still richer content.

The word closest to *anaphora* in the vocabulary of the West was doubt- less *illatio*, which in ordinary usage likewise had the meanings of "contri- bution" and "sacrifice." But this term was used, for practical purposes, only in the Visigothic Church. Even there, moreover, it referred properly only to the first part of the Eucharistic Prayer, the one corresponding to

---

15. Vigilius, *Ep.* 2, 5 (PL 69:18).

the Roman preface and to the Gallican *immolatio*, which suggested the Eucharistic sacrifice, or *contestatio*, which meant "witness" or "intense prayer" and could also be used of the profession of faith. But despite the restricted technical meaning, these various nouns could also be used of the Eucharistic Prayer in its entirety.

In the Roman rite custom imposed the name "Canon," which meant "rule" and seemed to have little relation to the Eucharistic Prayer. In fact, this Greek word was used first in the expression *canon actionis*, which occurs in the Gelasian Sacramentary. The expression says two things: that the Eucharist is an *actio*, a term that was preserved in the rubrics of the later (Latin) Roman Missal, *infra actionem* ("within the action"); and that the Eucharistic Prayer given in the Sacramentary was the "rule" to be followed in celebrating this "action." Only the first word, *canon*, became the regular name for the Eucharistic Prayer.

Another Roman name for the Eucharistic Prayer was *prex* ("prayer"), which occurs especially in St. Gregory the Great. The Eucharistic Prayer is the prayer *par excellence*, since it is supremely effective in bringing to pass the greatest of mysteries; as such, this *prex* needs no qualifying adjective.

It should be pointed out that the term *canon actionis* in the Gelasian Sacramentary is a title that precedes the *Sursum corda*, whereas not too long afterwards the Canon was said to begin only after the *Sanctus*.[16] In like manner, the term *praefatio*, which in St. Cyprian seems to apply to the introductory dialogue,[17] came to designate the entire variable section that, in Roman usage, constitutes the beginning of the anaphora.[18]

§2. The Introductory Dialogue

BIBLIOGRAPHY

H. Engberding, "Der Gruss des Priesters zu Beginn der Eucharistia in den östlichen Liturgien," *JLW* 9 (1929) 138–43.
J. Hausleiter, "Erhebung des Herzens," *RAC* 6 (1964) 1–22.
C. A. Bouman, "Variants in the Introduction to the Eucharistic Prayer," *Vigiliae Christianae* 4 (1950) 94–115.
E. Ferguson, "The Liturgical Function of the *Sursum corda*," in *Studia Patristica* 13 (TU 116; Berlin: Akademie Verlag, 1975), 360–63.

---

16. See p. 133.
17. St. Cyprian, *De dominica oratione* 31, ed. G. Hartel (CSEL 3, 1; Vienna, 1868), 289.
18. In the Gallican Liturgy the term *Praefatio* designates a formulary that is not a prayer but a kind of admonition in which, before the Eucharistic Prayer, the priest describes the feast or mystery of the day.

Everywhere in the tradition, the Eucharistic Prayer was preceded by a dialogue, inspired by Jewish practice, between president and congregation. It begins with a salutation that takes its simplest and certainly its oldest form in the Churches of the West and the liturgies of the Alexandrian type. "The Lord be with you [with you all; with all]. — And with your spirit."

In areas influenced by Antioch, the wish was replaced by a more or less modified version of 2 Cor 13:13: "The grace of the Lord Jesus Christ, the love of God, and the fellowship of the Holy Spirit be with all of you."[19]

The president then urges the congregation to adopt the spiritual attitude that will prepare it for the prayer of thanksgiving: "Lift up your hearts. — We have them lifted to the Lord."

This simple formula, which has been retained in the Latin liturgies, is certainly the oldest of the formulas. It is attested in the Jerusalem catecheses and is at times found even today in the East. In general, however, variants were used: "Let us lift up our hearts," "Lift up your spirits," "We lift up spirit and heart," to say nothing of the fuller development found among the Eastern Syrians.

Encouraged, as it were, by the response he has received from the congregation, the celebrant is able to urge them to say or perform the Eucharist (it is both a prayer and an action that they are entering into with Christ): "Let us give thanks to the Lord. — [It is] right and just."

This was the formula of Hippolytus, although later tradition at Rome added "our God" to the celebrant's exhortation. The East remained faithful to the original version, which is attested for Jerusalem, Antioch, Constantinople, and Alexandria. The response is found universally. The two adjectives, which are very close in meaning, capture the whole purport of the thanksgiving or, we might say (with the etymology of the Greek word *axios*, "right," in mind), its whole weight. The response is thus the high point of the entire dialogue. The priestly people are "with" their Lord, whose presence is symbolized by the celebrant who through ordination has received Christ's "spirit." The attention of all is focused on the "heights" where the risen Christ lives in glory; all are intent on entering with him into his passage "from this world to the Father" (John 13:1). The prayer that follows is linked to the introduction by its opening words: "It is truly right and just."

---

19. The Byzantine anaphoras reproduce the passage almost verbatim; others prefer to restore the usual order of persons in the Trinity by inverting the first two names (see the Anaphora of James) or even by attributing grace to the Father and love to the Son. For the response of the congregation see p. 50.

§3. Expression of Thanksgiving and *Sanctus*

BIBLIOGRAPHY

W. C. Van Unnik, "I Clem. 34 and the Sanctus," *Vigiliae Christianae* 5 (1951) 204–48.

B. Capelle, "Problèmes textuels de la préface romaine," in *Mélanges Lebreton* II = *RechSR* 40 (1952) 139–50.

L. Chavoutier, "Un libellus pseudo-ambrosien sur le Saint-Esprit," *SE* 11 (1960) 174–91.

E. Dekkers, "*Propheteia–Praefatio*," in *Mélanges . . . Christine Mohrmann* (Utrecht: Spectrum, 1963), 190–95.

E. Moeller, *Corpus praefationum* (5 vols. CCL 161–161D; Turnhout: Brepols, 1980–81). The first volume has an *Etude préliminaire* and an extensive bibliography (cliv–cxci).

I. "IT IS TRULY RIGHT AND JUST TO GIVE YOU THANKS"

The entire Eucharistic Prayer is a thanksgiving, but the thanksgiving found expression especially in the statement of the motives for it, which were always brought out at the beginning of the anaphora. Simplifying somewhat, we might say that the motives included, on the one hand, God himself, whose greatness and mercies we contemplate, and, on the other, the history of salvation in which God has performed his "marvelous deeds." The second motive implicitly included the first, which was not always developed. This was true of the *Vere dignum* ("It is truly right . . .") of the Roman Canon, the first of the variable prayers in this otherwise fixed formulary. Each *Vere dignum* mentioned only one of the motives for "blessing" the Lord (the one chosen depended on the feast being celebrated); the liturgical cycle as a whole brought out the various facets of the mystery of salvation, using concise formulas that refer almost exclusively to the essential, i.e., christological, dimension. The same was true of the *Illatio* or *Contestatio* of the Spanish-Gallican liturgy, despite the very different style and far greater prolixity of the latter.

The Eastern anaphoras, on the other hand, had no variable parts. Each tried to present a comprehensive view of the Christian "economy," perhaps developing the picture in great detail as in the Liturgy of St. Basil, perhaps outlining it in a rather sketchy form as in the Liturgy of St. Mark:

> It is truly right and just . . . to give you thanks *night and day* with lips that never cease speaking, lips that never fall still, and with hearts that are never silent. For *you made the heavens and all they contain, the earth and all that is in it*, the sea, the springs, the lakes *(and the rivers) and all that is in them. You made human beings in your image and likeness* and gave them the enjoyment of paradise. When they had broken your commandment, you did not despise and abandon them but in your goodness called them anew through the Law. You instructed them through the prophets.

> Finally, you restored and renewed them through this awesome, lifegiving and heavenly mystery. *And you did all this through him who is your wisdom and the true light, your Son, our Lord* and God *and Savior Jesus Christ* . . .[20]

This passage calls to mind the creation of both material things and human beings, then the fulfillment of this creative work by the incarnation, the way for which is prepared by the promises made after the Fall. The Euchologion (Prayer Book) of Serapion focuses less on the world that issued from the hands of the Most High than upon God himself, "uncreated, mysterious, incomprehensible to any and every creature." In some prayers these negative terms used in describing the Lord form a lengthy list; the composer finds it impossible to speak of him except by rejecting all the limitations found in our universe (a negative or "apophatic theology").

Many Antiochene anaphoras use the *Sanctus* as a climax for this vision of the Father who made heaven and earth and receives their adoration. After the song of the Seraphim these anaphoras then develop the various aspects of salvation in a kind of revitalized surge of thanksgiving. In Basil this thanksgiving consists of over fifty biblical citations linked together to form a vast fresco leading into the New Testament. The account of the Last Supper finds its natural place in this unfolding sacred history. The artistic development gives the whole both a unity and a Trinitarian structure in which, after the evocation of the Son, the epiclesis speaks of the Holy Spirit.

II. "HOLY, HOLY, HOLY LORD . . . ."

In the carefully elaborated anaphoras of which I have just spoken, the *Sanctus* fits in well. In many others, however, it gives the impression of being simply added on. And in fact the *Sanctus* does not seem to have belonged to the Eucharistic Prayer in its primitive form. The anaphora of the *Apostolic Tradition* does not have it.[21] This is not surprising, inasmuch as the Christian prayer of thanksgiving originated in the Jewish liturgy for meals, which did not have the *Sanctus*. The *Sanctus* came from the inaugural vision of Isaiah (Isa 6:3) and was used above all in the liturgy of the synagogue; thus, at least from the second century A.D. on, the *Shema Israel* in the morning office was preceded by a blessing (*Yotser*) for light and creation, in the course of which the *Sanctus* was recited. Was

---

20. The Anaphora of Mark expands upon a text that contains only the words in italics and is known through a papyrus fragment preserved at Strasbourg; ed. M. Andrieu and P. Collomp, "Fragment sur papyrus des l'Anaphore de S. Marc," *RevSR* 8 (1928) 489–515.

21. See p. 27.

it from here that the composers of the anaphoras took it? In any case, in the anaphoras heaven is always mentioned along with earth as being filled with the glory of God.

We find the *Sanctus* attested in the East as early as the third quarter of the fourth century,[22] while in Egypt the prayer of Serapion was built around the *Sanctus*. It is noteworthy, however, that when the Latin Fathers of this same period commented on the passage in Isaiah, they made no reference to its liturgical use. On the other hand, a short treatise on the Holy Spirit that was written in northern Italy around 400 says that the entire congregation joins the priest in singing this acclamation during Mass "in almost all the eastern Churches and in some western Churches."[23] Was Rome among the latter?[24] Perhaps, since in this period of anti-Arian conflict the text of Isaiah was given a Trinitarian interpretation. Thus in 484 a profession of faith by African bishops says: ". . . adoring and glorifying the Most Holy Trinity, as we do during the mysteries when we say 'Holy . . . .'"[25] In Gaul the song of the Seraphim was first introduced in festal Masses, since the Council of Vaison in 529 prescribes its use in every Mass.[26] Nonetheless, as late as the fifth and sixth centuries, even in the East, there were anaphoras that omitted it.[27]

The *Sanctus* was always introduced by a reference to the heavenly liturgy,[28] although this reference did not always follow smoothly upon what preceded it. Moreover, an acclamation taken from the gospel was added to the passage from Isaiah, except in the Egyptian and Ethiopian liturgies: "Blessed be he who comes in the name of the Lord! Hosanna in the highest [heavens]" (Matt 21:9; see Ps 117:26 LXX, Vg). In the West the

---

22. Gregory of Nyssa, *De baptismo* (PG 46:421); St. John Chrysostom, *In Eph. hom.* 14, 4 (PG 62:104). See also PG 56:97 and 158; 61:232; 62:104 and 363.

23. L. Chavoutier, "Un libellus pseudo-ambrosien sur le Saint-Esprit," *SE* 11 (1960) 189.

24. Chavoutier thinks Pope Damasus introduced the *Sanctus*, since he exchanged letters with St. Jerome on the Trinitarian significance of Isaiah's hymn (*ibid.*, 183–84).

25. Victor of Vita, *Historia persecutionum* II, 100, ed. M. Petschenig (CSEL 7; Vienna, 1881), 70–71. The same passage is found in Pseudo-Athanasius, whose tenth book is considered to be of Spanish provenance (CCL 9:145). Who copied whom?

26. Council of Vaison, can. 3, ed. C. De Clercq (CCL 148A), 79: "The *Sanctus* is always to be said, as it is in public Masses" (". . . semper Sanctus . . . quomodo ad missas publicas dicitur, dici debeat . . .").

27. Fragments have been discovered of Italian anaphoras that lacked the *Sanctus*: L. C. Mohlberg, *Sacramentarium Veronense*, 202 (see PL 138:883–84; *DACL* 1:2816). For the East see B. Botte, "Fragments d'une anaphore inconnue attribuée à S. Epiphane," *Le Muséon* 73 (1960) 311–15. See also *Testamentum Domini*, ed. I. E. Rahmani, 40–41.

28. The reference is inspired by Isa 6, but also by Ezek 10, Dan 7:10, and Rev 4:8-10. The connection with the passage in Daniel is already made in Clement of Rome, *Ad Corinthios* 34, ed. H. Hemmer (Textes et documents 10; Paris: Picard, 1926). This does not prove that Clement knew a Eucharist that included the *Sanctus*. See W. C. Van Unnik, "I Clem 34 and the Sanctus," *Vigiliae Christianae* 5 (1951) 204–48.

Benedictus verse made its appearance in St. Caesarius of Arles,[29] in the first half of the sixth century.

After the Sanctus the priestly prayer picked up again in a more or less artificial way. Thus in the Spanish-Gallican liturgy the priest began "Vere sanctus" ("Holy indeed") and said, in substance, ". . . Sanctus Iesus, qui pridie . . ." ("Holy is Jesus, who on the day before he suffered. . . ."). The same procedure was followed, though with wide variations, in many anaphoras. In the Alexandrian liturgy the linking idea was not holiness but fullness, which was better suited to lead into the epiclesis that followed: "Heaven and earth are filled with your glory. . . . Fill this sacrifice too. . . ." The Roman Canon, for its part, was unconcerned with establishing a link between the Sanctus and what immediately followed, namely, the "recommendation of the gifts," of which Innocent I spoke in 416.[30]

§4. The Account of Institution, the Anamnesis and Offering

BIBLIOGRAPHY

F. Hamm, Die liturgischen Einsetzungsberichte im Sinne vergleichender Liturgieforschung (LQF 23; Münster: Aschendorff, 1928).

A. Raes, "Les paroles de la consécration dans les anaphores syriennes," OCP 3 (1937) 484–504.

J. M. Hanssens, "Une formule énigmatique des anaphores éthiopiennes," OCP 7 (1941) 206–32.

A. Raes, "Le récit de l'institution eucharistique dans l'anaphore chaldéenne et malabare des Apôtres," OCP 10 (1944) 216–26.

B. Botte, "Problèmes de l'anamnèse," Journal of Ecclesiastical History 5 (1954) 16–24.

B. Capelle, "L'évolution du Qui pridie de la messe romaine," RTAM 22 (1955) 5–16 (= Travaux liturgiques 2:176–286).

J. Jungmann, "Das Gedächtnis des Herrn in der Eucharistia," Theologische Quartalschrift 133 (1963) 385–99.

L. Ligier, "Célébration divine et anamnèse dans la première partie de l'anaphore ou canon de la messe orientale," Gregorianum 48 (1967) 225–52; also in Eucharisties d'Orient et d'Occident 2 (Lex Orandi 47; Paris: Cerf, 1972), 139–78.

B. Botte, "Mysterium fidei," Bible et vie chrétienne no. 80 (1968) 29–34.

—————, " 'Et elevatis oculis in caelum.' Etude sur les rites liturgiques de la dernière Cène," in Gestes et paroles dans les diverses familles liturgiques (Bibliotheca EL, Subsidia 14; Rome: Centro Liturgico Vincenziano, 1978), 77–86.

V. Fiala, "Les prières d'acceptation de l'offrande et le genre littéraire du canon romain," in Eucharisties d'Orient et d'Occident 1 (Lex Orandi 46; Paris: Cerf, 1970), 117–33.

---

29. St. Caesarius of Arles, Serm. 73, 2, ed. G. Morin (CCL 103; Turnhout: Brepols, 1953), 307.

30. See p. 81.

J. Pinell, "Anámnesis y epíclesis en el antiguo rito gallicano," *Didaskalia* 4 (1974) 3–130.

G. Ramis, "El memorial eucarístico, concepto y formulación en los textos de la anáforas," *EL* 91 (1982) 189–208.

Once God had been blessed for all his wonderful deeds that culminated in the paschal mystery, the next step was to express, via the signs of the Eucharistic meal, the "today" of Christ's sacrifice. This was done through the account of institution and the anamnesis (or remembering), which, as I pointed out earlier,[31] were closely connected. Rarely were the two intermingled as in the prayer of Serapion. As a general rule, the evocation of the Supper preceded the expression of remembrance.

I. THE ACCOUNT OF THE INSTITUTION OF THE EUCHARIST

It is at this point that the various Eucharistic formularies resembled each other most closely, although we never find exactly the same wording twice, and the texts could range from the very sober to the very prolix. The liturgical account of institution also differed from the corresponding passages in the New Testament, since it issued from a tradition that had been independent of the Scriptures, although the latter eventually exercised an influence, especially in the direction of a greater symmetry between the ritual of the bread and that of the cup.

The special character of the liturgical account of institution shows itself in two points. First, the account is incorporated into a prayer, so that during it the celebrant continues to address God; in the Roman Canon, for example, he says *"Tibi gratias agens"* ("giving thanks to you, Father"). The liturgical account is thus anything but a Scripture reading added on in order to explain the action. Second, the liturgical account includes details not given in the account of the Last Supper. Some of these are taken from some other part of the gospel, e.g., "lifting his eyes to heaven, to you" (multiplication of the loaves). Others are nonbiblical, e.g., the observation on the hands of Christ (Roman Canon: *"in sanctas et venerabiles manus suas,"* "into his holy and venerable hands"; St. John Chrysostom: *"en tais hagiais autou kai achrantois kai amōmētois chersin"*); the mention of the water that is mixed with the wine (St. James: *"to potērion kerasas ex oinou kai hudatos,"* "having mixed water and wine in the cup"; "having mixed" is found in many anaphoras); the mention of the Savior being the first to drink from the cup (*geusamenos,* "Having tasted": Twelve Apostles, Alexandrian Anaphora of Basil); or the expression "the holy disciples and apostles."

---

31. See pp. 28 and 33–34.

In addition to these nonbiblical details, most of which are ancient, there are redundancies, since there is a tendency to multiply more or less synonymous verbs, adjectives, and nouns. Some terms carrying a theological significance are also introduced: Jesus "sanctifies" (*hagiasas*) the bread and cup; he "fills" the cup "with the Holy Spirit" (St. James: *"plēsas pneumatos hagiou"*).

The recall of the Supper always begins with a reference to the death of Christ: "When he was about to hand himself over," "On the night before he suffered," and ends (with some exceptions) with the Lord's command: "Do this in remembrance of me." In the East the anaphoras quite often add to the Lord's command the recommendation of St. Paul: "As often as you eat this bread and drink this cup, you proclaim my death until I come." This in turn is almost always accompanied by the gloss: "you confess my resurrection" and even (in Mark and Basil) "my ascension." I mentioned earlier the original form of the East Syrian Anaphora of Theodore: "Do the same, whenever you gather, in memory of me."[32]

II. THE ANAMNESIS

This command of the Lord is fulfilled in the liturgical action; remembering him, we offer his sacrifice. This was clearly expressed in the Roman Canon and in liturgies of the Antiochene type, which followed the same line as Hippolytus: *Unde et memores, Memnēmenoi oun* ("Calling to mind, therefore"). The object of the remembrance is the paschal mystery. The most concise texts went straight to the essential point: the death and resurrection. Many anaphoras, however, included other "events" as well, especially the ascension and the return at the end of time. The Roman Canon, for example, says:

> ". . . calling to mind the blessed passion of this same Christ, your Son, our Lord, and also his resurrection from the grave, and glorious ascension into heaven. . . ." The Syrian Anaphora of the Twelve Apostles departs here from the usual pattern and addresses Christ himself:
>
> As we remember, Lord, this salutary command and the entire plan which you carried out for us: your cross, your death, your burial, your resurrection from the dead on the third day, our ascension into heaven, your sitting at the right hand of the Father's Majesty, and your glorious second coming at which you will pass glorious judgment on the living and the dead and render to individuals according to their works. . . .

Offerimus, prospheromen ("we offer"). The gift offered to the Father is described in sacramental terms. The texts do not adopt a realistic stance

---

32. See pp. 33–34.

and say: "the body and the blood of Christ." They use, instead, symbolic language: "What is yours, (taken) from what is yours" (*Ta sa ek tōn sōn*: Basil, Chrysostom); "this awe-inspiring and unbloody sacrifice" (James); "we . . . offer . . . of the gifts you have bestowed on us, a perfect, holy, and unblemished Victim, the sacred bread of everlasting life and the chalice of eternal salvation" (Roman Canon). The gift which the Lord himself made of his life becomes "today" in the action of the celebrating Church. Notice, in the Roman Canon, the use of the first person plural, which is specified in the prayer of St. Gregory the Great as "we, your servants, and with us your holy people" (*nos servi tui et plebs tua sancta*).

The Roman formulary added a petition (the *Supra quae propitius*, "Be pleased to look") that the offering might prove acceptable to God. This prayer was already known to St. Ambrose in a shorter form: "We ask and implore you to accept this offering through the hands of your angel at your altar on high, as you deigned to accept the gifts of your servant Abel, the sacrifice of Abraham our father, and the sacrifice which Melchisedech the high priest offered to you."

This petition with its recall of the three sacrifices that the Bible assures us were acceptable to God, was peculiar to the Roman tradition.[33] The Byzantine anaphoras ended the anamnesis with an acclamation: "We praise you, we bless you, we thank you, we implore you."[34]

Once we move outside the Antiochene and Roman liturgies, we no longer find the same clear and meticulous structure. In the Alexandrian Anaphora of St. Mark, for example, the account of institution is linked to what follows not by the words "in remembrance of me" but by the phrases "you proclaim my death, you confess my resurrection": "As we proclaim the death of your only Son . . . and confess his resurrection . . . we set before you. . . ." Among the Eastern Syrians the Anaphora of Theodore uses as its springboard the words "Do the same, as often as you come together": ". . . we have come together . . . to celebrate . . . the great, holy, and awe-inspiring mystery by which salvation has been wrought . . . and we offer . . . ." Other expressions still less classical are to be found, even in the Gallican-Hispanic liturgy, although here the *Post pridie* prayer brings us back to familiar ground:

> Lord, we remember your Son . . . because, coming among humankind, he made the human condition his own; to redeem the human beings he had

---

33. This prayer is illustrated by the fine mosaic in Sant'Apollinare in Classe in Ravenna, in which we see Abel, Abraham, and Melchizedek as concelebrants at the same altar. See A. Baumstark, *Liturgia romana e liturgia dell'essarcato* (Rome: Pustet, 1904), 168.

34. This acclamation, which already occurs in the Anaphora of Addai and Mari, is also found in the Anaphora of the Twelve Apostles in place of the offering, which is not given expression after the anamnesis.

created he suffered the cross for human salvation; to conquer the death we had merited and to tread it under foot he handed himself over for our sake to the death he had not merited; he emptied hell in part by abandoning the wicked and taking up to heaven with him at his resurrection the saints who were detained there; by returning to heaven he opened the way for us to ascend to heaven; he will come to judge the living and the dead, to condemn the wicked and sinners to eternal torment, and to bestow his eternal glory on the faithful who have kept his commandments. Through him, Father Most High, we implore you to accept with good will this offering that is pleasing to you and that our hands present to you; we ask you to bless it and look upon it with kindly eye from your throne on high, so that all of us who share in it for our nourishment may derive from it salvation and the healing of soul and body.[35]

The final lines of this prayer turn our attention to a further component of the Eucharistic Prayer. To this I now turn.

§5. Invocation of the Fruits of the Eucharist upon the Communicants, and the Epiclesis

BIBLIOGRAPHY

A. Chavasse, "L'épiclèse eucharistique dans les anciennes liturgies orientales. Une hypothèse d'interprétation," *Mélanges de science religieuse* 2 (1946) 197–206.
B. Botte, "L'épiclèse de l'anaphore d'Hippolyte," *RTAM* 14 (1947) 241–51.
C. Callewaert, "Histoire positive du canon romain: Une épiclèse à Rome," *SE* 2 (1949) 95–110.
S. Salaville, "Epiclèse eucharistique," in *Catholicisme* 4 Paris: Letouzey et Ané, 1953), 302–7.
O. Burmester, "The Epiclesis in the Eastern Church and the 'Heavenly Altar' of the Roman Canon," in *Tome commémoratif du millénaire de la bibliothèque patriarcale d'Alexandrie* (Alexandrie, 1953), 277–96.
A. Sage, "Saint Augustin et la prière du canon *Supplices te rogamus*," *Revue des études byzantines* 11 (1953) 252–65.
B. Botte, "L'épiclèse dans les liturgies syriennes orientales," *SE* 6 (1954) 48–72.
J. Pinell, "Anámnesis y epíclesis en el antiguo rito gallicano," *Didaskalia* 4 (1974) 3–130.
I. H. Dalmais, "L'Esprit-Saint et le mystère du salut dans les épiclèses eucharistiques syriennes," *Istina* 18 (1973) 147–54, and *EL* 90 (1976) 262–71.
D. B. Spinks, "The Consecration Epiclesis in the Anaphora of St. James," *Studia Liturgica* (Rotterdam) 11 (1976) 19–38.

The prayer that follows the anamnesis in the Anaphora of St. Basil may be taken as the quintessential Eastern epiclesis:

---

35. *Liber mozarabicus sacramentorum* no. 34 (4th Sunday of Advent), ed. M. Férotin (Monumenta Ecclesiae liturgica 6; Paris: Firmin-Didot, 1912), 21–22.

May it please your goodness that your Holy Spirit come upon us and the gifts here offered, in order to bless and sanctify them and to consecrate this bread as the adorable body of our Lord, God and Savior Jesus Christ and this cup as the adorable blood of our Lord, God and Savior Jesus Christ that was shed for the life of the world. Grant, too, that all of us who share in the same body and the same cup may be united to one another in a sharing of the one Spirit.

An analysis of this passage shows the following components:
1. The Father is asked to send his Spirit
2. on "us" (those who have presented the gifts and will receive them back in communion), and
3. on the gifts offered
   a. in order that they may be blessed and sanctified
   b. and that the bread may be consecrated as the Body of Christ and the cup as the Blood of Christ.
4. As a result, sharing in the bread and cup will bring about a communion of all in the one Spirit.

If we look at the less developed formularies representative of the traditions that led up to the Basilian formulary, we find our attention drawn in three directions. First, the *Apostolic Tradition*: "Send your Holy Spirit on the offering of your holy Church, to bring together in unity all those who receive it. May they be filled with the Holy Spirit." Of the components of the Basilian formulary, as analyzed above, the Hippolytan prayer includes nos. 1, 3 (without a or b), and 4. The object of the prayer is the sanctification of the communicants, the bread and wine serving as vehicles of divine life.[36] No. 2 in the Basilian formulary seems intended to convey the same meaning, despite what follows there.

A second earlier formulary is the Anaphora of Addai and Mari, which contains, in addition, no. 3a.[37] Finally, there is the Prayer Book (Euchologion) of Serapion that also includes no. 3b. The formulary of Serapion has two further peculiarities. First, the consecration is attributed to the Logos; this is probably an archaic, theologically undeveloped way of speaking of the divine action in a matter that concerns Christ. Second, there is also a petition that precedes the account of institution: "Fill this sacrifice with your power and participation"; this, along with an explicit mention of the Spirit, would remain characteristic of the entire Alexandrian tradition.

Not surprisingly, the more profound theology of the Third Person of the Trinity that developed, especially in the Patriarchate of Antioch, led

---

36. See p. 28.
37. "May your Holy Spirit come, Lord, may he rest upon this offering (of your servants), may he bless and sanctify it, so that it may win for us. . . ."

to an enrichment of this prayer in the literature tributary to Hippolytus. Thus there is the gloss in the *Apostolic Constitutions*: "May he [the Spirit] make it clear (*apophēnē*, "manifest") that the bread is the body . . . the wine the blood." The Anaphora of the Apostles uses almost the same language, while adding the words "upon us." The liturgy of St. John Chrysostom replaces the language of "manifestation" with a more realistic terminology according to which the Spirit "makes" (*poiēson*) the bread be the Lord's Body and the wine his Blood.

One point is clear: We find everywhere a petition for a divine intervention that will affect the gifts so that those who share in them may be sanctified. Though the Roman Canon does not mention the Spirit,[38] it does have the petition that the participants in the Eucharist may receive its fruits. The petition is here mediated through the image of the two altars and the twofold movement associated with them: the offering of human beings ascends to God and then comes back in blessing upon those who approach the table of sacrifice. As in the Egyptian tradition, the account of institution is preceded by an invocation of divine consecratory power.[39]

In the Gallican-Hispanic liturgies the extensive collection of *Post Pridie* prayers contains some that resemble the prayers we have been examining from the other traditions.

The practice of the epiclesis would eventually give rise to the theological problem of the moment of consecration; we cannot go into it here. It must be noted, however, that for centuries the various Churches used the formularies created by their respective traditions, and yet this did not cause the slightest controversy among them.

§6. The Intercessory Prayers

BIBLIOGRAPHY

V. L. Kennedy, "The Pre-Gregorian *Hanc igitur*," EL 50 (1936) 349-58.
_____, *The Saints of the Canon of the Mass* (Studi di antichità cristiana 14; Vatican City, 1938).
B. Capelle, "*Et omnibus orthodoxis atque apostolicae fidei cultoribus*," in *Miscellanea historica Alberti de Meyer* 1 (Louvain, 1946), 137-50 (= *Travaux liturgiques* 2:258-68).
P. Borella, "S. Leone Magno e il *Communicantes*," EL 60 (1946) 93-101.

---

38. There is no basis for identifying the angel of this prayer with the Spirit; St. Ambrose speaks of "angels" and has only the ascending movement. See B. Botte, "L'ange du sacrifice et l'épiclèse de la messe romaine au moyen-âge," *RTAM* 1 (1929) 285-308.

39. Ambrose has the—less clearly epicletic—ancestor of this formula in *De sacramentis* IV, 21: "Fac nobis hanc oblationem scriptam, rationabilem, acceptabilem, quod est figura corporis et sanguinis Domini nostri Iesu Christi . . ." (ed. B. Botte, SC 25bis, pp. 114-15).

C. Callewaert, "S. Léon, le *Communicantes* et le *Nobis quoque peccatoribus,"* *SE* 1 (1948) 123–61.

P. Borella, "Memoriis sanctorum communicantes," Ambrosius 27 (1951) 75–76.

B. Capelle, "Problèmes du *Communicantes* de la messe," *Rivista liturgica* 40 (1953) 187–95 (= *Travaux liturgiques* 2:269–75).

A. Stuiber, "Die Diptychon-Formel für die Nomina offerentium im römischen Messkanon," *EL* 68 (1954) 127–46.

B. Capelle, "L'intercession dans la messe romaine," *RBén* 65 (1955) 181–91 (= *Travaux liturgiques* 2:248–57).

L. Eizenhöfer, "*Te igitur* und *Communicantes* im römischen Messkanon," *SE* 8 (1956) 14–75.

B. Botte, "*Communicantes,"* *QL* 38 (1957) 119–23.

C. Mohrmann, "*Rationabilis-logikos,"* in her *Etudes sur le latin des chrétiens* 1 (Rome: Edizioni di storia e letteratura, 1958), 179–87.

_____, "*Locus refrigerii lucis et pacis,"* *QL* 39 (1958) 196–214.

H. Engberding, "Das anaphorische Fürbittgebet der byzantinischen Chrysostomosliturgie," *OC* 45 (1961) 20–29; 46 (1962) 32–60.

_____, "Das anaphorische Fürbittgebet der Basiliusliturgie," *OC* 47 (1963) 16–52; 49 (1965) 18–37.

_____, "Das anaphorische Fürbittgebet der griechischen Markusliturgie," *OCP* 30 (1964) 398–446.

R. Berger, *Die Wendung "offerre pro" in der römischen Liturgie* (LQF 41; Münster: Aschendorff, 1965).

H. Engberding, "Das anaphorische Fürbittgebet der syrischen Basiliusliturgie," *OC* 50 (1966) 13–18.

_____, "Das anaphorische Fürbittgebet der älteren armenischen Basiliusliturgie," *OC* 51 (1967) 29–50.

The intercessory prayers, like the *Sanctus,* did not form part of the earliest structure of the Eucharistic Prayers. Hippolytus does not have them; in the Gallican and Spanish rites the "reading of names" took place "before the mysteries"[40] and never became part of the Eucharistic Prayer proper. All the other liturgical families did have the intercessory prayers but at different places; this would indicate that they were introduced only after the main components of the anaphora had been given their fixed order.

Liturgies of the Antiochene type inserted them at the end, between the epiclesis and the doxology; thus they did not interrupt the flow of the Eucharistic Prayer, which is so carefully arranged in the Byzantine formularies or the Anaphora of St. James. The Egyptian and Ethiopian liturgies placed these prayers between the expression of thanksgiving and the *Sanctus.*[41] The Roman Church located them in an original way after the hymn of the Seraphim. Here the intercessions begin with a petition that the gifts may be acceptable (a theme especially dear to this tradition) and continue

---

40. See p. 81.

41. Exceptions: the Euchologion of Serapion (showing that Egypt perhaps knew other methods as well), and formularies taken over from Syria.

in the *Memento*, the *Communicantes*, and the *Hanc igitur*. Then, at the end of the Canon, before the final prayer and doxology, there is a kind of resurgence of intercession in the *Nobis quoque*.[42] Among the Eastern Syrians the intercessory prayers were inserted between the anamnesis and the epiclesis, at least in the Anaphoras of Theodore and Nestorius.[43]

Two distinct but related and often convergent considerations seem to have been the source of the intercessory prayers:

A first intention was to recommend to God those who had contributed the bread and wine; expression was thus given to their participation in the fruits of the sacrifice,[44] but there was also a tendency to call special attention to those for whose sake the contributors had made their offering. The Roman Canon even had, in addition to the *Memento* ("Remember"), a formula, the *Hanc igitur* ("We therefore beg you to accept this offering"), that provided a place for mentioning in the Eucharist those Christians who were entering upon a new function or a new state of life in the Church: the newly baptized, the newly ordained, newly consecrated virgins, the newly married, and so on. Thus at the celebration of the sacraments of initiation those persons were mentioned "to whom you have deigned to grant rebirth through water and the Holy Spirit by forgiving all their sins."

A further intention was to give expression to ecclesial communion. In this context the celebrant named the local bishop, the patriarch, and the Roman pontiff. Omission of one of these names signified a break in unity, either on the part of a member of the hierarchy who had become heterodox and could no longer be named, or on the part of a community that had cut itself off from the rest of the faithful and their pastors. Moreover, brotherhood and sisterhood in Christ extended not only to the earthly Church but also, as the Anaphora of St. Basil (for example) puts it, to those

> who have been pleasing to you since the beginning of the world: the ancestors, fathers, patriarchs, prophets, apostles, preachers, evangelists, martyrs, confessors, and doctors, as well as every upright soul that has been justified by faith, and especially our Lady the Mother of God, Mary ever vir-

---

42. On the Memento of the dead see p. 135. The absence of this formulary in the early witnesses creates a problem for liturgical historians; some of them think the Memento occurred only in Masses celebrated for the deceased. See B. Botte, *Le Canon de la messe romaine* (Textes et études liturgiques 2; Louvain: Mont César, 1935), 67–69. The text itself is Roman in origin. See C. Mohrmann, "*Locus refrigerii,*" in B. Botte and C. Mohrmann, *L'ordinaire de la messe. Texte critique, traduction et études* (Etudes liturgiques 2; Paris: Cerf, and Louvain: Mont César, 1953), 123–32.

43. For the Anaphora of Addai and Mari see p. 29.

44. See p. 80. The word "diptychs" is sometimes used in this context. The reference is to two small tablets, hinged together, with the inner surfaces coated with wax for writing. They were used for recording the names of those to be mentioned during the liturgy.

gin, who is all holy and spotless and blessed above all women, as well as St. John the Precursor, St. _____ whom we remember, and all the saints.

The various categories of faithful who had achieved holiness were mentioned almost everywhere. Some of these individuals might be mentioned by name, and this practice sometimes led, as in the Jerusalemite Anaphora of St. James, to a list that amounted to a litany of the saints.[45] The Roman Canon contained two different lists: the first included the Virgin Mary, the Twelve Apostles (with Paul and without Matthias), and nine martyrs; the second included John (the Baptist), Stephen, Matthias, and Barnabas, along with eleven martyrs, of whom five were women. In both lists the saints named were honored at Rome from before the end of the fourth century, although not all of them were Romans. In addition, the *Communicantes* prayer ("In the unity of holy fellowship") had variable clauses for the principal feasts of the year.

In these intercessions, unlike the General Intercessions or prayer of the faithful (though at times these two different formularies exerted a reciprocal influence), only those persons were named with whom the celebrant and congregation shared the same faith within the one Church.

§7. The Final Doxology and the Amen of the Congregation

BIBLIOGRAPHY

C. Callewaert, "La finale du canon de la messe," *RHE* 30 (1943) 5–21.

M. Del Alamo, "La conclusión actual del canón de la misa," in *Miscellanea liturgica in honorem L. C. Mohlberg* 2 (Rome: Edizioni liturgiche, 1948), 107–13.

J. Brinktrine, "Über die Herkunft und die Bedeutung des Kanongebetes der römischen Messe *Per quem haec omnia*," *EL* 62 (1948) 365–69.

P. Borella, "La dossologia finale del canone . . .," *Ambrosius* 41 (1965) 183–200.

J. Pinell, "La grande conclusion du canon romain," *LMD* no. 88 (1966) 96–115.

The second intercession of the Roman Mass ended with the formula: "It is ever through him [Christ] that all good gifts, created by you, O Lord, are by you sanctified, endowed with life, blessed and bestowed upon us (*haec omnia, Domine, semper bona creas, sanctificas, vivificas, benedicis et praestas nobis*)." The words did not refer to the Body and Blood of Christ. They were a blessing of first fruits[46] (beans and grapes), the

---

45. In this context St. Augustine warns the faithful against a false notion of the veneration to be paid to the saints: "They are named in their proper place and order, but they are not invoked by the sacrificing priest" (*De civ. Dei* XXII, 10 [CCL: 48:828; PL 41:772]).

46. *Ge* no. 577 (beans); *Gr* nos. 630–31 (grapes), 333–34 (oil of the sick); *Le* no. 205 (milk and honey). — On the blessing of the oil of the sick see *The Church at Prayer* III.

oil of the sick, and, at Easter, milk and honey. As is clear from Hippolytus, Rome had a custom similar to that of which the Council of Carthage
in Africa spoke in 397.[47]

All the anaphoras end with a Trinitarian formula that is clearly doxo-
logical in character.[48] The same words recur: praise, glory, honor, blessing, adoration. Almost all of the Eastern formularies put the Three Divine
Persons on the same level; this was a consequence of the theological disputes of the fourth century and doubtless represented a shift from an older
type of formula. The West, on the other hand, kept the assertion of Christ's
mediatorial role. Compare, for example, the doxology in the Liturgy of
St. John Chrysostom and the doxology in the Roman Canon:

> And grant that we may with one voice and one heart glorify and praise
> your all-worthy and magnificent name, Father, Son, and Holy Spirit, now
> and always and forever and ever.

> Through him [Christ], with him, and in him all honor and glory is given
> to you, God, almighty Father, in the unity of the Holy Spirit, forever and
> ever.

Thus, at the end of the Eucharistic Prayer, the Roman Mass returns
to some extent to the theme of thanksgiving. The words are accompanied, moreover, by a gesture of offering that is described in *Ordo* I: the
bishop elevates the consecrated bread and with it touches the heavy chalice that the archdeacon at his side likewise elevates by its handles; the
two celebrants retain this posture until the Amen of the congregation has
died away.[49]

In all the liturgies the conclusion of the Eucharistic Prayer elicits this
participation of the faithful, which St. Justin emphasized long ago. The
Amen of the congregation is a meaningful expression of the priesthood
of the baptized as they unite themselves to the Eucharistic action. Dionysius
of Alexandria, in the third century, believed there was no need of baptizing a person who had long ago received the sacraments of initiation in
a heretical sect, because since then the person "had listened to the Eucharistic prayers and joined in the Amen (*synepiphthegxamenon to Amēn*)."[50]

---

47. *Traditio apostolica* 21 (Botte 56–57): milk and honey for the newly baptized; 6 (Botte
18): cheese and olives; 5 (Botte 18): oil. — Council of Carthage (397), can. 23 (CCL 149:40).

48. Except in the Anaphora of Addai and Mari. The conclusion of Serapion's euchologion
is not a doxology.

49. *OR* I, 89–90 (Andrieu, *OR* 2:96).

50. Letter to Pope Xystus, recorded in Eusebius, *The History of the Church* VII, 9, trans.
G. A. Williamson (Baltimore: Penguin Books, 1963), 291.

Chapter VI

The Communion

BIBLIOGRAPHY

P. Gy, "Les rites de la communion eucharistique," *LMD* no. 24 (1950) 141-60.

Once the Eucharistic Prayer was finished, the celebration reached completion through communion in the Body and Blood of Christ. But there was also a preparation for this action by means of elements found in all the liturgies: the breaking of the Eucharistic bread and the Our Father (in that order except in the Roman and Byzantine traditions where the order was reversed). Some Churches also included the kiss of peace and the presentation of the Blessed Sacrament to the faithful. Each of these main actions was accompanied by secondary rites. I shall follow here the order of the Roman liturgy.

§1. The Our Father

BIBLIOGRAPHY

C. Lambot, "Le Pater dans la liturgie apostolique d'après saint Grégoire," *RBén* 42 (1930) 265-69.

J. A. Jungmann, "Das Pater noster im Kommunionritus," *ZKT* 58 (1934) 552-71.

E. Griffe, "Saint Grégoire et Mgr Duchesne, à propos de la récitation du Pater à la messe," *Bulletin de littérature ecclésiastique* 55 (1954) 164-66.

L. Eizenhöfer, "Zur Pater noster-Einleitung der römischen Messe," *ALW* 4 (1956) 325-40.

I. H. Dalmais, "L'introduction et l'embolisme de l'oraison dominicale dans la célébration eucharistique," *LMD* no. 85 (1966) 92-100.

The exhortation that introduces the Our Father in the Roman liturgy echoes a passage of St. Cyprian: "Among the saving commandments (*praecepta*) and divine teaching (*monita*) that the Lord has left us for the salvation of his people, he has included a formula of prayer; he himself has taught us what we should ask for."[1]

But was Cyprian already referring to the Mass? It is risky to say he was, since the earliest known use of the Our Father was in prayer during the day.[2] There is no sure attestation of its use in the Eucharist until the end of the fourth century,[3] and even then the custom spread only gradually.[4]

St. Augustine seems to put the Our Father after the fraction (the breaking of the bread).[5] This was in fact the practice in all the liturgies.[6] In the time of Gregory the Great only the Byzantine tradition was an exception to this rule; as a result, the pope was suspected of imitating the Greeks when he altered Roman practice on this point. He wrote as follows to John of Syracuse in 598:

> Here is why we say the Lord's prayer right after the Canon (*mox post precem*). The custom of the apostles was to consecrate the sacrifice solely by means of the prayer of offering. It seemed to me quite inappropriate, on the one hand, to say over the offering a prayer composed by one or other writer (*scholasticus*) and, on the other, not to say over the redeemer's body and blood the prayer which he himself composed and which tradition has preserved for us. But, whereas among the Greeks the prayer is said by the entire congregation, among us the priest alone says it.[7]

The pope thus gives the Our Father a dignity comparable to that of the consecratory prayer; he notes, in addition, that in the tradition of his Church the celebrant alone says it. This was also the practice in Africa

---

1. St. Cyprian, *De dominica oratione* 2, ed. G. Hartel (CSEL 3, 1; Vienna, 1868), 267.

2. See *The Church at Prayer* IV, p. 163. But arguments have been offered in favor of a Eucharistic interpretation of the passage in Cyprian; see V. Saxer, *Vie liturgique et quotidienne à Carthage vers le milieu du IIIe siècle* (Studi di antichità cristiana 29; Vatican City: Pontificio Istituto di archeologia cristiana, 1969), 233–37.

3. See St. Ambrose, *De sacramentis* V, 24 (SC 25bis:132); St. Cyril of Jerusalem, *Catecheses mystagogicae* (SC 126:160–68); St. Augustine, *Ep.* 149, 16 (PL33:633). See also pp. 114–15 on the kiss of peace.

4. Theodore of Mopsuestia seems not to know it, and the Council of Toledo (633), ed. J. Vives, *Concilios visigóticos e hispano-romanos* (España cristiana, Textos 1; Barcelona-Madrid, 1963), 194–95, observes that some priests say the Our Father only on Sundays, even though of itself it is a "daily prayer."

5. See n. 3, above. Another passage, in *Serm.* 83 (PL 39:1101), seems to say the opposite, but perhaps the words "ubi est peracta sanctificatio" ("After the sanctification [= the Eucharistic Prayer] is completed") are not to be taken literally.

6. For Gaul see Pseudo-Germanus, I, 25 (Ratcliff 15). In the East today only the Byzantines, Armenians, and Maronites put the Our Father before the fraction.

7. St. Gregory the Great, *Ep. ad Ioannem Syracus.*, in *Registrum* IX, 26, ed. L. M. Hartmann, 2 (MGH *Epist.*, 2; 1889), 59–60. This practice becomes even more intelligible if the usage followed was already that described in OR I, where the pope presides over the fraction (and then says the Our Father that follows it) from his chair and not at the altar.

in Augustine's time.[8] The Eastern Churches, on the other hand, including the Byzantine, had the entire congregation say the prayer. The same custom seems to have been followed in Gaul.[9] In Spain, at least according to the later books, the congregation said an Amen after each of the petitions sung by the celebrant.[10]

The Lord's Prayer was often prolonged by an "embolism," that is, a fuller development of some part of the prayer. An example of this is the Roman *Libera* ("Deliver us, . . ."), which may go back to the time of St. Gregory. In the *Libera* the Apostle Andrew was associated, under the influence of Constantinople, with the Apostles Peter and Paul, who were buried in the Eternal City; these three, and all the saints, were asked to intercede, along with "the blessed and glorious ever-virgin Mary, Mother of God," in order that the faithful might enjoy peace as they partook of the sacrament. Many Eastern rites had similar prolongations of the Our Father.

In every instance the Our Father was regarded as a privileged form of preparation for communion. The patristic commentaries on the liturgical use of the Our Father sometimes take as their point of departure the mention of "our daily bread." In its first and obvious meaning, the reference is not to the Eucharist, but how could Christians fail to regard the sacrament, as St. Ambrose does,[11] as a true "substantial" food for Christian life? More frequently, however, the commentaries focus on the words "Forgive us . . . as we forgive." St. Augustine, for example, says: "As a result of these words we approach the altar with clean faces; with clean faces we share in the body and blood of Christ."[12]

§2. The Fraction (Breaking of the Bread)

BIBLIOGRAPHY

M. Andrieu, *Immixtio et consecratio* (Paris: Picard, 1924), *passim*, esp. 1–19, and OR 2:56–64.

B. Capelle, "Le rite de la fraction dans le messe romaine," *RBén* 53 (1941) 5–40 (= *Travaux liturgiques* 2:287–318).

---

8. St. Augustine, *Serm.* 58, 10 (PL 38:399): "This prayer is said at the altar . . . and the faithful listen to it."

9. Gregory of Tours, *De virtutibus s. Martini* II, 30, ed. B. Krusch (MGH, *Script. rer. merov.*, 1; 1885), 620: a mute woman is healed at the moment of the Our Father and "begins to sing it with the others."

10. *Missale mixtum* I, 4 (PL 85:119).

11. See St. Ambrose, *De sacramentis* VI, 21 (SC 25bis:95).

12. St. Augustine, *Serm.* 17 (PL 38:127). See St. John Chrysostom, *In Gen. hom.* 27, 8 (PG 53:251); *De capto Eutropio* 5 (PG 52:396).

J. P. De Jong, "Le rite de la commixtion dans la messe romaine," *RBén* 61 (1951) 15–37.

J. A. Jungmann, *"Fermentum,"* in *Colligere fragmenta. Festschrift A. Dold* (Beuron: Beuroner Kunstverlag, 1952), 185–90. See also Jungmann, *Pastoral Liturgy* (New York: Herder and Herder, 1962), 287–95.

B. Capelle, "Fraction et commixtion, aménagements souhaitables des rites actuels," *LMD* no. 35 (1953) 75–94 (= *Travaux liturgiques* 2:319–31).

J. P. De Jong, "L'arrière-plan dogmatique du rite de la commixtion dans la messe romaine," *ALW* 3 (1953) 81–98.

B. Capelle, "L'oraison *Haec commixtio et consecratio* de la messe romaine," in *Mélanges en honneur de Mgr M. Andrieu* (Strasbourg: Palais universitaire, 1956), 65–78 (= *Travaux liturgiques* 2:332–43).

J. P. De Jong, "Le rite de la commixtion dans ses rapports avec les liturgies syriennes," *ALW* 4 (1956) 245–78; 5 (1957) 33–79.

V. Janeras, "El rito de la fracción en la liturgia hispánica," in *Liturgica* 2 (Scripta et documenta 10; Montserrat, 1958), 217–47.

P. Borella, "Frazione, confractorium e commistione nell'antica messa ambrosiana," *Ambrosius* 38 (1962) 303–11.

J. P. De Jong, "Der ursprüngliche Sinn von Epiklese und Mischungsritus nach der Eucharistielehre des heiligen Irenäus," *ALW* 9 (1965) 28–47.

I. THE "BREAD BROKEN" AND THE "LAMB OF GOD"

The action of Christ at the Supper that gave the early Christians their name for the Eucharist ("the breaking of bread"), was continued in the liturgy. St. Paul himself supplied a catechesis on the rite: "The bread which we break, is it not a participation in the body of Christ? Because there is one bread, we who are many are one body, for we all partake of the one bread."[13]

It is not surprising, therefore, that this rite should have been given a certain solemnity in *Ordo* I: bishops and priests break all the consecrated loaves, which acolytes carry in linen sacks to these various celebrants at their places.[14] The rite was a practical necessity in view of distributing Communion, and it took some time when the congregation was a large one. The rite was accompanied by the singing of the *Agnus Dei*, introduced at the end of the seventh century by a Syrian pope, Sergius I.[15] Thus the symbolism of the slain Lamb of the new Passover was added to the sign of the father of the family giving food to his children, as at Jewish meals.[16]

It is not impossible that the fraction had already been provided with a vocal accompaniment at an earlier date, even when the action preceded the Our Father. In Milan, where it is still performed at this point, varia-

---

13. 1 Cor 10:16b–17.
14. *OR* I, 101–2 (Andrieu, *OR* 2:100).
15. *LP* 1:376.
16. Rev 5:6 and 13:6. See John 1:9 and 36.

ble antiphons have been preserved as an accompaniment to the rite on feast days; similar compositions are attested for Spain and Gaul.[17] These compositions, intended to punctuate psalmody, doubtless originated in the East.[18]

The rite itself is attested in all the Churches.[19]

II. BODY AND BLOOD REUNITED IN THE CUP

The rite of "commingling" consists of placing a bit of the consecrated bread into the chalice. The action perhaps had various meanings.

1. *The* fermentum

In Rome, priests were obliged on Sundays to celebrate Mass for their congregations in their own churches (the "titles") and therefore could not take part in the solemn papal Mass. A sign was used, however, to bring out the unity of the one Christian community. Pope Innocent I wrote of this in 416 in a letter to Bishop Decentius of Gubbio:

> With regard to the *fermentum* [literally: leaven] which we send on Sundays to the various "titles": . . . The priests of those churches cannot join us in celebrating on that day because they must take care of their own people; therefore acolytes bring them the *fermentum* which we have consecrated, so that on that day, of all days, they may not feel separated from communion with us.[20]

We do not know just when this custom was introduced[21]; moreover, after the seventh century it was retained only at the Easter Vigil. Its retention on this feast occasioned a description of the rite: the porter of the

---

17. M. Huglo, "Antifone antiche per la *fractio panis*," *Ambrosius* 31 (1955) 85–95. — The Antiphonary of León gives antiphons under the title *Ad confractionem panis*, and Pseudo-Germanus (I, 24b; Ratcliff 15) speaks of antiphons in the Gallican Mass (whence perhaps comes this prayer that has remained part of the Liturgy of Lyons: "Come, people, to the immortal holy sacrificial mystery. Let us approach with fear and faith. With clean hands let us share in the gift of repentance. The Lamb of God is set before us as a sacrifice offered for our sakes to the Father. Let us adore him alone; let us join the angels in glorifying him with Alleluias").

18. The *Octoechos* of Severus of Antioch has similar compositions "before communion" (PO 6–7).

19. See the *Euchologium Serapionis* 16 (Funk 2:176–78); Theodore of Mopsuestia, *Homiliae catecheticae* 16 (2nd on the Mass) (Tonneau-Devreesse 159–61); St. John Chrysostom, *In Ep. I Cor. hom.* 14, 2 (PG 61:200); etc.

20. Innocent I, *Ep. 25 ad Decentium*, ed. R. Cabié, *Lettre d'Innocent Ier à Decentius de Gubbio* (Bibliothèque de la RHE 58; Louvain: Publications universitaires, 1973), 26–27. See *ibid.*, 50–53.

21. Historically valueless entries in the *LP* attribute the custom to Miltiades and Siricius, popes of the fourth century (*LP* 1:168 and 216).

papal church was given the fragment of consecrated bread after the fraction, and the priest of the titular church received it and put it into his chalice at the same point in his own Mass.[22]

2. *The* Sancta

After the Eucharistic liturgy was finished, some of the consecrated bread was kept in order to give Communion to the dying. This portion of bread was the *Sancta* of which *Ordo* I speaks: the bread was brought up and presented to the pope who "greeted" it at the beginning of the celebration and approved the quantity as adequate; the bread was then entrusted to a subdeacon and placed in the chalice after the Our Father.[23] The action was thus seemingly the same as that performed by a priest who received the *fermentum* in his own church. The action made sense when the bishop of Rome was prevented from celebrating and was replaced by someone else. The latter, according to *Ordo* II,[24] performed the rite with a piece of consecrated bread (likewise called *fermentum*) from a previous Mass of the bishop of the local Church. Once again, the piece of consecrated bread was a sign of unity with the local bishop (as well as a temporal link between successive Sunday Eucharists).

But what was the meaning of the action when the bishop himself performed it? Should we see in it an extension of what was done in his absence? Or was it simply a means of renewing the reserved sacrament, while at the same time making the bread, now soaked in wine, easier to swallow (the bread would have hardened, since there was not as yet any question of unleavened bread)?[25]

3. *A sign of resurrection*

These various testimonies applied only to Rome, and Innocent I expressly stated that there was no question of a *fermentum* for "the rural parts of dioceses, since the sacraments should not be carried to distant places."[26] Yet the "commingling" took place almost everywhere.

Although no explanation of the rite is completely convincing, the most likely one is to be found in the symbolism of the two species. According to the Semitic mind, the separate giving of the body and blood by Christ

---

22. See *OR XXX* (Andrieu, *OR* 3:474), a late Frankish compilation based on Roman sources. — On the *fermentum* see J. A. Jungmann, *"Fermentum,"* in *Colligere fragmenta. Festschrift Alban Dold* (Beuron: Beuroner Kunstverlag, 1952), 185-90.

23. *OR* I, 48 and 95 (Andrieu, *OR* 2:82 and 98).

24. *OR* II, 6 (Andrieu, *OR* 2:115).

25. *OR* I (Andrieu, *OR* 2:56-64).

26. Innocent I, *Ep. 25 ad Decentium* (Cabié 26-27): "per parrochias fieri debere non puto, quia nec longe portanda sunt sacramenta."

at the Supper signified his death, since his life (his blood) was no longer in his body. In order, therefore, to signify that the Savior is now alive, it was quite natural to mix the bread and wine. This is the point which Theodore of Mopsuestia seems to be making with regard to the rite: "The entire human body is one with its blood; the blood mingles with every part. . . . That is how it was with the Lord's body before his passion."[27]

The formula that accompanies the action in *Ordo* I—"May this mingling and consecration (*commixtio et consecratio*) of the Body and Blood of our Lord Jesus Christ be for us who receive it a source of eternal life"— has given rise to a great many controversies. The formula is probably to be compared with the one in the Syrian liturgy: "It is united and sanctified and rendered complete." Both formulas refer to the joining of body and blood as bringing to completion, at the level of signs and with a view to communion, what the consecration had accomplished.

4. The "fervor of a faith that is filled with the Spirit"[28]

A similar meaning, it seems, is to be given to another rite of uncertain origin that is practiced by the Byzantines: the rite of the *Zeon* or warm water that is poured into the chalice. As a result of this action, the blood that is drunk is warm—another sign of life. Moreover, as the warmth fills the cup, so the life-giving Spirit uses the Eucharistic food to fill the faith of Christians by pouring out on them the graces of Christ's Passover and the pledge of their own resurrection.

§3. The Kiss of Peace

BIBLIOGRAPHY

F. Cabrol, "Baiser," *DACL* 2 (1910) 117–30.

L. Brou, "L'oraison *ad pacem* dans les anciennes liturgies latines," in *XXXV. Congreso eucarístico internacional. Sesiones de estudios* 1 (Barcelona, 1952), 699–704.

M. Huglo, "L'invito alla pace nelle antiche liturgie beneventana e ambrosiana," *Ambrosius* 30 (1954) 158–61.

The kiss of peace was practiced everywhere in much the same manner described in the *Apostolic Constitutions*: "Let the bishop greet the congregation with the words: 'May the peace of Christ be with all of you.' And the entire congregation is to respond, 'And with your spirit.' The

---

27. Theodore of Mopsuestia, *Homiliae catecheticae* 16, 15 (Tonneau-Devreesse 557).

28. "Zesis pisteōs plērēs Pneumatos Hagiou." See J. M. Hanssens, *Institutiones de ritibus orientalibus* 2:235–40. — P. De Meester, "Les origines et les développements du texte grec de la liturgie de saint Jean Chrysostome," in *Chrysostomika. Studi e ricerche intorno a san Giovanni Crisostomo* (Rome: Pustet, 1908), 348–49.

deacon then says to all: 'Greet one another with a holy kiss.' Let the clergy then embrace the bishop, laymen laymen, and laywomen laywomen."[29]

Depending on the tradition in question, however, the rite took place either before communion or at the time when the gifts were placed on the altar.

I. AT THE BEGINNING OF THE EUCHARISTIC LITURGY

In most of the Christian liturgies it was before the preparation of the gifts, and usually after the general intercessions, that the faithful were asked to greet one another. The Lord's exhortation in Matt 5:23-24 ("If you are offering your gift at the altar . . .") served, of course, as the basis for catechetical instruction on the liturgical gesture.[30] In the Churches of Gaul and Spain the rite included a presidential prayer, the *Collectio ad pacem* ("Collect at the kiss of peace"), for which numerous formularies have been preserved in the liturgical books.

In his letter to Bishop Decentius of Gubbio, Innocent I refers to this manner of practicing the kiss of peace: "With regard to the kiss of peace: you say that among you certain ministers announce it to the people before the celebration of the mysteries and those who are priests give it to one another."

II. BEFORE COMMUNION

Innocent I goes on to say: "It is after that of which I may not speak that peace should be proclaimed according to rule. For it is clear that the people thereby give their consent to everything . . . that has gone before, since the peace puts its seal on the conclusion [of the Eucharistic Prayer]."[31]

This is an authoritative statement of the Roman tradition: the gesture of peace is made after the canon ("*post omnia quae aperire non debeo*," "After all that of which I may not speak") as a seal marking its conclusion. This image had already been used by Tertullian: "*osculum pacis, quod est signaculum orationis*" ("the kiss of peace, which is a seal set upon the prayer").[32]

---

29. *Constitutiones apostolorum* VIII, 11, 8–9 (Funk 1:494). See II, 57, 17 (Funk 1:165).
30. See Cyril of Jerusalem, *Catecheses mystagogicae* V, 3 (SC 126:148-50).
31. Innocent I, *Ep. 25 ad Decentium* (Cabié 20-21); see Cabié 36-40.
32. Tertullian, *De oratione* 18, 1 (CCL 1:267).

But of what prayer is Tertullian speaking? Did the practices attested for Rome and Africa[33] at the beginning of the fifth century already exist in the third? It seems doubtful. Justin and Hippolytus mention the greetings exchanged at the beginning of the Eucharistic liturgy,[34] and Cyprian connects the *pax* with the gifts carried to the altar. On the other hand, Justin and Hippolytus speak of the *pax* only in connection with initiation or ordination. In addition, Cyprian is commenting on the gospel and not on the liturgical celebration; moreover he does so in a treatise on the Lord's Prayer, and it was probably this prayer that Tertullian had in mind.[35]

Since we do not know just when the Our Father became part of the Mass, we are limited to probabilities with regard to the shift of the kiss of reconciliation from before the Eucharistic liturgy to the position it acquired at Rome.[36] The Milanese liturgy, however, does offer a clue, since the invitation *Pacem habete* ("Be at peace") remains like a vestigial organ before the offertory.[37]

We may note finally (though it is perhaps only a coincidence) that the kiss of peace was exchanged before communion in Churches in which the preparation of the gifts involved a procession of the faithful to the sanctuary.

§4. The Blessing of the Faithful and the Presentation of the Blessed Sacrament

I. THE BLESSING OF THE FAITHFUL BEFORE COMMUNION

BIBLIOGRAPHY

G. Morin, "Le canon du concile d'Agde sur l'assistance à la messe entière," *EL* 49 (1935) 360–66.

E. Moeller, *Corpus benedictionum pontificalium* (4 vols.; CCL 162, 162A, 162B,

---

33. St. Augustine, *Serm.* 227 (PL 38:1101).

34. St. Justin, *Apologia I* 65 (see p. 14); *Traditio apostolica* 4 and 21 (Botte 11 and 55).

35. See n. 32. Tertullian continues: "When is the exchange of peace with our brothers and sisters more appropriate than when our prayer, made more acceptable by our actions, ascends to heaven?"

36. Some liturgical historians offer a dual hypothesis: the Our Father was already part of the Mass in the time of Cyprian and even of Tertullian and was initially the conclusion of the General Intercessions. The combined Our Father and kiss of peace would subsequently have been moved to its present place after the Eucharistic Prayer. See E. Dekkers, *Tertullianus en de geschiedenis der liturgie* (Catholica IV, Liturgie 2; Brussels–Amsterdam, 1947), 59; Saxer, *Vie liturgique* (n. 2, above), 137–243.

37. P. Borella, *Il rito ambrosiano* (Milan: Morcelliana, 1964), 202.

162C; Turnhout: Brepols, 1971-79). Vol. 162B has a history of the blessings and a very extensive bibliography.

G. Boffa, "A proposito della cosidetta 'Benedizione episcopale,'" *EL* 91 (1982) 253-64.

In sixth-century Gaul, Caesarius of Arles ordered all the faithful to remain in church "until the Lord's Prayer has been said and the people have received a blessing."[38] A blessing usually marks the end of a celebration. As a matter of fact, at a very early period the faithful fell into the habit of approaching the Lord's table only rarely, and it was judged better to let non-communicants leave at this point. Gregory of Tours even speaks of the people "beginning to receive the Most Holy Body of the Redeemer *expletis missis* [after the dismissal]."[39]

The blessing was a solemn one when given by a bishop; it varied from feast to feast and had a tripartite structure modeled on the great priestly blessing of the Old Testament (Num 6:22-26). The tripartite blessing, each part followed by an Amen, formed a unified whole—a majestic, cadenced paragraph that ended in the usual doxology. The people were very appreciative of this blessing, and the custom remained widespread throughout the Middle Ages.[40]

In Eastern liturgies of the Antiochene type the fraction was preceded by a prayer over the people, who were asked to bow their heads, but this prayer does not seem to have had the same function as the Latin blessing. In the Roman tradition the congregation was dismissed only after communion. Before communion, however, the archdeacon announced the time and place of the next assembly and made various other announcements; this practice suggests that some of the faithful left the church immediately afterwards.[41]

II. "HOLY THINGS TO THE HOLY."

BIBLIOGRAPHY

J. M. Hanssens, *Institutiones liturgicae de ritibus orientalibus* 3 (1932), 499-503.

M. Arranz, "Le *Sancta sanctis* dans la tradition liturgique des Eglises," *ALW* 15 (1973) 31-67.

---

38. St. Caesarius of Arles, *Serm.* 73, 2 (CCL 103:307).

39. Gregory of Tours, *De virtutibus sancti Martini* II, 47 (Krusch 626); *idem, Historia Francorum* IX, 3, ed. Poupardin (Paris: Picard, 1913), 346, where King Gontran approaches the altar to receive Communion *peracta solemnia* ("when the celebration has ended").

40. It continued down to our time in some French dioceses, and the recent reform has restored it as an optional formula on certain privileged days. According to Pseudo-Germanus I, 26 (Ratcliff 16), if it is a priest who presides, he uses a simpler formula.

41. *OR* I, 108 (Andrieu, *OR* 2:102); *Ge*, no. 1260, p. 186.

From a very early period all the Eastern liturgies had the rite that is described as follows in the *Apostolic Constitutions*: "The deacon says, 'Give heed!' and the bishop addresses the people with the words, *'Ta hagia tois hagiois'* ['Holy things to the holy']; the people answer, *'Heis hagios, heis Kyrios, Iesous Christos, eis doxan Theou Patros'* ['One alone is holy, one alone is Lord, Jesus Christ, to the glory of God the Father']."[42]

St. John Chrysostom comments: "When we say 'Holy things to the holy,' the meaning is that someone who is not holy should not approach."[43] The response of the people—"One alone is holy, one alone is Lord, Jesus Christ"—allays the fears that such a strict requirement might rouse.[44] Sometimes, as in Theodore of Mopsuestia, the acclamation takes on a Trinitarian form that distorts the meaning: "A single holy Father, a single Son . . . ."[45] The exhortation and acclamation generally precede the fraction and are always accompanied, except among the Eastern Syrians, by an elevation of the bread and cup so that the faithful may see them.

During the period under discussion here there is no mention of this rite in the Western Churches. But the Latin formulas—*Sancta sanctis* and *Unus sanctus, unus Dominus Iesus Christus in gloria Dei Patris*—are found in some fifth-century documents[46]; they were therefore perhaps being used in some communities.

§5. The Communion Ritual

BIBLIOGRAPHY

H. Leclercq, "Communion (rite et antienne)," *DACL* 3 (1914), 2427–65.
P. Browe, "Die Kommunion in der gallikanischen Kirche," *Theologische Quartal-schrift* 102 (1921) 22–54.
_____, "Kommunionriten früherer Zeiten," *Theologie und Glaube* 24 (1932) 592–607.
J. M. Hanssens, "Le cérémonial de la communion eucharistique dans les rites orientaux," *Gregorianum* 41 (1960) 30–62.

Here again the *Apostolic Constitutions* summarizes the various elements that are found almost identically in all the liturgical traditions:

---

42. *Constitutiones apostolorum* VIII, 13, 11–13 (Funk 1:516).
43. St. John Chrysostom, *In Ep. ad Heb. hom.* 17, 5 (PG 63:133). He compares this warning to that of the herald at the Olympic Games as he ordered the departure of slaves, thieves, and people of unworthy life.
44. St. Cyril of Jerusalem, *Catecheses mystagogicae* V, 19 (SC 126:168–69).
45. Theodore of Mopsuestia, *Homiliae catecheticae* 16, 21–23 (Tonneau-Devreesse 565–69).
46. See G. Morin, "Formules liturgiques orientales en Occident aux IVe-Ve siècles," *RBén* 40 (1928) 136–37. — L. Brou, "Le *Sancta sanctis* en Occident," *JTS* 46 (1945) 160–78; 47 (1946) 11–29.

After this [the *Sancta sanctis*], the bishop communicates, and then the priests and deacons . . . and finally the entire congregation in good order, respectfully and adoringly, and without noise. The bishop gives a share in the sacrificial victim, saying, "The body of Christ"; the one receiving it says "Amen." Then the deacon extends the chalice and gives it, saying, "The blood of Christ"; again the person drinking says "Amen." Psalm 33 is to be said during the communion of the congregation.[47]

I. "THE BODY . . . THE BLOOD OF CHRIST. — AMEN"

1. *The profession of faith*

In the intensely communal atmosphere created by the Our Father, the kiss of peace, the fraction, and the processional song, an eminently personal action takes place, as each believer approaches the Lord and professes faith in the Eucharist. St. Ambrose writes: "Not without reason do you say 'Amen,' for you acknowledge in your heart that you are receiving the body of Christ. When you present yourself, the priest says to you, 'The body of Christ,' and you reply 'Amen,' that is, 'It is so.' Let the heart persevere in what the tongue confesses."[48]

The act of receiving also represents a commitment to live in conformity with the reality that one confesses. St. Augustine makes this point to those whom he has just finished baptizing:

> If you are the body and members of Christ, then what is laid on the Lord's table is the sacrament (*mysterium*) of what you yourselves are, and it is the sacrament of what you are that you receive. It is to what you yourselves are that you answer 'Amen,' and this answer is your affidavit. Be a member of Christ's body, so that your 'Amen' may be authentic."[49]

This dialogue would subsequently be replaced by formulas that, unfortunately, no longer called for a response from the communicant. This development took place in Rome as early as the sixth century.[50]

2. *The two species*

While Communion under the species of bread alone was always the rule in cases where Communion was received apart from Mass (the absent, the sick), both species were received during the celebration itself. Here the symbolism of bread for the journey and of sharing in one table

---

47. *Constitutiones apostolorum* VIII, 13, 14–17 (Funk 1:516–18).

48. St. Ambrose, *De sacramentis* IV, 25 (SC 25bis:117).

49. St. Augustine, *Serm.* 272 (PL 38:1247). — See P. T. Camelot, "Un texte de Tertullien sur l'Amen de la communion," *LMD* no. 79 (1964) 108–13.

50. See Paul the Deacon, *Sancti Gregorii Magni vita* 23 (PL 75:52–53): "May the body of our Lord Jesus Christ bring you the forgiveness of sins and eternal life."

was completed by reception of the chalice, which symbolized both the covenant that had been sealed in blood and the joy of the eschatological banquet. Drinking from the cup was surely the most expressive form of reception of the blood, but in some cases, for reasons of hygiene or convenience, recourse was had to a drinking straw or to "intinction" (a piece of the consecrated bread was dipped into the Precious Blood).

II. "THE BISHOP, THE PRIESTS AND DEACONS, AND THE ENTIRE CONGREGATION"

In the Christian economy, the Lord's presence has never been signified solely by things, however sacred, independently of a ministry entrusted to human beings. Even the privileged act of receiving the sacred species requires the service of ministers who bring the sacrament from the altar and give it to their brothers and sisters. The dialogical formula which we saw a moment ago presupposes this mediation. As a result, in all the liturgies the president receives Communion first, then the rest of the clergy, and finally the faithful. In normal circumstances the bishop or his priests distribute the bread, and deacons present the cup.[51]

This ministerial mission brings with it a responsibility in relation to the Eucharist. St. John Chrysostom says: "I turn now to you who very carefully distribute these gifts. No small punishment awaits you if you know a person is a sinner and nonetheless admit him or her to a share in this table."[52]

The hierarchy is itself of the sacramental order; it is a sign of the Church as being a body with different members, in which God has willed to make use of human beings in the service of the community. That is the sole meaning of the hierarchical order. Here again is John Chrysostom, bishop of Constantinople, stressing this point.

> I do not have a greater share in the Lord's table and you a lesser; we participate equally. I come first; what difference does that make? Among children, the eldest is the first to reach for the food, but he does not get a larger share. . . . I do not receive from one Lamb, you from another; we all share together in the one Lamb.[53]

---

51. See St. Augustine, *Serm.* 304, 1 (PL 38:1395), where he says of St. Lawrence, a deacon, that "he administered the sacred blood of Christ"; St. Ambrose, *De officiis* I, 41 (PL 16:84–85). *Traditio apostolica* 21 (Botte 56) has priests administering the chalice, but it adds that "if there are not enough priests, deacons may do it."

52. St. John Chrysostom, *In Matt. hom.* 82, 5–6 (PG 58:744–45).

53. St. John Chrysostom, *In Ep. 2 ad Thess. hom.* 4, 4 (PG 62:492). — On the "Lamb" see n. 55, p. 144.

III. "RESPECTFULLY, ADORINGLY"

The attitude of the communicant is carefully described in the Jerusalem Catecheses (*ca.* 400):

> When you approach, do not extend your hands with palms upward and fingers apart, but make your left hand a throne for your right hand, since the latter is to receive the King; then, while answering "Amen," receive the body of Christ in the hollow of your hand. Next, carefully sanctify your eyes through contact with the sacred body; then take it in your mouth, being watchful that nothing of it is lost. If you were to lose part of it, it would be like losing one of your own members. If someone were to give you some flakes of gold, would you not guard them very carefully and see to it that you did not lose any and suffer a loss? Should you not therefore watch far more carefully over an object more valuable than gold or precious stones, lest you lose a crumb of it? Then, after receiving the body of Christ, approach his blood. . . .[54]

The actions here described were practiced all over the Christian world.[55] The faithful lifted their joined hands to their mouths in the manner indicated. Women sometimes covered their hands with a veil.[56] Devotional acts, such as touching the eyes with the Body of Christ, are often mentioned.[57]

In order to receive Communion, the faithful came forward to the entrance of the sanctuary and perhaps even, in some places, to the altar itself (if the expression *ad altare*, "to the altar," is to be taken literally). The exhortations to orderliness show that jostling was not always avoided.[58]

IV. THE COMMUNION SONG

BIBLIOGRAPHY

> P. Vila-Abadal, "El salmo 33 como canto de comunión," in *XXXV. Congreso eucarístico internacional. Sesiones de estudios* 1 (Barcelona, 1952), 725-31.

---

54. St. Cyril of Jerusalem, *Catecheses mystagogicae* V, 27 (SC 126:170-73).

55. See Theodore of Mopsuestia, *Homiliae catecheticae* 16, 27 (Tonneau-Devreesse 577); St. Augustine, *C. Ep. Parmen.* II, 13 (PL 43:58); St. John Damascene, *De fide orth.* IV, 13 (PG 94:1149); etc.

56. St. Caesarius of Arles, *Serm.* 229, 4 (CCL 103:908); Council of Auxerre (end of sixth century), can. 42 (CCL 148A:270).

57. See St. John Chrysostom, *In diem natalem DNIC* 7 (PG 49:361-62); Aphraates, *Hom.* 7, 8, ed. G. Bert (TU 3/4), 125; Isaac of Antioch, *Carmen* XVII, ed. G. Bickel 1 (Giessen, 1877), 9; St. John Damascene, *ibid.*

58. St. John Chrysostom, *Hom. in Bapt. Christi* 4 (PG 49:370); St. Nilus († 430), *Ep.* 294 (PG 79:346).

A. Rose, "Les antiennes et les psaumes de communion," *Revue diocésaine de Namur* 11 (1957) 280–86, 289–305, 420–32, 539–48, 698–708; 12 (1958) 52–58.

P. Borella, "Il transitorium de la messa ambrosiana," *Ambrosius* 38 (1962) 231–38.

E. Moneta-Caglio, "Significato del nome Transitorium," *Ambrosius* 40, Supplem. to no. 4 (1964), 26–30.

B. Velat, *Etudes sur le Me'eráf* (PO 33; Turnhout: Brepols, 1966), 9.

Earlier, in discussing the preparation of the gifts, I noted the parallelism of the offertory and communion processions (a point emphasized by St. Augustine) and of the psalmody accompanying them.[59] According to the Jerusalem Catecheses, "you hear the cantor inviting you, by means of a divine melody, to communion in the holy mysteries: 'Taste and see how good the Lord is.' "[60] There are numerous witnesses in East and West to the use of Psalm 33 [34] at this same period. The Antiphonary of León shows that the custom was observed in Spain; the antiphon is there called the *Ad accedentes* antiphon ("At the procession"), a title that recalls another verse of the same psalm: *"Accedite ad eum et illuminamini"* ("Come to him and be enlightened": Ps 33:6 Vg).

Other psalms could be used, however, and eventually it became customary in Rome to follow more or less strictly the order of the psalter.[61] In the East the psalms were generally replaced by poetic compositions, often biblically inspired, such as the Byzantine troparia. The latter were perhaps the source of many of the Milanese *Transitoria.*

§6. The Concluding Rites

BIBLIOGRAPHY

C. Callewaert, "Qu'est-ce que l'*oratio super populum?*" *EL* 51 (1937) 310–18.

J. A. Jungmann, "*Oratio super populum* und altchristliche Büssersegnung," *EL* 52 (1938) 77–96.

L. Eizenhöfer, "Untersuchungen zum Stil und Inhalt der römischen *Oratio super populum,*: *EL* 52 (1938) 258–311.

B. Botte, "*Ite missa est,*" in B. Botte and C. Mohrmann, *L'ordinaire de la messe* (Etudes liturgiques 2; Paris: Cerf, and Louvain: Mont César, 1953), 145–49.

C. Mohrmann, "Missa," *Vigiliae Christianae* 12 (1958) 67–92.

R. Falsini, *I postcommuni del Sacramentario leoniano* (Bibliotheca Pont. Athenaei Antoniani 13; Rome, 1964).

M. Augé I Benet, *La oración "Super populum" en el Sacramentario Veronese. Estudio de su forma i contenido* (Rome: Claretianum, 1968).

---

59. See p. 78.

60. St. Cyril of Jerusalem, *Catecheses mystagogicae* V, 29 (SC 126:168–71).

61. During Lent the numerical sequence (Ps 1–26 [27]) was rather strictly followed. The refrain was a verse from the psalm that could provide an allusion to the Eucharist; later on it was often a passage from the gospel.

I. POSTCOMMUNION SONGS

As communions became increasingly infrequent, a confusion arose between songs meant to accompany the communion procession and others meant to come after communion. A typical example of the second type is the Gallican *Trecanum*, which is probably to be interpreted as a profession of faith.[62]

Patriarch Sergius of Constantinople is said to have introduced in 624 the following song to be sung while the remaining sacred species were being transferred: "Fill my mouth with praise of you, Lord, so that we may celebrate your glory for having deigned to admit us to your sacred mysteries. Preserve us throughout the day in your holiness as we meditate on your holy justice."[63]

II. THE CONCLUDING PRAYER

In Egypt the Euchologion of Serapion gives a "Prayer after the communion of the congregation,"[64] and a similar prayer is found elsewhere in the East.[65] The sacramentaries of the Roman liturgy have a prayer *Post communionem* ("After communion"), which the Gregorian Sacramentary calls the *Ad complendum* ("Concluding prayer"). It asks that the congregation receive the fruits of the Eucharist and especially of the final act of the celebration: the reception (various words for receiving, sharing, being filled: *sumpsimus, suscepimus, percepimus, accepimus, communicavimus,* or *vegetati, satiati, inebriati, repleti, participes effecti*) of the Body and Blood of Christ (various words for food, or for table, meal, or for aid, medicine, etc.: *panis, potus, esca, alimonia, cibum, dapes, viaticum,* or *mensa, calix, convivium, cena,* or *deliciae, subsidia, medicina, pignus vitae aeternae*).[66]

III. THE BLESSING AND DISMISSAL

BIBLIOGRAPHY

P. Borella, "La benedizione della messa," *Ambrosius* 43 (1967) 1-36.

---

62. Pseudo-Germanus I, 28a (Ratcliff 16).

63. *Chronicon Paschale* (PG 92:1001).

64. *Euchologium Serapionis* 16 (Funk 2:176).

65. St. Cyril of Jerusalem, *Catecheses mystagogicae* V, 22 (SC 126:172). Compare the Byzantine *Opisthambonos* (Prayer from behind the ambo) which in the ancient manuscripts includes several formularies.

66. See J. M. Sustaeta, *Misal y Eucaristía* (Series Valentiniana 3; Valencia: Facultad de teología S. Vicente Ferrer, 1979), 131-41.

It was the deacon's role to announce the ending of the assembly. The Roman liturgy used a formula of a juridical kind (*ite missa est*) that had no religious significance; it is as though the deacon were saying: "The meeting is concluded." There is no witness to its use in the liturgy prior to *Ordo* I,[67] although the term *missa* had long been in use for the dismissal of the congregation.[68] The Eastern Churches had various expressions; the one in general use was "Go in peace."

In most Churches this deaconal announcement was immediately preceded by a blessing from the celebrant.[69] In Rome, however, according to *Ordo* I, there was no blessing; as the pope was returning to the sacristy he would simply say "May God bless us" (*Benedicat nos Deus*") to the petition, "Bless us, Lord" ("*Iube, Domine, benedicere*") of the various categories of people he met on his way.[70] In the Leonine Sacramentary, however, the concluding prayer of the Mass is followed by another formula that seems to be part of the regular structure of the Mass. It is a true blessing of the people or *oratio super populum* ("prayer over the people"). The later liturgical books have it only on certain days.[71]

It is to be noted that a recessional song was not used anywhere.

---

67. *OR* I (Andrieu, *OR* 2:107).

68. See *Itinerarium Egeriae* 26, 32, 34, and *passim* (CCL 175:72, 78, etc.).

69. See *Constitutiones apostolorum* VIII, 15, 6–9 (Funk 1:520), and the "prayer while bowing" of the Eastern rites.

70. *OR* I, 126 (Andrieu, *OR* 2:108).

71. The Gregorian Sacramentary, which uses the title *Super populum*, has these formularies for the weekdays of Lent; the Gelasian also gives them (under the rubric *Ad populum*) for Christmas, Epiphany, and the Sundays of Lent.

DEVELOPMENTS AND ADAPTATIONS IN THE LITURGY OF THE MASS FROM ABOUT THE EIGHTH CENTURY TO VATICAN COUNCIL II

Chapter I

The Mass in the Middle Ages
(Eighth to Fifteenth Century)
New Perspectives[1]

BIBLIOGRAPHY

V. Leroquais, *Les sacramentaires et les missels manuscrits des bibliothèques publiques de France* (4 vols.; Mâcon: Protat, 1924).

Pontifical Romano-Germanique, XCII: *Ordo missae*, ed. C. Vogel and R. Elze, 1 (ST 226; Vatican City: Bibliotheca Apostolica Vaticana, 1963), 329–42.

OR IV–IX (Andrieu, *OR* 2:229–348).

Martène, Liber I, cc. 3–5, M 463–596.

A. Ebner, *Quellen und Forschungen zur Geschichte und Kunstgeschichte des Missale Romanum im Mittelalter. Iter Italicum* (Freiburg: Herder, 1898; repr. 1959).

A. Franz, *Die Messe im deutschen Mittelalter. Beiträge zur Geschichte der Liturgie und des religiösen Volksleben* (Freiburg: Herder, 1902).

N. Maurice-Denis and R. Boulet, *Eucharistie* (Paris: Letouzey et Ané, 1953), 173–95.

B. Luykx, *De Oorsprong van het gewone der Mis* (Utrecht: Spectrum, 1955). German translation: *Der Ursprung der gleichbleibenden Teile der heiligen Messe* (Maria Laach, 1961).

C. Vogel, *Introduction aux sources de l'histoire du culte chrétien au moyen âge* (Biblioteca degli "Studi medievali" 1; Spoleto: Centro italiano di studi sull'alto medioevo, 1966).

P. Salmon, *Analecta liturgica. Extraits des manuscrits liturgiques de la Bibliothèque Vaticane. Contribution à l'histoire de la prière chrétienne* (ST 273; Vatican City, 1974).

E. Costa, "Tropes et séquences dans le cadre de la vie liturgique au moyen âge," *EL* 92 (1978) 260–322, 440–71.

---

1. This chapter will describe the essential characteristics of the development of the Mass in the Middle Ages. The next chapter will show how the various elements in the Order of Mass prepared the way for the Missal of 1570.

§1. The Expansion of the Roman Mass

BIBLIOGRAPHY

G. Prado, *Historia del rito mozárabe* (Silos, 1928).
Andrieu, *OR* 2:xvii–xlix.
J. Deshusses, *Le sacramentaire grégorien* 2. *Textes complémentaires pour la messe* (Spicilegium Friburgense 24; Fribourg: Editions universitaires, 1979).

Even before the Carolingian period the liturgy of the Apostolic See had exercised an influence outside its own proper area; by and large, it had become the liturgy of the Churches of England and Germany, which were founded by papal missionaries. In the sixth century the Roman books were copied for use in the Suevian kingdom of Galicia. But the most important territories conquered by this liturgy were the Churches of Gaul (eighth century) and those of the Iberian Peninsula (eleventh century).

I. THE INTRODUCTION OF THE ROMAN MASS INTO GAUL

A pressing need of reform was felt in Gaul in the last part of the Merovingian period; the lack of copyists had left only tattered old manuscripts, and the ignorance of the clergy made the use of these manuscripts even more difficult. Moreover, there was no longer any authority that could convoke the kind of councils that had created Gallican usage in the time of Caesarius of Arles. Beginning in the seventh century, however, private initiatives led to the introduction of the Roman sacramentaries, which were extensively used to supplement such local books as the *Missale Gothicum*.[2]

These measures were insufficient. In view, therefore, of the difficulties attendant on a restoration of local rites, the monarchs of the new dynasty decided on a more radical solution. Thus Pepin the Short favored the introduction of the Roman mode of chanting (the *"cantilena romana"*) and accomplished it primarily with the aid of the bishops of Metz and Rouen; this shift led to the adoption of many of the texts sung at Rome. Moreover, at the king's instigation a reformed Frankish sacramentary was compiled at the abbey of Flavigny in Burgundy. Its basis was the Roman presbyteral sacramentary known as the "Old Gelasian," which had entered Gaul as early as the end of the seventh century. The compilers also made use of a sacramentary of the Gregorian type, and, of course, of the existing Gallican books. The resulting compilation is known as the "Eighth-

---

2. *Missale Gothicum*, ed. H. M. Bannister (HBS 52 and 54; London: Henry Bradshaw Society, 1917–19); ed. L. C. Mohlberg (REDMF 5; Rome: Herder, 1961).

century Gelasian"; it was constantly recopied (and therefore used) until the eleventh century.[3]

Charlemagne, in his turn, determined on an even more radical solution: he acquired from Pope Hadrian a copy of the Gregorian Sacramentary and had copies made of it by competent scribes under the watchful eyes of the bishops.[4] However, the work that was finally delivered to Aix-la-Chapelle and was intended for the episcopal liturgy could not meet all the needs of the Christian communities. Therefore experts like Alcuin and Benedict of Aniane effected a new integration of the Hadrian Sacramentary with Roman usages already known in the land and a small number of local usages they were unwilling to sacrifice. The emperor's authority ensured the swift spread of this "new liturgy," which eventually triumphed over all competing usages.

II. THE INTRODUCTION OF THE ROMAN MASS INTO SPAIN

In the Province of Narbonne (southern Gaul), which at that time included five dioceses located south of the Pyrenees,[5] the Carolingian rite was adopted in an original form, since it was combined with ancient usages that were still being followed in the rest of Spain.[6] It was in this manner that Roman influence was exerted on the Spanish marches.

In the following century, under pressure from Pope John X, the central part of the Roman Canon was accepted, although it was not given a place in the books being used. Only at the end of the eleventh century did Gregory VII succeed in imposing his discipline on the whole of the peninsula, which he dreamed of turning into a fief of the Holy See. He was helped in his project by the Cluniac abbeys (he himself had been a Cluniac monk). A council held at Burgos in 1085 proclaimed the abolition of the Spanish tradition. This reform was applied only two centuries later in the region of Valencia, since the latter was at this time occupied by the Arabs. The reform also encountered such strong resistance at Toledo

3. A. Chavasse, "Le sacramentaire gélasien du VIIIe siècle: Ses deux principales formes," *EL* 73 (1959) 249–98; J. Deshusses, "Le sacramentaire de Gellone dans son contexte historique," *EL* 75 (1961) 193–210; *idem*, "Les sacramentaires. Etat actuel de la recherche," *ALW* 24 (1982) 19–46. See *The Church at Prayer* I, where these questions are discussed in greater detail.

4. See the various ordinances of Charlemagne beginning in 789, in MGH, *Capitularia Reg. Francorum* 1, ed. A. Boretius (1883). Other books, the *Ordines* in particular, would subsequently come from Rome.

5. These dioceses were attached to the capital of Narbonne, because the see of Tarragona was in Arab hands at this period.

6. The result was what may be called the Catalan-Languedoc Liturgy. See *Liturgie et musique (IX[e]-XIV[e] s.)* (Cahiers de Fanjeaux 11; Toulouse: Privat, 1982).

that the old rite succeeded in keeping its place; it was reorganized in the eleventh century and is known as the Mozarabic Liturgy.

§2. The Romano-Frankish Mass (Ninth and Tenth Centuries)

I. LITURGICAL CHANT

Copies of the "Gregorian" antiphonary have come down to us from the eighth century, but the manuscripts of that time contain no notation; a first attempt at musical notation appears only in the next century. The text is Roman in origin, but it is difficult to establish the provenance of the melodies after the Roman method of chanting had appeared on the scene (under Pepin the Short, when cantors from Italy came and taught it to the Franks).

In any case, psalmody during Mass gradually took the form of long-winded antiphons that left little room for verses. In addition, there is evidence of tropes and sequences being used from the middle of the ninth century on. According to E. Costa, these chants

> represent a development, both textual and melodic, of the compositions in the Gregorian repertory. Tropes are characterized by numerous ways of interpolating chants from the "Proper" and the "Ordinary" of the Mass. . . . Sequences use two different techniques: first, a text is combined with the notes of certain extended melodic sounds (*prosula*); this type of composition, however, gradually develops into an entirely independent form that has its own structures (the "sequence" in the narrower sense).[7]

II. PRIVATE PRAYERS OF CELEBRANT AND MINISTERS

BIBLIOGRAPHY

Martène, Liber 1, c. 4, M 547 (*Missa Illyrica*).
F. Cabrol, *Apologies*, DACL 1 (1907), 2591–2601.
B. Luykx, *Der Ursprung der gleichbleibenden Teile der heiligen Messe* (Maria Laach, 1961).
P. Borella, "Le *apologiae sacerdotis* negli antichi messali ambrosiani," *EL* 63 (1949) 27–41.
P. Salmon, *Analecta liturgica. Extraits des manuscrits liturgiques de la Bibliothèque Vaticane. Contribution à l'histoire de la prière chrétienne* (ST 273; Vatican City, 1974), 195–221.

7. E. Costa, "Tropes et séquences dans le cadre de la vie liturgique au moyen âge," *EL* 92 (1978) 266.

The manuscripts of the Carolingian period attest to the appearance and multiplication of personal prayers for the celebrant. These are known as *apologiae* and consist of self-accusations and confessions by which the celebrant intends to humble and purify himself both before approaching the altar and in the course of the liturgy. The most extensive development of these prayers came in the tenth and eleventh centuries. Then they disappeared almost suddenly, despite the persistence of some formulas; the reason for this phenomenon may have been the evolution of sacramental confession, which now became more frequent.

In addition to the *apologiae,* prayers were introduced to accompany actions originally done in silence.

A manuscript dating from the second half of the ninth century and known as the Amiens Sacramentary was the first to introduce into the official text a complete set of private prayers for the celebrant and ministers, from the beginning of the Mass to its end.[8]

These prayers appear throughout the celebration, but they are more numerous at certain points that were favorable to their introduction: the entrance rites, when the celebrant reaches the sanctuary; the preparation of the gifts, when he is beginning the "sacred mysteries"; the approach of communion, when he is about to share in the sacred meal. The prayers are taken from the most varied sources, ranging from the old Roman or Gallican sacramentaries to the books of private devotion that made their appearance in certain strata of society beginning in the Carolingian period.

III. THE CREED

BIBLIOGRAPHY

B. Capelle, "Le Credo," in *Cours et conférences des Semaines liturgiques* 6 (Louvain: Mont César, 1927), 171-84.

_____, "L'origine adoptianiste de notre texte du symbole de la messe," *RTAM* 1 (1929) 7-20 (= *Travaux liturgiques* 3:47-59).

_____, "Alcuin et l' histoire du symbole de la messe," *RTAM* 6 (1934) 249-60 (= *Travaux liturgiques* 2:211-21).

_____, "L'introduction du symbole à la messe," in *Mélanges J. de Ghellinck* 2 (Louvain, 1951), 1003-27 (= *Travaux liturgiques* 3:60-81).

It was during the confused struggles against Arianism that the Creed, which had its original liturgical place in the rite of baptism, made its way into the Mass. As we shall see further on, it appeared in the East in the first quarter of the sixth century. It appeared in the West at the time when

---

8. V. Leroquais, "L'*Ordo missae* du Sacramentaire d'Amiens BN lat. 9432," *EL* 41 (1927) 435-45.

the Visigoths renounced Arianism and a Council of Toledo (589) decided to imitate Eastern usage; the Council put the Creed just before the Our Father.[9]

The adoptianist controversy led Charlemagne, Alcuin, and Paulinus of Aquileia, in 794, to introduce the Constantinopolitan Creed after the gospel[10]; they also inserted the word *Filioque*, which was not in the Greek text. Via the antiphonaries the innovation made its way abroad from the court at Aix-la-Chapelle. Pope Leo III disapproved of the addition of the *Filioque*, but he allowed it to remain. Only in 1014, and under pressure from St. Henry,[11] did the Church of Rome accept the Creed, which, however, never became a part of every Mass. The Milanese, like most Easterners, placed the Creed immediately before the Eucharistic Prayer; they adopted it in the ninth century under the name *Symbolum dominicale*.

IV. UNLEAVENED BREAD

BIBLIOGRAPHY

J. M. Hanssens, *Institutiones liturgicae de ritibus orientalibus* 2:121–265.
P. Browe, "Mittelalterliche Kommunionsriten," *JLW* 15 (1935 = 1941) 23–66.

The use of unleavened bread, already practiced by the Armenians,[12] became general in the West in the eleventh century; this presupposes that it had been introduced here and there a little earlier.[13] The faithful received Communion only infrequently, and the donation of a liturgical gift from their own tables had lost its meaning.[14] Practical reasons, having to do especially with the reservation of the species, must have played a part, but were joined to considerations from the gospel (the Last Supper took

---

9. Third Council of Toledo, Capitula 2 (Vives 125).

10. This Creed is already found in the Stowe Missal before the offertory, but it lacks the *Filioque*; see G. F. Warner, *The Stowe Missal* 2 (HBS 32; London: Henry Bradshaw Society, 1915), 8.

11. We are told this by an eyewitness: Berno of Reichenau, *De quibusdam rebus ad missae officium spectantibus* 2 (PL 142:1060).

12. In the time of Emperor Maurice (582–602) Catholicos Moses II refused to journey to Constantinople: "God grant . . . I may never eat baked bread or drink warm wine" (*Narratio de rebus Armeniae*, PL 132:1248–49).

13. Rhabanus Maurus († 856), *De institutione clericorum* I, 31 (PL 107:318), speaks of "unleavened bread" ("panem infermentatum"). The testimony of Alcuin, *Ep.* 90 (PL 100:289), can be invoked ("the body of Christ is consecrated without the addition of any other agent"—"absque fermento ullius alterius infectionis"), but it is only indirect, since what he is opposing is the use of salt.

14. Survivals of the offertory process remained, but without organic connection with the Eucharist; see Jungmann, *The Mass of the Roman Rite* 2:11ff., especially n. 61.

place in the Jewish week of unleavened bread). From this time on, the Latin theologians condemned the use of leavened bread; the result was bitter disputes with the Eastern Churches.[15]

V. THE CANON SAID IN A LOW VOICE AND THE "SECRET"

BIBLIOGRAPHY

E. De Moreau, "Récitation du canon de la messe à voix basse," *Nouvelle revue théologique* 51 (1924) 65–94.

J. A. Jungmann, "Praefatio und stiller Kanon," *ZKT* 53 (1929) 247–71.

C. A. Lewis, *The Silent Recitation of the Canon of the Mass* (Bay St. Louis: Divine Word Missionaries, 1962).

At Rome in the time of *Ordo* I, the Eucharistic Prayer could still be heard by the congregation; this observation does not seem to be contradicted by the rubric, *"Surgit pontifex solus et intrat in canone"* ("The pope arises by himself and enters into the canon").[16] But when the same liturgy was celebrated in Frankish territory, probably in the second half of the ninth century, the relevant *Ordo* adds: "in a low voice" (*"tacito intrat in canonem"*).[17] The formula used suggests the high priest entering alone into the Holy of Holies.

The rubric was placed after the *Sanctus*. What precedes was still sung or read aloud. The variable nature of what would come to be called the "Preface" led to its being distinguished in the books from the ensuing fixed part, and the latter alone was regarded henceforth as constituting the canon.[18]

The trend to silence affected other prayers as well. Thus the Roman prayer *Super oblata* ("over the gifts") acquired the name *Secreta*, which was already used in the Old Gelasian Sacramentary. Was the name of

---

15. See the letters of Michael Cerularius, Patriarch of Constantinople (1043–58) and the replies of Pope Leo IX (1054), then of Cardinal Humbert (PL 143:555 and 793, and 143:744, 773, and 927). The various councils that attempted to effect a union of the two Churches tackled the question of unleavened bread: the Second Council of Lyons in 1274 said only: "The Roman Church confects the Eucharist with unleavened bread" (*ex azymo*) (DS 860), while the Council of Florence in 1439 said more specifically: "The body of Christ is truly consecrated with wheaten bread, whether leavened or unleavened; priests must consecrate the Lord's body in one or other of these ways, each following the practice of his own Church, whether Western or Eastern" (DS 1303).

16. OR I, 88–89 (Andrieu, OR 2:95–96), short recension. OR XV (3:103), which was compiled in Frankish territory, says that the celebrant changes his tone: "in a different voice so that he can be heard only by those standing at the altar."

17. OR V, 58 (Andrieu, OR 2:221).

18. The illuminations that turned the first letter of *Te igitur* into a picture of the cross also helped distance this part of the Mass from what preceded.

Gallican origin? Quite possibly.[19] It cannot, however, be said with certainty that the custom of saying this prayer in a low voice, like the canon of which it seems to be the prelude, did not begin in Rome.

VI. ADAPTATIONS OF THE ROMAN CANON

BIBLIOGRAPHY

B. Capelle, *"Et omnibus orthodoxis atque apostolicae fidei cultoribus,"* in *Miscellanea historica Alberti de Meyer* 1 (Louvain, 1946), 137–50 (= *Travaux liturgiques* 2:258–68).

B. Botte, *Le Canon de la messe romaine* (Textes et études liturgiques 2; Louvain: Mont César, 1938).

B. Botte and C. Mohrmann, *L'ordinaire de la messe* (Etudes liturgiques 2; Paris: Cerf, and Louvain: Mont César, 1953).

Some additions were quickly made to the text of the Eucharistic Prayer that was contained in the sacramentary sent to Charlemagne from Rome. The additions are easily recognizable in the manuscripts adapting the papal liturgy to a new context:

a) At the beginning of the canon, mention of the pope was followed by *"et antistite nostro illo et omnibus orthodoxis atque Catholicae et apostolicae fidei cultoribus"* ("and our bishop N. and all faithful guardians of the catholic and apostolic faith").[20] The *cultores* ("guardians") in question are the bishops.[21] This change in the canon was evidently due to the fact that the Roman Eucharistic Prayer was now being used in other Churches.

b) In the Memento of the living the phrase *"qui tibi offerunt"* ("who offer to you") became *"pro quibus tibi offerimus vel qui tibi offerunt"* ("for whom we offer to you or who offer to you"). We noted earlier, in discussing the intercessory prayers, the tendency to lay the emphasis on those for whom the offering was being made.[22] The mentality of the time fostered such a tendency.

---

19. For the Gelasian we have in fact only a copy made in Gaul, and the Bobbio Missal already uses the term *secreta*, among other Gallican titles, for prayers borrowed from Rome. It is to be noted that *OR* XI, 33, transcribes as *secreto* ("secretly") the term *secreta* which it takes from *Ge* I, 26 (Mohlberg, no. 194). On the other hand, the Catalan-Languedoc liturgy has the word *sacra*, which was probably due to a misinterpretation of an abbreviation.

20. B. Botte and C. Mohrmann, *L'Ordinaire de la messe* (Etudes liturgiques 2; Paris: Cerf, and Louvain: Mont César, 1953), 76–77. The first words "et antistite nostro" were in the Gelasian; the following words were to be found only in Irish manuscripts.

21. B. Botte, *Le canon de la messe romain* (Textes et études liturgiques 2; Louvain: Mont César, 1938), 55.

22. Botte, *ibid.* 62–65; see p. 104. This addition is not found in any manuscript before this period.

c) The anamnesis, which formerly had two verbs in the present tense, *memores sumus* and *offerimus* ("we remember . . . we offer"), was reformulated with a single verb, *memores . . . offerimus* ("Calling to mind . . . we offer"). The change meant closer agreement with most of the Eastern anaphoras.

d) A Memento of the dead henceforth began the second series of intercessions. What is difficult to explain here is not the addition but the absence of this Memento in earlier documents, since it has all the earmarks of being a rather ancient Roman text[23] and since the *Nobis quoque peccatoribus* seems to be in continuity with it. Perhaps it was an ancient prayer that had to some extent disappeared; one eighth-century witness has it in Masses for the dead.[24] Gallican usage, which in the past had listed the dead in every Eucharist, although before the canon, probably led to a departure from Roman usage, which was more reticent in its mention of the dead.[25]

VII. THE TRANSFORMATION OF THE COMMUNION RITUAL

BIBLIOGRAPHY

P. M. Gy, "Quand et pourquoi la communion dans la bouche a-t-elle remplacé la communion dans la main dans l'Eglise latine?" in *Gestes et paroles dans les diverses familles liturgiques* (Bibliotheca *EL*, Subsidia 14; Rome: Centro liturgico Vincenziano, 1978), 117–22.

It was more or less around the time when unleavened bread was introduced that the custom also began of receiving Communion on the tongue, a custom already followed in exceptional cases, in particular in dealing with the sick. The new practice was sanctioned by a Council of Rouen in the reign of Louis the Pious: "The Eucharist is not to be placed in the hands of any layman or laywoman but only in their mouths."[26] This was certainly understood at the time as a mark of respect. The new practice probably led in turn to the custom of the faithful kneeling to receive Communion, since this made it easier for the priest to put the host

---

23. See C. Mohrmann, "*Locus refrigerii*," in Botte and Mohrmann, *ibid.* 123–33; *idem,* "*Locus refrigerii lucis et pacis*," *QL* 39 (1958) 196–214. This formula is linked to the popular Latin of the catacombs.

24. M. Andrieu, "L'insertion du Memento des morts au canon romain," *RevSR* 1 (1921) 151–54.

25. The Memento of the dead was therefore not inserted into an earlier text but rather restored after having been dropped from the episcopal Mass, probably because the reading of the names had become tedious.

26. Council of Rouen, can. 2 (Mansi 10:1199).

in their mouths. The new posture only gradually made its way, however, since contrary practices are found down to the end of the Middle Ages. Reception of the chalice through intinction, that is, by wetting the consecrated bread in the Precious Blood, existed in the East, but the practice was rejected in the West by the Council of Braga in 675. This conciliar decree was picked up in the eleventh century by John of Avranches and then by the Synod of Clermont in 1095.[27]

§3. Medieval Devotion (Eleventh to Thirteenth Century)

BIBLIOGRAPHY

E. Dumoutet, *Le désir de voir l'hostie et les origines de la dévotion au Saint-Sacrement* (Paris: Beauchesne, 1926).
P. Browe, *Die häufige Kommunion im Mittelalter* (Regensburg: Pustet, 1938).
J. A. Jungmann, *The Mass of the Roman Rite* 1:103–27.
V. L. Kennedy, "The Moment of Consecration and the Elevation of the Host," *Mediaeval Studies* 6 (1944) 120–50.
_____, "The Date of the Parisian Decree on the Elevation of the Host," *Medieval Studies* 8 (1946) 87–96.
F. Pérez, "La participación activa de los fieles en la liturgia eucarística en las liturgias occidentales durante la edad media," *Liturgia* (Silos) 7 (1952) 143–55.
O. Nussbaum, *Kloster, Priestermonch und Privatmesse* (Theophaneia 14; Bonn: Hanstein, 1961).
P. Salmon, *Les manuscrits liturgiques latins de la Bibliothèque Vaticane* 2 (ST 253; Vatican City, 1969).
A. Haussling, *Mönchskonvent und Eucharistiefeier. Eine Studie über die Messe in der abendländischen Klosterliturgie des frühen Mittelalters und zur Geschichte der Messhäufigkeit* (LQF 58; Münster: Aschendorff, 1973).
C. Vogel, "Une mutation cultuelle inexpliqués = le passage de l'eucharistie communautaire à la messe privée" *Rev SR* 54 (1980), 231–50.

I. THE "COMPLETE MISSAL" AND PRIVATE MASSES

During the eleventh century the first examples of the "complete missal" made their appearance. A "complete missal" was a book in which all the texts of the songs, readings, and prayers were given in the order in which they were to be used during the Mass. The book in this form was a novelty, but it had more or less distant precursors in the sacramentaries, insofar as the latter carried in the margins the incipits of the songs and readings,[28] and in manuscripts that, beginning in the ninth century,

---

27. Council of Braga III, 1 (Vives 372–73). — John of Avranches, *De ecclesiasticis officiis* (PL 147:36–37). — Council of Clermont (Mansi 20:818).
28. See Codex Ottoboni 313 of the Vatican Library: H. A. Wilson, *The Gregorian*

gave the complete text of votive Masses and Masses for the dead that were in common use.

Private Mass, that is, a Mass celebrated by a priest in the presence of a few persons or even of a single server, likewise became a regular practice with the aid of missals, which were in general use by about 1200. The private Mass was the Mass celebrated by priests outside the cities, who did not have the helps available to a bishop in his cathedral. The lack of singers and the smallness of the congregations led to a reduction in the solemnity of the celebration. The private Mass was also the Mass celebrated by monks as more and more of them were ordained to the priesthood.[29]

In time, the private Mass exerted a deleterious influence on the public Mass. In a twelfth-century Order of Mass for the Lateran we see the celebrant for the first time reciting the opening songs with his ministers, and the deacon, after having read the epistle, bringing it to the bishop for him to read.[30] The change represented the intrusion of priestly "asides," no longer simply in the form of personal prayers but in the practice of having the celebrant read texts that properly belonged to other agents in the celebration.

II. THE ELEVATION OF THE SPECIES

The first years of the thirteenth century saw the appearance of a practice that would profoundly alter the external aspect of the old Roman anaphora: the elevation of the host after the consecration. The faithful now rarely received Communion; in compensation they had a great desire to see the sacrament of the Body of Christ. They regarded as important the action by which the priest took the bread into his hands when beginning the account of institution, for it enabled them to see the sacrament; some celebrants tended to perform this action in such a way that the con-

---

Sacramentary under Charles the Great (HBS 49; London: Henry Bradshaw Society, 1915). The Bobbio Missal (seventh century) combines pericopes for reading and presidential prayers, something unparalleled at this period: E. Lowe, *The Bobbio Missal. Text* (HBS 58; London: Henry Bradshaw Society, 1920); *idem, The Bobbio Missal. Notes and Studies* (HBS 61; London: Henry Bradshaw Society, 1924), 156–59.

29. The part played by monks in the origin of the multiplication of Masses is still disputed. In Häussling's view, the monks of Rome sought to make their abbeys an image of the city with its many churches: the stational Mass was represented by the community celebration, and the Masses in the "titles" by Masses in the monastery chapels. According to Nussbaum, the ordination of monks made the Eucharist central in their lives, with each ordained monk representing as it were the entire assembly of believers.

30. L. Fischer, *Bernhardi cardinalis . . . Ordo officiorum ecclesiae Lateranensis* (Historische Forschungen und Quellen 2–3; Munich: Datterer, 1916), 80–81.

gregation might see it more easily. The practice became the object of a decree of the bishop of Paris shortly after 1200: "When priests take the host in their hands as they begin the *Qui pridie*, they are not immediately to elevate it very high so that the congregation can see it. Rather, they are to hold it in front of their breast until they have said the words 'This is my body,' and only then raise it higher so that all can see it."[31]

Note the use of the term "host," from the Latin *hostia*, meaning "victim." The word "offering" (*oblatio*), which had been the one most frequently used in earlier centuries, had gradually disappeared from current liturgical language. The elevation of the host spread rapidly throughout the West; the elevation of the chalice is attested only beginning in the last quarter of the century.[32]

III. THE COMMUNION OF THE FAITHFUL

1. *The infrequency of reception.* Despite the reaction of thirteenth-century theologians and mystics in favor of communion for the laity, the latter approached the holy table only very rarely.[33] Fear, the (then new) obligation of prior confession, and the demand that married people observe continence in preparation, had considerably reduced the frequency of reception. Moreover, some authors claimed that the priest received in behalf of the entire congregation and that the faithful were therefore excused from approaching the sacrament.

2. *The abandonment of participation in the chalice.* Practical convenience, the danger of spilling the Precious Blood, distaste for the practice, the danger of spreading disease—all these considerations prompted various ways of receiving under the species of wine. Perhaps the reservations, already pointed out, that were felt in the West in regard to intinction also played a role in the adoption of a more radical solution. In any case, the custom of withholding the chalice from the faithful gradually prevailed during the thirteenth century; by the time St. Thomas Aquinas († 1274) was finishing his *Summa*, he could describe the new practice as

---

31. *Statuts synodaux de Paris*, no. 80, ed. O. Pontal, *Les Statuts synodaux français du XIIIᵉ siècle* 1 (Collection de documents inédits sur l'histoire de France, serie in 8°, vol. 9; Paris: Bibliothèque Nationale, 1971), 83. This decree is generally attributed to Eudes of Sully († 1208).

32. William Durandus, *Rationale* IV, 41, 52; manuscript missals in Rome, Archivio de Stato, San Salvatore 1001, and Archivio de S. Maria Maggiore, BB II, 15. See S. Van Dijk and J. H. Walker, *The Origins of the Modern Roman Liturgy* (Westminster, Md.: Newman, 1960), 361.

33. The Lateran Council of 1215, cap. 21, obliged the faithful to receive Communion at least at Easter (DS 812).

a custom prudently observed by some Churches.[34] From that time on, however, communion under one species quickly became the general rule; the ensuing centuries witnessed only a few survivals of the older practice.[35]

IV. THE DECLINE IN PARTICIPATION BY THE FAITHFUL

The infrequency of communion was not the only sign of the progressive decline through the Middle Ages in active participation of the faithful in the Eucharist. Many other factors contributed to increasing the distance between sanctuary and nave: the abandonment of a donation of the gifts by the faithful (the use of unleavened bread prevented any return to the old custom), the multiplication of private Masses, and the use of a language increasingly different from that spoken by the people (although Latin remained the official means of communication in civil society and the schools).

To these causes must be added the monastic and canonical character that the liturgy had gradually acquired. Chanting became an increasingly complex matter and therefore the prerogative of canons, trained bodies of singers, and cantors, as the "choir" replaced the congregation. This element of substitution was aggravated in cathedrals and abbeys by the installation of roodscreens, which, from the fourteenth century on, often became more or less opaque partitions between the faithful and the few individuals who were the sole agents in the Eucharistic celebration. All these factors turned the laity into onlookers so passive that the liturgical books no longer even mentioned their presence.

§4. Instructional Treatises and Rubrics

BIBLIOGRAPHY

Amalarius, *Amalarii episcopi opera liturgica omnia*, ed. J. M. Hanssens (3 vols.; ST 138–40; Vatican City, 1948–50). The *Expositiones missae* are in 1:283–338.
A. Wilmart, "Expositio missae," *DACL* 5 (1922), 1014–27.
A. Franz, *Die Messe im deutschen Mittelalter* (Freiburg: Herder, 1902), 331–740.
A. Wilmart, *Auteurs spirituels et textes dévots du moyen âge latin* (Paris: Bloud et Gay, 1932).
F. Brovelli, "Expositio missae canonicae," *Archivio Ambrosiano* 35 (1979).

---

34. St. Thomas Aquinas, *Summa theologiae* III, 80, 12.

35. Among the Cistercians, communion under both kinds was restricted to ministers at the altar in the thirteenth century; this custom was suppressed in 1437. — Survivals: in the papal Mass on Easter in the fourteenth and fifteenth centuries (*OR* Mab 15, no. 85; PL 78:1332), and in the Mass for the coronation of an emperor or king (Louis XV was probably the last to receive under both kinds at his coronation).

I. ALLEGORICAL COMMENTARIES

Ever since the mystagogical catecheses of Christian antiquity, every age had provided itself with explanations of the ceremonies of the Mass. At an early date, however, writers ceased being satisfied with the basic sacramental symbolisms; in order to instruct or to edify they added more or less extrinsic interpretations, assigning new meanings to the rites, even to those that originally had had a purely utilitarian significance. Historians of liturgy describe this approach as allegorical. The tendency can be seen at work as far back as Theodore of Mopsuestia, and in fact it developed first in the East, in Pseudo-Dionysius (for example) and, later on, in Germanus of Constantinople. But it also spread in the West; Isidore of Seville († 636) was one of its principal representatives.

In the Middle Ages this literary genre flourished in the form of short treatises known from the ninth century on as *Expositiones missae* ("Explanations of the Mass").[36] These supplied material for the meditation of the faithful and were at the same time manuals of theological and moral formation that took as their point of departure the mysteries being celebrated. A pioneer in the use of this method was Amalarius of Metz (775–852). Despite some critics, among them Deacon Florus of Lyons, this literature became very popular in the ensuing centuries. It contained some well balanced productions, such as the commentary written by the future Pope Innocent III.[37] Other authors, however, superimposed on the parts of the Mass various episodes from the life or passion of Christ that had no real connection with the actualization of salvation in the "today" of the liturgy.[38] Because of their very popular character, all these works found a wide readership.[39]

II. THE RUBRICS OF THE MASS

During this period the *Ordines Romani* continued to evolve along two different lines.

---

36. The earliest witness to this literature is probably the anonymous *Primum in ordine*, ed. A. Wilmart, *EL* 50 (1936) 133–39.

37. *De sacro altaris mysterio libri sex* (PL 217:774–914).

38. For Amalarius the entrance song images forth the choir of prophets as they announce the Messiah; the *Kyrie* suggests the Old Testament; the *Gloria* introduces the New Testament (song of the angels at Bethlehem); the collect is related to the manifestation of Jesus in the temple at the age of twelve; the readings before the gospel recall the preaching of John the Baptist; and so on. Certain notions are even bolder: when the priest ascends the altar, he represents Jesus ascending Calvary; when he moves from one side of the altar to the other, he is Christ going from Caiaphas to Pilate; and so on.

39. This doubtless sheds light on the meaning of some of the medieval "mystery plays"; see O. Hardison, *Christian Rite and Christian Drama in the Middle Ages* (Baltimore, 1965).

In France and Germany they assimilated local elements and to the description of rites added the formulas of the prayers. The end result was the Romano-Germanic Pontifical, a compilation made at Mainz in the middle of the tenth century. This new book was then brought to Rome, where it provided the basis for the Roman Pontifical of the twelfth century and then for the thirteenth-century Pontifical of the Roman Curia. As it passed through these stages, the Pontifical gradually omitted all that had to do with the Mass and limited itself strictly to other episcopal functions. At the end of the thirteenth century, however, the great liturgist William Durandus, bishop of Mende, used the Pontifical of the Curia as the basis for a book that better met the needs of a diocesan bishop and described in detail the episcopal Mass, the functions of other ministers, and the use of insignia.[40]

In Rome, meanwhile, the rubricists of the twelfth and thirteenth centuries were producing *Ordines* of a quite different character. These gave full descriptions of the practices for Mass and the liturgical year, and reported all the variants in the actual usage of the pope. Neither the transfer of the papal court to Avignon nor the difficulties the papacy encountered in the fifteenth century interrupted the painstaking work of these men.[41] The documents continued to develop and climaxed in the work entitled *Rituum ecclesiasticorum sive sacrarum ceremoniarum S. Romanae ecclesiae* ("The ecclesiastical rites and sacred ceremonies of the Holy Roman Church, in three books"), which was composed in 1488 by Johannes Burckard, Agostino Patrizi, and Paride Grassi.[42]

As far as the essentials inherited from the ancient Roman tradition were concerned, the entire Latin world used just about the same liturgy. But the introduction of private prayers, as well as the gestures that had been made part of the celebration, allowed some freedom of movement in certain parts of the Mass: the opening prayers and offertory prayers, the

---

40. Andrieu, *PR* 3:631-62. The Pontifical printed in 1485 reproduces Durandus almost verbatim.

41. A list of these *Ordines* and their editions is given in P. Salmon, *Les manuscrits liturgiques latins de la Bibliothèque Vaticane* 3 (ST 260; Vatican City, 1970), ix-xii and 101-45; complementary information in B. Schimmelpfennig, *Die Zeremonienbücher der römischen Kirche im Mittelalter* (Tübingen: Niemeyer, 1973), and M. Dykmans, *Le cérémonial papal de la fin du moyen âge à la Renaissance* (3 vols.; Bibliothèque de l'Institut historique belge de Rome 24-25; Rome, 1977-83).

42. M. Dykmans, *L'oeuvre de Patrizi Piccolomini ou le cérémonial papal de la première Renaissance* (ST 293-94; Vatican City, 1980-82). — This book was published in Venice in 1516 by Cristoforo Marcello, Archbishop of Corcyra; it was reprinted in 1750 with a commentary by Giuseppe Catalani and until recent years was normative for papal ceremonies. The same Roman tradition, adapted to bishops of other sees by Paride Grassi, served as the basis for the *Caeremoniale episcoporum* promulgated by Clement VIII in 1600. See P. Borella, *San Carlo e il Ceremoniale dei vescovi* (Varese: Tipografia Varese, 1937).

preparation for communion, the concluding rites. In the thirteenth century each diocese established its own set of customs, which then tended to become stereotyped. In fact, the same elements (with some variants) were used in many places, but the wide range of ways in which they were combined gave an impression of very great diversity.

At this same period, however, the various mendicant orders each adopted a common practice for convenience' sake, because the members moved about a great deal. As a result, the Friars, who traveled widely and worked in many places, created in the people at least a desire for some degree of unity. The Dominicans, for example, carried with them the usages of Paris,[43] the Franciscans those of the Roman Curia,[44] and the Carmelites elements of the rite that had been established in the Latin Patriarchate of Jerusalem.[45]

§5. The Evolution of the Mass in the Eastern Churches

BIBLIOGRAPHY

F. E. Brightman, *Liturgies Eastern and Western* I. *Eastern Churches* (Oxford: Clarendon Press, 1896).

J. M. Hanssens, *Institutiones liturgicae de ritibus orientalibius* 2 (Rome: Gregorian University, 1930), 475–512: "De ordine missae orientalis a s. IX. ad praesentem aetatem."

N. Maurice-Denis and R. Boulet, *Eucharistie* (Paris: Letouzey et Ane, 1953), 87–125.

I. SANCTUARY AND NAVE

BIBLIOGRAPHY

A. Raes, *Introductio in liturgiam orientalem* (Rome: Pontificio Istituto Orientale, 1947), 30–39: "De divisione interna ecclesiae" (with bibliography).

---

43. Their liturgy resembled that of many other French and English dioceses. In 1256, Humbert of Romans, Dominican Master-General, definitively revised all the liturgical usages of the Friars Preachers. See G. Sölch, *Die Eigenliturgie der Dominikaner* (Düsseldorf: Albertus Magnus Verlag, 1957).

44. See V. L. Kennedy, "The Franciscan *Ordo missae* in the Thirteenth Century," *Mediaeval Studies* 2 (1940) 204–22; S. Van Dijk, *Sources of the Modern Roman Liturgy* (Leiden: Brill, 1963). — There is evidence of private Masses at the papal court beginning with the pontificate of Honorius III (1216–27). Sixteen years after this pope's death Haymo of Faversham established the first complete Order of Mass for the Roman private Mass; it was for the use of the Franciscans and began with the words *Indutus planeta*. It was replaced, for low Mass, only by that of Johannes Burckard.

45. *Ordinale Ordinis Carmelitarum saec. XIII*, ed. Patrick de Saint-Joseph, in *Etudes Carmélitaines*, 1912–13.

In most present-day Eastern churches the sanctuary is separated from the nave by an opaque partition that is decorated with icons in accordance with strict rules and is therefore called the "iconostasis" (*eikonostasis* or *eikonostasion*).[46] A central door, which remains shut during a large part of the liturgy, and two side doors provide for communication between the *bêma* and the rest of the building. This arrangement appeared only at the end of the fourteenth century in the Slavic countries and spread from there throughout the Churches of the Levant. It is therefore not an expression of the medieval mentality. The only explanation for its success is that it was in harmony with a conception of the liturgical celebration that was familiar to the Eastern faithful.

As early as the eighth century we find the space around the altar being described as the "Holy of Holies" and therefore "accessible only to priests"; the people, on the other hand, remain on the other side of grills known as chancels (*kagkella*).[47] The deacons, whose ministry is compared to that of the angels,[48] spend part of the time within the sanctuary, assisting the celebrant, and part of the time outside, where they lead the faithful in prayer, especially by means of litanies that recur throughout the celebration. The deacons ascend and descend the ladder of Jacob, as it were,[49] and act as a link between the faithful and the image of heaven that is the sanctuary.

II. THE PREPARATION OF THE GIFTS

BIBLIOGRAPHY

Hanssens 3:17–31.

Except for the Armenians, who had begun using unleavened bread at an early date,[50] the Eastern Churches have continued to use leavened bread. In time, however, the Churches were no longer content to use the bread that the faithful ate at home; instead, priests and other ministers were charged with baking the bread for the Eucharist, to the accompaniment of suitable prayers.[51]

More importantly, beginning in the eighth century, and perhaps even earlier, the preparation of the gifts was transferred from the beginning

---

46. Other names are also used: *druphakta, diasyla, kionia, stēthea*, etc.
47. Germanus of Constantinople (Borgia 13).
48. Borgia 17. — See S. Salaville and G. Nowack, *Le rôle du diacre dans la liturgie orientale* (Archives de l'Orient chrétien 3; Paris: Institut francais d'études byzantines, 1962).
49. Gen 28:12.
50. See n. 12, p. 132.
51. Hanssens, *Institutiones* 2:206–17.

of the Eucharistic liturgy proper to the beginning of the entire celebration.[52] In most of the Churches, this ceremony takes place at the altar, where it is more or less felicitously integrated with the entrance rites.[53] Among the Byzantines, however, it is a private ceremony, but also one of no little complexity: it is performed by a priest, with the assistance of a deacon, and in a place equipped for the purpose, on a table called the "prothesis" (*prothesis*).[54] The ceremony is known as the "proscomide" (*proskomidē*) and its ritual was organized between the twelfth and fourteenth centuries.[55]

This Byzantine practice has made it possible to retain the procession with the bread and wine at the beginning of the Eucharistic liturgy proper. The "Great Entrance" has kept its solemn character due to the singing of the Cherubic Hymn (*Cheroubikon*),[56] to which have been added private prayers of the celebrant and an intercession for the ecclesiastical hierarchy.[57] In the other Eastern rites the gifts are already present on the table of sacrifice,[58] and though a processional antiphon or hymn may still be sung, it has lost its original function. In the twelfth century the Alexandrian liturgy of St. Mark still had a transfer of the gifts,[59] but nothing is now left of this except a procession with the gifts around the altar at the beginning of the celebration.

---

52. The existence of the proscomide is attested in about 820 by Gregory of Decapolis, *Sermo* (PG 100:1201-4).

53. In the Western Syrian rite and among the Maronites the deacon played an important role in this preparation, a fact that probably helped to integrate it in a fairly satisfactory way into the entrance rites.

54. The rite is also found among the Armenians, but in a much more modest form.

55. With a small lance the priest incises a cross in the *prosphora* (bread to be offered), as well as the letters IC.XC.NI.KA; the result is to detach one portion, called the *Amnos* (Lamb), which will be consecrated. The remainder of the bread is cut into small pieces that are arranged on the diskos (paten) according to precise rules, in memory of the saints and of the intentions for which the sacrifice is to be offered. The chalice is filled, the offerings are incensed and covered with veils.

56. See p. 79.

57. Among the Armenians a deacon fetches the offerings without any solemnity and brings them to the altar.

58. Among the Eastern Syrians it is at this point that the ministers come to the altar, the first part of the Mass having been celebrated on the tribune, which occupies the center of the nave. The Nestorians, unlike the Chaldeans, do not prepare the offerings before the Mass, but at this point.

59. Codex Rossanensis, Bibl. Vat., ms. grec 1970; ed. C. A. Swainson, *The Greek Liturgies* (London: Clay, 1884), 22-24.

III. THE CREED

BIBLIOGRAPHY

B. Capelle, "Le Credo," in *Cours et conférences des Semaines liturgiques* 6 (Louvain: Mont César, 1928). 171–84.

_____, "L'introduction du symbole à la messe," in *Mélanges J. de Ghellinck* 2 (Louvain: Museum Lessianum, 1951), 1003–27 (= *Travaux liturgiques* 3:60–81).

_____, "Le pape Léon III et le *Filioque*," in *1054–1954, L'Eglise et les Eglises* Chevetogne, 1954), 309–22 (= *Travaux liturgiques* 3:35–46).

It was in the East that the Creed originally made its appearance in the Mass. Patriarch Timothy of Constantinople (512–18) "decided that it was henceforth to be said at every synaxis."[60] At Antioch it was probably introduced even earlier, at the end of the fifth century, under Patriarch Peter the Fuller. The Churches of the East quickly adopted it (this Creed evidently did not contain the *Filioque*[61]). In most of these Churches it is said immediately or almost immediately before the anaphora. Among the Byzantines and Copts it follows the kiss of peace and is connected with it. Depending on the Church in question, it is recited by the priest alone or by the entire congregation. Among the Armenians, who were influenced by the West on this point, the deacon proclaims it immediately after reading the gospel; he holds the Book of Gospels aloft as he does so.

Despite the controversies it has caused, the Creed remains in the West a response to God's word and in the East a means of purifying one's faith before celebrating the sacred mysteries. It shows that all the Churches are united in submission to divine Wisdom.

IV. THE SILENT EUCHARISTIC PRAYER

BIBLIOGRAPHY

Hanssens 3:481–85.

The tendency to read the Eucharistic Prayer in a low voice appeared very early in some of the Eastern Churches, since we find Emperor Justinian ordering priests, in 565, to say "the divine offering . . . not quietly, but in a voice loud enough to be heard by the faithful."[62] This custom was probably still fairly widespread a century and a half later, because

---

60. Theodore the Reader, *Historia ecclesiastica* II, 32 (PG 38:201).

61. The addition is accepted by the Melkites, Ruthenians, and Italo-Greeks, but has not been imposed on all the Churches united with Rome.

62. Novella 137, ed. G. Krueger and T. Mommsen, *Corpus Iuris Civilis* (Berlin, 1891), 699.

John Moschus feels it necessary to explain that in some places (he is speaking of the region of Apamea in Syria) celebrants habitually say the anaphora aloud.[63]

Silence (the use of a low voice) does not take the same form as in the Roman liturgy. After the opening dialogue, the first part of the Eucharistic Prayer (corresponding to the Latin Preface) is said in a low voice down as far as the "ecphonesis" (a prayer "spoken aloud"), with which the *Sanctus* is connected; other interventions of the congregation are introduced in the same manner. Differently than in the Roman Canon, some parts are sung, as, for example, the account of institution, each consecration being followed by an Amen of the congregation.

V. THE QUESTION OF THE EPICLESIS

BIBLIOGRAPHY

M. Jugie, *De forma eucharistiae, de epiclesibus eucharisticis* (Rome: Officium libri catholici, 1943).
A. Chavasse, "L'épiclèse eucharistique dans les anciennes liturgies orientales. Une hypothèse d'interprétation," *Mélanges de science religieuse* 2 (1946), 197–206.
A. Raes, "L'epiclesi nelle liturgie orientali," in *Incontro ai fratelli separati di Oriente* (Rome, 1945), 331–41.
S. Salaville, "Epiclèse eucharistique," in *Catholicisme* 4 (1953), 302–7.
E. Boularand, "L'épiclèse au Concile de Florence," *Bulletin de littérature ecclésiastique* 60 (1959) 241–73.

Is it the account of institution or the epiclesis that "makes" the Eucharist? Such were the terms of a problem that arose in the confrontation between East and West during the Middle Ages. It is noteworthy that this difficulty was not brought up in the controversies between the two Churches in the ninth and eleventh centuries. By the fourteenth century, however, Nicholas Cabasilas, the great Byzantine liturgist, was aware of Latin opposition to the teaching of the Eastern tradition, and he undertook to justify the latter.[64]

The question was debated at the Council of Florence in 1439, but the Council asked the Byzantines only for an official verbal declaration on the point. The projected decree said that the consecration was effected solely by the words of Christ, but Pope Eugene IV eliminated this state-

---

63. John Moschus, *Pratum spirituale* 196 (PG 87:3080–81); trans. Rouet de Journel, SC 12 (Paris: Cerf, 1946), 266.
64. Nicholas Cabasilas, *A Commentary on the Divine Liturgy*, trans. J. M. Hussey and P. A. McNulty (London: SPCK, 1960), chapters 29–30.

ment from the text to be signed, lest (he said) the Eastern Churches be insulted by the implication that they had hitherto professed a contrary view.[65] The pope wished to affirm the doctrine, while at the same time recognizing that the liturgical usages of the two Churches (the Greeks relied on their usages to defend their thesis) could not by themselves resolve a question that had not arisen in these terms at the time when the prayers were being composed.

Bossuet in the seventeenth century made the same point in some wise observations:

> The intent of liturgies and, in general, of consecratory prayers, is not to focus our attention on precise moments, but to have us attend to the action in its entirety and to its complete effect. . . . It is to render more vivid what is being done that the Church speaks at each moment as though it were accomplishing the entire action then and there, without asking whether the action has already been accomplished or is perhaps still to be accomplished.[66]

VI. ALLEGORICAL EXPLANATIONS OF THE LITURGY

BIBLIOGRAPHY

N. Borgia, *Il commentario liturgico de s. Germano patriarca costantinopolitano e la versione latina di Abastasio Bibliotecario* (Grottaferrata, 1912).

G. Gharib, "Nicolas Cabasilas et l'explication symbolique de la liturgie," *POC* 10 (1960) 114–33.

R. Bornert, *Les commentaires byzantins sur la liturgie divine du VIIᵉ au XVᵉ siècle* (Archives de l'Orient chrétien 9; Paris: Institut français d'études byzantines, 1966).

N. Cabasilas, *A Commentary on the Divine Liturgy,* trans. J. M. Hussey and P. A. McNulty (London: SPCK, 1960).

R. Bornert, "L'anaphore dans la spiritualité liturgique de Byzance. Le témoignage des commentaires mystagogiques du VIIᵉ au XVᵉ siècle," in *Eucharisties d'Orient et d'Occident* 2 (Paris: Cerf, 1970), 241–63.

Explanations of the Mass have not been lacking in the East, from the *Mystagogy* of Maximus the Confessor (*ca.* 628–30) to quite recent works. Landmarks along the way have been the work of Germanus of Constantinople, patriarch from 715 to 730,[67] the *Protheoria* from about the middle

---

65. *Concilium Florentinum, Documenta et scriptores* V, 2 (Rome: Oriental Institute, 1953), 448–51.

66. J. B. Bossuet, *Explication de quelques difficultés sur les prières de la messe* 45, ed. F. Lachat, *Oeuvres* 17 (in the L. Vives ed., 1864), 74–75.

67. Questions remain regarding the author and text of this commentary. It seems that Germanus was the author of a first redaction that was later subjected to numerous interpolations.

of the eleventh century,[68] and the writings of Nicholas Cabasilas († 1350) and Symeon, bishop of Thessalonica from 1410 to 1429, to mention only Byzantine writers.

The Eastern allegorical interpretations differ clearly from those of the Latin Middle Ages. They are built around a basic symbolism: the "Divine Liturgy" is, in a sense, heaven come down to earth and the focal point of a cosmic vision of reality. Here the entire universe is transfigured by the Holy Spirit in the offering of the sacred gifts. The Byzantine writers adopt this perspective throughout as they comment on the rites of the Mass: thus the singing echoes the singing of the angelic choirs; the reading of the gospel effects the presence of Christ who shows the invisible God to human beings; the dismissal of the catechumens suggests the sheep who are not yet included in the fold; the bringing of the gifts to the altar recalls the pyre of Isaac and the cross of the risen Lord; and so on.

---

68. The *Protheoria* has come down in two recensions, one attributed to Nicholas, the other to Theodore, both of them bishops of Andida in Pamphilia. The second seems to be a corrected re-edition of the first.

Chapter II

The Medieval Origins of the 1570 Order of Mass

BIBLIOGRAPHY

A. Ebner, *Quellen und Forschungen zur Geschichte und Kunstgeschichte des Missale Romanum im Mittelalter. Iter Italicum* (Freiburg: Herder, 1898; repr., 1959).

A. Franz, *Die Messe im deutschen Mittelalter. Beiträge zur Geschichte der Liturgie und des religiösen Volksleben* (Freiburg: Herder, 1902).

V. Leroquais, "L'*Ordo missae* du Sacramentaire d'Amiens, BN. Lat. 9432," *EL* 41 (1927) 435–45.

B. Luykx, *Der Ursprung der gleichbleibenden Teile der heiligen Messe* (Maria Laach: Verlag Ars liturgica, 1961).

P. Salmon, *Analecta liturgica. Extraits des manuscrits liturgiques de la Bibliothèque Vaticane. Contribution à l'histoire de la prière chrétienne* (ST 273; Vatican City, 1974), 195–221: "L'*Ordo missae* dans dix manuscrits du Xe au XVe siècle."

The Order of Mass found in the Missal of St. Pius V (published in 1570)[1] represents both the end result and a critical revision of medieval developments. When we locate it in this dynamic perspective, we can see mirrored in it the history of each part of the Mass from the eighth century on. Such a history is made all the easier by the fact that while in theory the reform of 1570 was binding on all the Churches of the West, an exception was made for customs that could claim to have existed for two hundred years. Thanks to this exception, survival was ensured for the Ambrosian liturgy of Milan and the Mozarabic liturgy of Toledo, which represent other traditions. Survival was also ensured for properly Roman rites that were distinguished from the new Order of Mass only by adaptations subsequent to the Carolingian period: secondary actions and, above all, private prayers of the ministers.

---

1. On the reform decreed by the Council of Trent and on the Missal of Pius V see p. 173.

§1. The Preliminary Rites

BIBLIOGRAPHY

Martène, Liber I, cap. 4, a. 1–3; M. 468–85.
Jungmann, *The Mass of the Roman Rite* 1:261–390.

I. BEFORE MASS

1. The "Preparation for Mass"

Personal preparation was not necessarily expressed in formulas nor set down in writing; of itself it was not a part of the liturgy. Gradually, however, the celebrant's preparation did in fact become part of the Order of Mass. We find prayers for this purpose in tenth-century documents in the East[2] and in the eleventh-century sacramentaries of the West. The psalms and prayers given in the latter become more numerous in the thirteenth-century Missal of the Papal Chapel and pass from the latter into the Roman Missal.[3]

2. Vesting prayers

Prayers also accompanied the vesting of the celebrant, giving an allegorical explanation of each garment; the prayers differed for bishops and presbyters. In the Carolingian period there was an almost endless variety of these prayers, but they are not of great interest. In some medieval usages the celebrant robed, or finished robing, at the altar.[4]

II. THE CELEBRANT'S ENTRANCE

1. The Introit and prayers at the foot of the altar.

When Mass was sung it began with an entrance psalm (the Introit psalm), which was now reduced to a single verse and a doxology, along

---

2. Hanssens, *Institutiones* 3:1–7.

3. Psalms 84, 85, 86, 116, and 130 with the antiphon *Ne reminiscaris* ("Do not remember"), and followed by the *Kyrie*, the Our Father, some verses, and seven prayers—a real Little Office meant to be said in a group. The first three psalms and the first prayer are already found in the eleventh century books. The Roman Missal subsequently has a "Prayer of St. Ambrose" that is divided according to the days of the week. The prayer is in fact probably from the eleventh century and may be the work of John of Fécamp; see A. Wilmart, *Auteurs spirituels et textes dévots du moyen âge latin* (Paris: Etudes augustiniennes, 1971²), 101–25.

4. Comparable prayers occur in the Eastern liturgies; deserving of mention are those of the Byzantine rite, which are accompanied by blessings, and those of Syrian rite, which are solemnly sung when a bishop presides.

with an antiphon, the ornate melody of which was sung twice, making it long enough to accompany the celebrants to the altar.

During their procession the celebrants said alternately some verses of the psalms and some *apologiae*, which, in the eleventh century, took the form of a *Confiteor*. This last made its appearance in the Mass, the Office, and the sacrament of penance.[5] There were various versions of it, but all contained two parts: an acknowledgment of sin before God and before the Church of heaven and earth, and a petition for the intercession of the brethren. The saints mentioned could be more or less numerous, and the list might or might not be repeated in the second part.[6] One of the simplest texts remained in use in the Dominican rite: "I confess to almighty God [and to Blessed Mary ever virgin and St. Dominic, our father] and to all the saints and to you, brethren, that I have sinned exceedingly in thought, word, deed, and omission, by my own fault; I ask you to pray for me."

Since the distance to the altar was usually rather short, the prayers continued at the foot of the altar. In low Masses, the whole process even began there, with a sign of the cross to introduce these private devotions of the ministers.

From among the current formularies the Missal of Pius V chose one of the longest, since it was widespread in Italy. In it the "confession" was fuller, and, above all, Psalm 43 was said in its entirety.[7]

2. The ascent of the altar

The prayers at the foot of the altar were followed by one or several prayers said, still in a low voice, while ascending the steps. The most widely

---

5. The *Confiteor* is followed by the *Misereatur* ("May almighty God have mercy on you") and a formula that was used for sacramental absolution, *(Indulgentiam) absolutionem . . .* ("May the almighty and merciful God grant us pardon, absolution . . ."). — On the various texts of the *Confiteor* see M. Bernard, "Un texte inédit, le Confiteor lyonnais," *EL* 83 (1969) 459–81.

6. The Eastern Churches (except for the Armenians, who took it over from the Friars Preachers) have nothing comparable to the *Confiteor*, but they do say silent prayers of self-accusation and psalms. It is to be noted that these Churches did not experience the development of penitential practice associated with the Latin Middle Ages.

7. Psalm 43 was chosen in function of the verse that serves as an antiphon: "I will go to the altar of God." In the fourth century the newly baptized sang this psalm as they approached the altar, where they would share in the Eucharist for the first time; as they went they were filled with all the freshness and joy of the grace bestowed on them ("to God who gives joy to my youth"). See St. Ambrose, *De sacramentis* IV, 7 (SC 25:79–80). — The Dominican Missal has only two psalmic verses: "Confitemini Domino quoniam bonus" and "Adjutorium nostrum," which serve as a frame for the *Confiteor*. Similarly the Carthusian rite: "Pone, Domine, custodiam ori meo" and "Adjutorium nostrum," which the priest says while turned to the server.

used of these prayers was the *Aufer a nobis* ("Take away our sins"). The prayer was put to this use in the eleventh century, but it came from the older Roman euchology.[8] The Gregorian Sacramentary made it part of the ceremony for the transfer of relics, a fact not irrelevant to its use at the beginning of Mass, since it is followed here by the kissing of the altar. This gesture, used in the Eastern Churches of the Antiochene tradition, was originally addressed simply to the table of sacrifice and sometimes to the Book of Gospels that rested on it. But it came in time to be addressed to the relics of the martyrs that were customarily deposited in the altar stone as in a tomb.

In solemn Masses a blessing of the incense and a first incensation followed at this point.

III. THE SONGS AND PRESIDENTIAL PRAYERS

In churches that faced east the missal was placed on the south side of the altar. It was there that the celebrant read the Introit, even this had already been sung by the choir. There too, after the *Kyrie*, the *Gloria* (if it was to be said), and the salutation, he read the collects. There were now usually several collects, since those of some other office or for intentions for which the celebrant wanted to pray were often introduced into the Mass of the day.[9]

§2. The Liturgy of the Word

I. THE READINGS

BIBLIOGRAPHY

Martène, Liber I, cap. 4, a. 4–5; M 486 and 486bis.
Jungmann, *The Mass of the Roman Rite* 1:391–494.

The first reading, called the "Epistle" even if it was not always taken from the apostolic letters, was read at the same side of the altar. The gospel was read at the northern side.[10] Its reading was accompanied by two pri-

---

8. *Le* 985; *Ge* 84; *H* (Hadrianum) 194.

9. In the ninth century Amalarius, *Liber officialis*, Prooemium 1–2 and 10 (Hanssens 2:13 and 15), recommended, after inquiring into the practice of the Roman clergy, that there be but one collect; but this was not accepted by the Gauls and Franks who preferred greater prolixity.

10. The northward position recalled the unbelief of the nations to whom the preaching of the apostles was directed.

vate prayers: before it the *Munda cor* ("Cleanse my heart"), which was an interior preparation of the minister, and after it the *"Per evangelica dicta deleantur nostra delicta"* ("By the words of the gospel may our sins be forgiven"). In some places, moreover—a custom kept by Pius V—each reading was followed by a response said half aloud by a cleric (*"Deo gratias,"* "Thanks be to God," and *"Laus tibi, Christe,"* "Praise to you, O Christ"). These responses were never sung in solemn liturgies.

The Word of God was proclaimed in a language that had become a foreign one for the congregation. As a result, the people were aware less of the content of the Word than of the external circumstances of its proclamation, especially at the reading of the gospel. Here there was an opening acclamation derived from the Gallican liturgy: *"Gloria tibi, Domine"* ("Glory to you, O Lord"); signs of the cross made on the book and by the people on themselves before and after the reading. In solemn Masses there were in addition the incensation of the book, the arrangement of the ministers in a sign of the cross, and so on.

II. THE SONGS

BIBLIOGRAPHY

> P. Wagner, *Origine et développement du chant liturgique jusqu'à la fin du moyen âge* (Tournai: Desclée, 1904). The book was translated from a German original of 1895; Wagner published a 3rd ed. in 1911.
> R. J. Hesbert, *Antiphonale missarum sextuplex* (Brussels: Vromant, 1935), xxxv–lxxix.
> A. Manser, "Sequenz," *Lexikon für Theologie und Kirche* 9 (1937) 482–85. (First ed. of the *Lexikon*.)
> R. Crocker, *The Early Medieval Sequence* (Berkeley: University of California Press, 1977).
> E. Costa, "Tropes et séquences dans le cadre de la vie liturgique au moyen âge," *EL* 92 (1978) 261–332, 440–71.

1. *The Gradual*

The gradual retained nothing of its responsorial form, except that, of the two verses making it up, only the second was designated as such.

2. *The Alleluia and Tract*

The alleluia was often accompanied by a text that was not from the psalms or even from the Bible. In Lent it was replaced by the tract (*tractus*), the origin of which is still disputed; the tract consisted of a section of a psalm without any refrain.

3. *The Sequence*

On feast days there was added to the alleluia a poetic composition in free rhythm, but often rhymed, that was called a sequence or "prose."[11] This custom had become increasingly frequent in the twelfth century. The simple melodies for these compositions enabled the people to sing them, and they became very popular. Unfortunately, they also turned attention from the proper function of this part of the celebration. The Missal of Pius V eliminated a large number of these superfluous poems and kept only four sequences[12]: the *Victimae paschali* ("To the Paschal victim"),[13] the *Veni Sancte Spiritus* ("Come, Holy Spirit"),[14] the *Lauda Sion* ("Laud, O Zion"),[15] and the *Dies irae* ("Day of wrath!").[16]

At the end of the Middle Ages it was at this point that the preparation of the gifts took place in many areas. These were brought ceremoniously to the bench on the south side of the sanctuary, where the priest was seated.

III. THE SERMON

The advent of the mendicant orders brought a revival of preaching in the Middle Ages, but the preaching tended to be unconnected with the liturgy. The place for the sermon was no longer the sanctuary but the pulpit, which was located in the nave. Most of the time the discourse was not a homily but an explanation of dogma or moral principle; too often it sacrificed substance to rhetoric and could just as easily be delivered apart from the celebration of Mass.[17]

---

11. The sequence perhaps originated in the tropes with which the alleluia was adorned.

12. The *Stabat Mater*, which is rare in medieval missals, entered the Roman Missal in the eighteenth century, when Benedict XIII extended the feast of Our Lady of the Seven Sorrows to the universal Church. These five sequences were kept in the Missal of Paul VI, but were placed before the alleluia.

13. For Easter Sunday. The sequence is made up of two different parts: the first is marked only by assonance, the second has an Eastern flavor. See E. Arens, "Wipos Oster-Sequenz," *Theologie und Glaube* 18 (1926) 149–54.

14. On this sequence see A. Wilmart, *Auteurs spirituels et textes dévots du moyen âge latin* 37–45.

15. For the feast of Corpus Christi. The poem seems to have been composed by St. Thomas Aquinas in 1263, but the attribution has often been challenged.

16. For Masses of the dead. See M. Inguanez, "Il *dies irae* in un codice del secolo XII," *Rivista liturgica* 18 (1931) 277–88.

17. On the creed see p. 131.

IV. THE PRAYERS OF THE PRONE

BIBLIOGRAPHY

J. B. Molin, "L'*oratio fidelium*, ses survivances," *EL* 73 (1959) 310–17.

_____, "Enquêtes historiques," in J. B. Molin and T. Maertens, *Pour un renouveau des prières du prône*, (Bruges: Apostolat liturgique, 1961), 11–44.

_____, "Les prières du prône en Italie," *EL* 76 (1962) 39–42.

_____, "L'*oratio communis fidelium* au moyen âge en Occident du Xe au XVe siècle," in *Miscellanea liturgica . . . Lercaro* 2 (Rome: Desclée, 1967), 313–468.

G. Landotti, "Nuove testimonianze sulla 'Preghiera dei fedeli' nel medioevo," *EL* 99 (1985), 206–8.

It was a Mass without any General Intercessions that reached Gaul in the Carolingian period when the Roman liturgy was adopted there. It seems that at least in some regions people did not forget a practice that had subsisted until then in local usages. Thus at the end of the tenth century we find the people being exhorted after the sermon on Sundays and feast days to pray for various intentions by saying an Our Father in a low voice, while the priest added a prayer appropriate to each intention.[18] This custom became widespread in the Middle Ages; it is attested in many dioceses of France, England, Germany, and even Italy. At the end of this period these intentions and prayers became part of what is known as the "prone," where it is preceded by announcements and followed by an instruction. The pastoral renewal initiated by the Council of Trent gave this practice a very wide extension, perhaps under the influence of St. Peter Canisius, who drew up a formulary of intentions in the mid-sixteenth century.[19]

In order not to have to return to this topic in the next chapter I shall cite here by way of example the text found in the ritual of a reforming bishop of southern France.

> Knowing that God is pleased by prayer from a contrite and humble heart, we will offer him our very humble prayers, that he would teach us to do his holy will. Then, not only today and in the coming week but throughout our lives, we will be able to render him pleasing service and, being solidly founded in authentic faith, we will be able to have a holy hope of salvation by observing his commandments with the help of his grace.
>
> We will pray also for the peace and unity of the Church, for a deepening of Catholic, apostolic, and Roman faith, for the extirpation of heresies, and for the conversion of unbelievers, heretics, schismatics, and all those who are separated from us, that God may be acknowledged, served, and worshiped in every place.

---

18. See Regino of Prüm († 915), *De synodalibus causis* 190 (PL 132:224).

19. See P. F. Saft, "Das 'Allgemeine Gebet' des heiligen Petrus Kanisius im Wandel der Zeiten," *Zeitschrift für Aszese und Mystik* 13 (1938) 215–23.

We will pray for all of the Church's prelates and pastors and especially for our holy father the Pope and our most revered father in Christ, bishop N., our prelate, and for all pastors in charge of souls, that God will give them the grace of so exercising their ministry as to lead themselves and the people entrusted to them in the way of salvation to eternal life.

We will pray also for the peace and tranquillity of this realm, for unity among Christian princes, and especially for our Most Christian King and the entire royal family. We will also pray for the Lord (or: Lady) of this place that by his (her) authority, admonitions, and good example, he (she) will lead us all to the careful observance of the commandments of God and the Church, and may preserve us in salutary peace.

We will pray for all the benefactors of this church, especially those who provide the blessed bread today, and for those who have made offerings and given of their goods to adorn and maintain the building. We will pray for them that God in his goodness and mercy may reward them in this world and the next.

We will pray for all widows and orphans, for those who are ill, and for the captive and the oppressed, that God will console them and deliver them from their afflictions or give them patience in their sufferings.

We will pray for pregnant women that God will keep them safe and bring their children to the holy font of baptism.

We will pray for all those in the state of grace that God may keep them in it, and for those in mortal sin that being enlightened and converted by his grace they will acknowledge their sins and truly repent of them.

We will pray also for all our relatives and for friends absent or traveling, that God will keep them safe from every danger and give them a joyous and healthy homecoming.

We will pray, too, for all the people of this diocese and especially of this parish, that God will join them in mutual concord so that they will bear with one another and show charity in mutual aid.

Finally, we will pray that God will give us good weather, suited to keep us in bodily health and preserve the fruits of the soil, so that when these have been harvested in due season we may use them to his honor and help the poor in their needs.

For all these intentions and, more generally, for all the intentions for which the Church is accustomed to pray, you will join in prayer and say the following: [Ps 123, verses and three prayers].

Since sacred scripture attests and the Church has always believed that it is a holy and salutary thought to pray for the deceased faithful, we will add solemn prayers for them and especially for the souls of the founders and benefactors of this church, for our deceased fathers, mothers, brothers, sisters, relatives, friends, and benefactors, whose bodies rest in the church or cemetery of this parish, and, more generally, for all the souls in purgatory, that God in his goodness and mercy will deliver them from their sufferings and bring them into the kingdom of paradise. To this end you will join your prayers to ours and we will say together [Ps 130, verses and three prayers and, after announcements if any, the Our Father, Hail Mary, Creed, and commandments of God and the Church].[20]

The intentions are evidently close in kind to those of the ancient General Intercessions, although they bear the mark of the "Christendom" in which they are offered, being now intercessions for Christians alone.

§3. The Eucharistic Liturgy

I. THE OFFERTORY

BIBLIOGRAPHY

Martène, Liber I, c. 4, a. 6–7; M 487–509.

Jungmann, *The Mass of the Roman Rite*, 2:1–464.

P. Salmon, "Les prières et les rites de l'offertoire de la messe dans la liturgie romaine au XIIIe et au XIVe siècles," *EL* 43 (1929) 508–19.

B. Capelle, "Pour une meilleure intelligence de la messe. L'offertoire," *QL* 17 (1932) 58–67.

P. Borella, *Il rito ambrosiano* (Milan: Morcelliana, 1964), 165–71.

A. Hadlein, *Aquae et vini mysterium. Geheimnis der Erlösung und Geheimnis der Kirche im Spiegel der mittelalterlichen Auslegung des gemischten Kelches* (LQF 57; Münster: Aschendorff, 1975).

P. Tirot, "Histoire des Prières d'Offertoire dans la liturgie romaine du VIIIe au XVIe siècle, *EL* 98 (1984) 148–97, 323–91.

The offertory was a privileged place for private prayers of the priest (we saw how these multiplied in the Middle Ages); it was also, therefore, the point in the Mass at which the greatest local differences showed themselves and indeed continued to exist in the rites that the reform of Pius V left untouched. The best way of illustrating the divergences is to show some of the arrangements in parallel columns.[21]

We find, to begin with, that the same formulas, with variants, occur in several columns, though perhaps at different points. This is true of the prayers *In spiritu humilitatis* (R[oman Missal], L[yons], C[arthusians]), D[ominicans]), the *Suscipe, sancta Trinitas* (R, L, D), the *De latere* (L, C), not to mention the *Orate, fratres*, which is found everywhere, and the *Lavabo* (Ps 26), the verses of which are used in varying numbers (R, 6–12; D, 6–8; L, 6–7).

---

20. *Rituel à l'usage du diocèse d'Alet* [published by Bishop Nicolas Pavillon] (1667), 252–66.

21. See the table of parallels below in the text. The table does not include the Ambrosian rite, since this cannot be numbered among the Roman rites; it would be of interest, however, to extend the comparison so as to include it.

Roman Missal of Pius V	**Lyons Missal**

The priest uncovers the chalice

The priest uncovers the chalice: What return shall I make to the Lord for all his blessings?

He raises the paten with the bread: Receive, O holy Father, almighty and eternal God, this spotless host which I, your unworthy servant, offer to you, my living and true God, for my own countless sins, offenses, and negligences; and for all present here, as well as for all faithful Christians both living and dead, that it may profit me and them as a means of reaching salvation in the eternal life. Amen.

He extends his hands over the bread: Jesus said to his disciples: I am the living bread that has come down from heaven. Whoever eats this bread will live forever.

He puts wine, then water, in the chalice: O God, you wondrously ennobled human nature in creating it and even more wondrously restored it. Grant that through the mystery of this water and wine we may be made partakers of his divinity, who condescended to share our humanity, Jesus Christ, your Son, our Lord, Who lives and reigns with you in the unity of the Holy Spirit, God, forever and ever. Amen.

He puts wine and water in the chalice: At the moment of his death blood and water flowed from the side of our Lord Jesus Christ, signifying the mystery of the Blessed Trinity. John the evangelist saw it and bore witness to it, and we know that his testimony is true.

He raises the chalice: We offer to you, O Lord, the chalice of salvation, humbly begging your mercy that it may arise before your divine majesty as a pleasing fragrance for our salvation and for that of the whole world. Amen.

He raises the bread and chalice: Almighty God, receive this offering with kindness, we pray you, and forgive the sins of those who offer it to you and of those for whom it is offered.

He bows: In humility, with contrite heart, may we be acceptable to you, O Lord, and may our sacrifice be so offered in your sight this day as to be pleasing to you, O Lord God.

He adds: In humility, with contrite heart, may we be acceptable to you, O Lord, and may our sacrifice be so offered in your sight this day as to be pleasing to you, O Lord God.

Come O Sanctifier, almighty and eternal God, and bless this sacrifice prepared for the glory of your holy name.

Carthusian Missal	**Dominican Missal**
The priest uncovers the chalice	*The priest uncovers the chalice*
The bread and wine were prepared during the Creed	*The bread and wine were prepared after the epistle (before Mass in private Masses)*
While putting water in the chalice: From the side of our Lord Jesus Christ blood and water flowed for the forgiveness of sins.	*While putting water in the chalice:* In the name of the Father (+) and of the Son and of the Holy Spirit. Amen.
He raises the bread and chalice: In humility, with contrite heart, may we be acceptable to you, O Lord, and may our sacrifice be so offered in your sight this day as to be pleasing to you, O Lord God.	*He raises the bread and chalice:* What return shall I make to the Lord for all his blessings? I will take the chalice of salvation and call upon the name of the Lord.
He makes a sign of the cross with the bread and chalice: In the name of the Father and of the Son and of the Holy Spirit.	Receive, O holy Trinity, this offering which I make in remembrance of the passion of our Lord Jesus Christ; may it arise before you and be pleasing to you, and may it win my salvation and that of all the faithful. Amen.

Roman Missal of Pius V	**Lyons Missal**
He washes his hands: I wash my hands in innocence, and I go round your altar, O Lord, giving voice to my thanks, and recounting all your wondrous deeds. O Lord, I love the house in which you dwell, the tenting-place of your glory. Gather not my soul with those of sinners nor with men of blood my life. On their hands are crimes, and their right hands are full of bribes. But I walk in integrity; redeem me, and have pity on me. My foot stands on level ground; in the assemblies I will bless the Lord. Glory . . .	*He washes his hands:* I wash my hands in innocence, and I go round your altar, O Lord, giving voice to my thanks, and recounting all your wondrous deeds.

He adds: Come, Holy Spirit, fill the hearts of your faithful and enkindle in them the fire of your love. |
He bows: Receive, O holy Trinity, this offering which we make in remembrance of the passion, resurrection, and ascension of Jesus Christ, our Lord; and in honor of blessed Mary, ever Virgin, blessed John the Baptist, the holy apostles Peter and Paul, of these [the saints whose relics are on this altar] and of all the saints; that it may add to their honor and aid our salvation; and may they be pleased to intercede in heaven for us who honor their memory here on earth. Through Christ our Lord. Amen.	*He bows:* Receive . . . in remembrance of the incarnation, passion . . . our Lord, as well as of the consolation which the Holy Spirit gives us; and in honor of . . . Virgin, of all the saints who have been pleasing to you since the beginning of the world, of those whose feast we celebrate today, of those whose names and relics are here; that it may . . . here on earth. Through Christ our Lord. Amen.
He addresses the other ministers: Brethren, pray that my sacrifice and yours may be acceptable to God the Father almighty.	*He addresses the other ministers:* Brethren, pray for me that my sacrifice and yours may be acceptable before the face of God.
They answer: May the Lord receive the sacrifice from your hands to the praise and glory of his name, for our welfare and that of all his holy Church.	*They answer:* May the almighty Lord receive the sacrifice from your mouth and hands, for the welfare of his holy Church, the salvation of all Christian people, and the healing of all the faithful departed.
Prayer over the gifts (Secret)	*Prayer over the gifts (Secret)*

Carthusian Missal

Dominican Missal

(He has already washed his hands after the gospel.)

He washes his hands: I wash my hands in innocence, and I go round your altar, O Lord, giving voice to my thanks, and recounting all your wondrous deeds. O Lord, I love the house in which you dwell, the tenting-place of your glory.

He adds: See the lowliness of our souls and the repentance of our hearts; welcome us, O Lord, receive our sacrifice today and let it be pleasing to you.

He addresses the other ministers: Brethren, pray for me, a sinner, before the Lord our God.

He addresses the other ministers: Brethren, pray that my sacrifice and yours may be acceptable to God the Father almighty.

Prayer over the gifts (Secret)

Prayer over the gifts (Secret)

In these diversely organized liturgies we can distinguish between:

1. *Prayers that accompany actions*

I do not cite above the prayers said during the incensation that is found in all the liturgies, and I set aside the elevation of the paten and the chalice, since these are doubtless gestures suggested by the formulas themselves. Prayers accompanying the actions begin at Lyons from the moment when the priest uncovers the chalice.

We must attend especially, however, to the ritual of the pouring of water into the chalice, since the prayers inflect its meaning in three different directions. It can be a simple blessing (D), done with a sign of the cross, which is found in fact in all the liturgies; this sign of the cross originated in the rubric in *OR* I: "He pours water into the chalice in the form of a cross," a gesture probably intended to secure a better mingling of the water with the wine. Another liturgy has recourse to the Christmas collect of the ancient Roman tradition, adapted here to its new context (R) and meant to bring out the "marvelous exchange" of which Augustine spoke long ago in connection with the bringing of gifts by the faithful.[22] Finally, use may be made of the symbolism (already given a Eucharistic application by the Fathers) of the water that came, mixed with blood, from Christ's side on the cross (L, C). Mention must also be made of the *Lavabo*, which the verses from Psalm 26 interpret as a sign of purification; here we are already in the realm of the *apologiae.*[23]

2. Apologia *formulas*

Protestations of unworthiness and repentance are not lacking: "I, your unworthy servant . . . for my own countless sins, offenses, and negligences" (R), "in humility, with contrite heart" (R, L, D), "forgive the sins . . . of all who make offering" (L). The *Orate, fratres* belongs to the same category: it is first and foremost a petition for the celebrant himself, as the Lyons Missal ("Pray for me, brethren") and the Carthusian ("For me a sinner") show, and its intent is to render acceptable to God the ministry of a sinner. The formula is addressed to the other ministers, whose

---

22. See p. 78.

23. These formulas are written in the first person singular; the celebrant speaks in his own name. There are, however, two exceptions in the Roman Missal: the *Offerimus tibi* ("We offer to you"), which celebrant and deacon say together at the offering of the chalice, and the *Suscipe sancta Trinitas* ("Receive, O holy Trinity"), where the plural perhaps occurs for the same reason, since the formula makes an offering of both bread and cup. The singular is attested for the *Suscipe sancta Trinitas* in the ninth-century Sacramentary of Saint-Thierry and the eleventh-century Sacramentary of Saint-Denis.

response, which exists only in the Roman and Lyons rites, picks up the same theme: "from your hands" (R), "from your mouth and hands" (L).

3. *Anticipations of the Eucharistic Prayer*

The most striking thing about these prayers is the way they anticipate the Eucharistic Prayer that is to follow. Thus, even though it is simply bread and wine that lie on the altar at this point, the prayers speak of "this spotless host (victim)" and "the chalice of salvation" (R); the bread and wine are already looked upon as what they will in fact become only through the consecration.[24]

We should not be surprised, therefore, to find prayers that duplicate the anaphoral prayers and, especially, that give expression to the act of offering. "Receive . . . this spotless host" (R), "We offer to you . . . the chalice of salvation" (R), "Receive . . . this offering which I (we) make" (L, R). The "our sacrifice" to which reference is made is the sacrifice of the Body and Blood of Christ, and not some other sacrifice that would precede it as a preparation or a condition. The presentation of the gifts, the "offering" of them ("offering" in our everyday sense of a gift or present), has attracted to itself the thought of the real sacrificial oblation that the presentation does not effect, even though it is a preparation for that oblation and a first step toward it. The ministers, for their part, ask the Lord that they may be pleasing to him as ministers, so that the mystery, of which they are only servants, may be celebrated: "May we be acceptable to you, O Lord, and may our sacrifice be so offered in your sight" (R, L, C, D).

It is in the same spirit that we should understand the anamnetic elements found in the prayers of the offertory: "in remembrance of the passion" (D), "in remembrance of the passion, resurrection, and ascension" (R); "in remembrance of the incarnation, nativity, passion, resurrection, and ascension" (L). Similarly for the anticipations of an epiclesis: "Come, O Sanctifier" and "bless this sacrifice" (R), "Come, Holy Spirit" (L). And even for the intercessions: "for all present here, as well as for all faithful Christians both living and dead" (R), "for our salvation and for that of the whole world" (R), "of those who offer it to you and of those for whom it is offered" (L), "for our welfare and that of all his holy Church" (R), "for . . . the salvation of all Christian people, and the healing of all the faithful departed" (L), "may it win my salvation and that of all the faithful" (D), or, again: "in honor of blessed Mary, ever Virgin, blessed John the Baptist, the holy apostles Peter and Paul" (R), "and of all the saints who have been pleasing to you since the beginning of the world, of those

---

24. This was a new manifestation of an already ancient tendency; see p. 79.

whose feast we celebrate today, of those whose names and relics are here" (L), "that it may add to their honor" (R).

4. *The incensation*

The incensation at the offertory is the oldest and most important one in the Roman Mass. It did not originate in Rome, however, where they were content simply to carry incense in an incense box. The incensation was limited at first to the altar, but it appeared in a more developed form as early as the Pontifical of Sées in the eleventh century. At this same period John of Avranches had a good deal to say about it in his commentary *De ecclesiasticis officiis*. The ritual was further encumbered by private prayers of the celebrant[25] and was made lengthier than it need have been by the fact that all the important members of the clergy were incensed individually.[26]

II. THE CANON

BIBLIOGRAPHY

Martène, Liber I, c. 4, a. 8; M 510–14.
Jungmann, *The Mass of the Roman Rite* 2: 101–274.

The text of the Roman Canon was now fixed and immutable; the only alteration the Church allowed itself to make was to add saints' names to the *Communicantes* and *Nobis quoque*. The old Frankish manuscripts mention Hilary and Martin, who were venerated throughout Gaul, as well as the Doctors of the Church, whose cult flourished during this period: Augustine, Jerome, Gregory; or, again, the patron saints of local communities.

I have already spoken at length of what was most noteworthy about the Canon[27]: the Eucharistic Prayer was enveloped in silence, or more or less drowned out by singing; and the elevation of the sacred species played an important role in popular devotion, a role underscored by the ringing of the bells at this point. In solemn Masses there were processions of cler-

---

25. These private prayers were preceded by a blessing of the incense "through the intercession of Michael the archangel"; the texts of the tenth and eleventh centuries always have "Gabriel" for "Michael," the allusion being to the appearance of Gabriel to Zechariah.

26. The gifts are also incensed in the Eastern rites. Among the Byzantines they are incensed three times: at the prothesis, at the Great Entrance, and as they lie on the altar. The Syrians, who have numerous "incense prayers" (*etro*) in the course of all liturgical actions, have an especially extensive incensation of the gifts during the Creed.

27. See pp. 133 and 137.

ics carrying torches and making their way around the altar[28]; the swinging of thuribles, and so on. For the rest, only the priest's attitudes at prayer and his gestures could be seen by the faithful (assuming that the choir screen did not hide even these from their sight): signs of the cross, bows, arms crossed after the consecration, and so on. It is noteworthy, however, that the final doxology always ended in a loud voice. This was in order that the "Amen" might ring out, even though it no longer gave expression to the unanimity felt in earlier times.

III. THE COMMUNION

BIBLIOGRAPHY

Martène, Liber I, c. 4, a. 9–10; M 515–40.
P. Browe, *Die häufige Kommunion im Mittelalter* (Regensburg: Pustet, 1938).
──────, "Mittelalterliche Kommunionriten," *JLW* 15 (1935 = 1941) 44–48.
J. Jungmann, *The Mass of the Roman Rite* 2:275–426.

1. *The Our Father, Kiss of Peace, and Fraction*

As I noted earlier, these various rites encroached on one another to some extent. In the Middle Ages they underwent amplifications that varied according to place: repeated genuflections, repeated elevations, kisses bestowed on host or chalice, and so on. It will be enough here to call attention to essential points.

a) In the eleventh century it was decided to say the embolism of the Our Father in a low voice. The singing of it survived only at Milan and Lyons and, in the Roman rite, in the Good Friday service.

b) The gesture of peace was no longer the greeting given one another by all the members of the congregation after the deacon had proclaimed it. It was initially restricted to communicants; then it was further restricted to the clergy, where it took the form of a message, so to speak, that passed down the line to one after another among them. The priest kissed the altar, or sometimes the consecrated bread, before "giving the *pax*" to the deacon. The latter then "brought" it to the clergy who passed it from one to another among them, while using appropriate formulas. The sign lost its expressive character when, beginning in the thirteenth century, use was made, in some cases, of an "instrument of peace," that is, a finely worked metal plate that each of the clergy kissed in succession.[29]

---

28. The *"Sanctus* candle" was made obligatory by the general rubrics in the Missal of Pius V, but the practice nonetheless fell into disuse.

29. In the East, where it has kept its place at the beginning of the Eucharistic liturgy, the gesture of peace is still practiced by all the faithful, except among the Byzantines, who limit it to celebrant and deacon. The form of the gesture has changed, however, probably

c) The fraction kept its meaning until the thirteenth century; the laity communicated rarely, but when they did, they usually received a piece of a host that the priest had broken. This custom disappeared, however, once the practice arose of using small hosts cut in advance, with the priest himself always eating the two parts of the bread he had broken.

2. *The Priest's Communion*

Like the offertory, preparation for communion was a time that lent itself in a special way to silent prayers of the celebrant; we find the same diversity in both parts of the Mass. The Missal of Pius V subsequently provided three prayers that are addressed to Christ and are couched in the first person singular. The first of the three precedes the kiss of peace, which is separated by the *Agnus Dei* from the wish that introduces it (the kiss);[30] this first prayer, "Lord Jesus Christ, who said . . ." (*"Domine, Iesu Christe, qui dixisti . . ."*) made its appearance in Germany at the beginning of the eleventh century.[31] The second, which was also the most widespread one in the Middle Ages,[32] was found as early as the ninth century in the Sacramentary of Amiens; this is the prayer "Lord Jesus Christ, Son of the living God. . . ." (*"Domine Iesu Christe, Fili Dei vivi . . ."*). The third prayer, "Let not the partaking of thy body . . ." (*"Perceptio corporis tui . . ."*), goes back to the tenth century.

These prayers have the same origin as the *apologiae* and originally belonged to collections of prayers for the use of the faithful.[33] The same resources for private devotion supplied the formula addressed to the Father that has been preserved in the rites of Milan and Lyons[34]; it is to be found

---

due to cultural developments: among the Copts, for example, each person bows to the neighbor and touches the neighbor's hand, while among the Maronites, each joins his hands together and, before raising them to his lips, slips them between the joined hands of the neighbor.

30. The link thus established between the *Agnus Dei* and the kiss of peace caused the final *Miserere nobis* to be replaced by *Dona nobis pacem*. The Carthusian tradition has but a single *Agnus Dei*.

31. This is the prayer that introduces the rite of peace in the new Sacramentary: "Lord Jesus Christ, you said to your apostles. . . ." The other two are given (one or other to be said) as private prayers of the celebrant before communion.

32. This is the only prayer kept by the Carthusians and Dominicans; it is unknown in the rites of Milan and Lyons.

33. See A. Wilmart, "Prières pour la communion en deux psautiers du Mont-Cassin," *EL* 43 (1929) 320–28, and "Le manuel de prières de saint Jean Gualbert," *RBén* 48 (1936) 295 and n. 2. See *Libellus precum* of the Abbey of Fleury (PL 101:1408).

34. *Liber precationum* of Charles the Bald, ed. F. Ninguarda (Ingolstadt, 1583), 115: "Lord, holy Father, almighty everlasting God, grant me so to receive the body and blood of Christ, your Son and our Lord, that I may thereby win the forgiveness of my sins and be filled with your Holy Spirit. For you are God, and the godhead is in you, and beside you there is no other, and your reign is everlasting." This prayer is preceded by the first of the three mentioned in the text.

in the prayer book of Charles the Bald. Other, less widely used texts also had a place in the various Ordinaries of the Mass. The accents are always the same: "Do not look upon my sins. . . . Rescue me. . . . If I make bold to receive your body despite my unworthiness, let this not bring judgment or condemnation upon me."

The priest's communion was accompanied by other words often taken from the psalms or the gospels,[35] over and above those that are parallel to the formulas used for the faithful: "May the Body . . .," "May the Blood . . . ."[36] Once the sacred species had been consumed, there were other prayers said during the purification of the vessels: "May we possess with a pure heart what we have taken as food. . . ." (*"Quod ore sumpsimus . . ."*) and "May your body, O Lord, which I have eaten . . ." (*"Corpus tuum quod sumpsi . . ."*),[37] both of which entered the Roman Missal, and others like them.

3. *The Communion of the Faithful*

Communion of the faithful became increasingly rare, to the point where the Order of Mass no longer provided for reception by the congregation. When, therefore, the theologians and mystics of the twelfth century turned the tide and inspired the laity to approach this sacrament, it became necessary to introduce into the Mass a ritual that would meet the new need.[38] Liturgists then had recourse to the ritual used in communion of the sick[39]: the *Confiteor*, followed by the *Misereatur* and absolution, to which were added the *Ecce Agnus Dei* (John 1:29), which the priest said while showing the host to the communicants, and the threefold *Domine, non sum dignus*, which the communicants said in response and which is the prayer of the centurion in slightly revised form (Luke 7:6-7).

---

35. See the composite citation of Psalm 116:12-13 and Psalm 18:3 in the Missal of Pius V: "What return shall I make . . . . I will call upon the Lord in praise . . . ." This citation led to the formation of a formula symmetrical with it: "I will take the chalice of salvation and invoke the name of the Lord." — See also the "Lord, I am not worthy" (Matt 8:8); elsewhere we find Matt 18:26; Luke 15:18-19; Luke 18:13; John 6:55; etc.

36. Some rites have but a single formula for the bread and the cup together; *e.g.*, the Dominican rite: "May the body and blood of our Lord Jesus Christ preserve me for everlasting life."

37. The first of these two formulas is a Roman postcommunion prayer (*Le* 521); the second is from the Gallican tradition: see *Missale Gothicum*, Vigil of Christmas, ed. Bannister, 3.

38. Among the Premonstratensians at the end of the thirteenth century the communion of the brothers was still part of the Mass, as it had been in antiquity: P. Lefèvre, *L'Ordinaire de Prémontré d'après les manuscrits du XIIᵉ siècle* (Bibliothèque de la RHE 22; Louvain, 1941), 59. — The early Dominican liturgical books, on the other hand, already provide a special ceremonial for such communions.

39. Pius V, *Ritus servandus* X, 8: "If any are to receive communion during Mass . . . ."

The communion of the faithful could now be regarded as a kind of alien body that had worked its way into the Eucharistic celebration, and churchmen did not hesitate, for reasons of convenience, to communicate the faithful with hosts consecrated at an earlier Mass and reserved in the tabernacle. However, the rubric in the Missal of Pius V supposes that the hosts destined for those approaching the holy table have been consecrated during the Mass in which they are participating.[40]

§4. The Concluding Rites

I. *ITE MISSA EST* OR *BENEDICAMUS DOMINO*

After the postcommunion, which, like the collect and secret, might include several prayers, the *Ite missa est* would normally announce the end of the assembly. But this formula was in competition with another, the *Benedicamus Domino*, which seems to have originated in Gaul and which served initially to conclude services other than Mass. From the eleventh century on, the *Ite missa est* was used in Masses in which the *Gloria* was said, while *Benedicamus Domino* was used in other Masses. Was the point that on days when the *Gloria* was sung, a mark of festivity, the congregation was so large that it needed an explicit exhortation to withdraw, while this was not the case on other days? Possibly—although all Sundays, even those on which the *Gloria* was not said or sung, would have had a large congregation. In any case, the *Ite missa est* must have struck a note of solemnity that was judged incompatible with prayer for the deceased, since the formula was replaced by a trite *Requiescant in pace* in Masses for the dead.

II. PROLONGATIONS OF THE CELEBRATION

The dismissal of the assembly was normally the final act of the celebration, and it continued to be so until the Middle Ages, when appendixes came to be added.

1. *The final homage to the altar*

The text of the Ordinary of Mass used by the Friars Preachers ended with the *Ite missa est*, even though the *Modus et ritus dicendi missam* (Manner and ritual for saying Mass) that was inserted at the beginning of the missal prescribed an ending like that found in the Roman Missal.

---

40. *Ibid.*: "The priest . . . is to place the particles in a ciborium or, if only a few are to receive, on a paten, unless they have been in a ciborium or other vessel from the beginning."

The formula with which the people were dismissed was preceded only by a private prayer, the *"Placeat tibi, sancta Trinitas"* ("May the homage of my service be pleasing to you, O holy Trinity"). This prayer, the style of which suggests a Gallican origin, came only gradually into general use, but it is found as early as the ninth century in the Sacramentary of Amiens, with the rubric: "He is to kiss the altar, saying . . . ." At the end of the Mass, as at the beginning, the altar was greeted with a kiss (the later repeated kissings of the altar during the celebration had not yet been introduced). The practice calls to mind the words that the Syrian liturgy bids its priests say at this moment: "Abide in peace, holy altar of God. I do not know whether I will be allowed to approach you again. May the Lord deign to let me see you in the heavenly Church."[41]

In the Missal of Pius V the prayer *"Placeat"* and the kissing of the altar follow upon the *Ite missa est* and precede the blessing; this order presupposes a rearrangement of the entire complex.

2. *The blessing*

The blessing at the end of the celebration was a late addition and still has no place in the Carthusian rite. This is not surprising if we remember that the Mass of *Ordo* I had no blessing save those given by the pope as he made his way to the sacristy and that the Gallican tradition placed the blessing before communion.[42] The solemn formula of blessing used by bishops made its appearance in the Roman Pontifical only in the fourteenth century.[43] The priest's blessing is found in various forms as early as the thirteenth century, but it is not possible to determine whether it was an integral part of the Order of Mass or was rather regarded as a devotional act after the Mass had concluded. In any case, the Tridentine Missal gave it the status it still has today.

3. *The last gospel*

The beginning of the Gospel According to John had been suggested to the celebrant as a private prayer after Mass; the custom then spread of having the priest recite it as he was leaving the altar, as indeed bishops continued to do in pontifical Masses down to the recent reform. Only in the thirteenth century did celebrants begin to make the Prologue a part of the Mass itself; thus, even though the Missal of Pius V kept the practice, it was still unknown in many diocesan Ordinaries of the eighteenth century, while the Carthusians never adopted it. The Prologue must be acknowledged as an incomparable formula for use in the period of recollec-

---

41. See V. Janeras, "Notes sur la prière syrienne d'adieux à l'autel," *OS* 5 (1960) 476–78.
42. See p. 116.
43. *OR* Mab 14, no. 53 (PL 78:1169).

tion after communion; it was, however, simply a devotional formula, and the faithful should not have been allowed to think of it as a kind of beginning of a new Liturgy of the Word.

As a help to continuing the celebrant's thanksgiving after Mass, the liturgical books offered a "Thanksgiving after Mass" that went back probably to the tenth century and was similar in character to the "Preparation for Mass," including as it did psalms, verses, and prayers. Later formulas, attributed to St. Thomas Aquinas and St. Bonaventure, were added to it.

§5. Conclusion

The Missal of Pius V gave the Order of Mass a new form that would put its stamp on the Roman rite for centuries to come and would be carried by the Church's missionary expansion to all the continents. The newness, however, was quite relative. As we saw, the contributions of the medieval period enriched the various parts of the celebration; these were retained, once their most questionable elements were eliminated. But amid the proliferation of the usages current, it was the tradition of the Roman Curia that was rendered sacrosanct by the Tridentine Missal. For this Missal was in fact largely dependent on the "Order of Mass according to the usage of the Roman Curia,"[44] as reproduced in the Roman Missal that was printed for the first time at Milan in 1474 and went through numerous editions in the following decades.[45]

The success of this work was doubtless due in large part to the fact that the Friars Minor had adopted the usage of the Curia and had broadcast it on their journeys[46]; the Franciscan Missal was based in all likeli-

---

44. Re-edited by R. Lippe, *Missale Romanum* . . . 1 (HBS 17; London: Henry Bradshaw Society, 1899). It goes back to the Missal made obligatory for Rome by Pope Nicholas III (1277). See M. Andrieu, "Le missel de la chapelle papale à la fin du XIIIᵉ siècle," in *Miscellanea Ehrle* 2 (ST 38; Vatican City, 1924); *idem*, "L'authenticité du missel de la chapelle papale," *Scriptorium* 9 (1955) 17–34. — S. Van Dijk, "The Legend of the Missal of the Papal Chapel," *SE* 8 (1956) 76–142; *idem*, "The Authentic Missal of the Papal Chapel," *Scriptorium* 14 (1960) 257–314.

45. R. Lippe, *Missale Romanum* . . . 2 (HBS 33; London, 1907), gives the variants from a good many manuscripts, but says nothing of the six incunabula in the Bibliothèque Nationale, which range from 1477 to 1495; see also A. Frutaz, "Due edizioni rare del Missale Romanum pubblicate a Milano nel 1482 e nel 1492," in *Miscellanea Mons. Giulio Belvederi* (Rome, 1954), 55–107.

46. V. L. Kennedy, "The Franciscan *Ordo missae* in the Thirteenth Century," *Mediaeval Studies* 2 (1940) 204–22; — S. Van Dijk and J. H. Walker, *The Origin of the Modern Roman Liturgy* (Westminster, Md.: Newman, 1960); — S. Van Dijk, *Sources of the Modern Roman Liturgy* (2 vols.; Leiden: Brill, 1963); — S. Van Dijk, *The Ordinal of the Papal Court from Innocent III to Bonifacius VIII and Related Documents* (Spicilegium Friburgense 22;

hood on a pontifical Ordinary of the first half of the thirteenth century.[47] Going further back, we may mention the commentary on the Mass written at the end of the previous century by the future Pope Innocent III.[48] In it he distinguishes between ceremonies proper to bishops and those suitable for priests, asserts the legitimacy of concelebration, is familiar only with communion under both species, and mentions no private prayer except the psalm *Judica me* and the *Confiteor*, at the beginning of the celebration (two prayers already part of Italian usage).[49]

During this period the rules governing the Mass of bishops acquired a set form, culminating in the *Caeremoniale episcoporum* of 1600. One of the principal prerogatives of the pastor of the diocese was to preside over the Liturgy of the Word from his chair (*cathedra*), whereas priests celebrated it at the altar. Also to be noted is the presence around the bishops of the various dignitaries of his Church, each robed in accordance with his rank.

The Order of Mass of Pius V was not, however, simply the end product of developments that had occurred in the Middle ages, nor did it represent a simple updating of usages in accordance with the desires for reform that did in fact manifest themselves in the sixteenth century. It was also the result of a Council that had been convoked in order to meet the most serious crisis the Western Church had yet known: the challenge of the Reformers to essential points in traditional Eucharistic doctrine. It was extremely important for the Church to pass unscathed through this time of intense attack, when quite legitimate calls for reform were confronted by a real hatred of the Mass formulas that had taken possession of many minds. We must turn, therefore, to the decrees of the Council of Trent if we are to understand the impact of this Council on the celebration of the sacred mysteries during the four centuries that have since passed.

Fribourg: Editions universitaires, 1975); — M. Dykmans, *Le cérémonial papal de la fin du moyen âge à la Renaissance* (3 vols.; Bibliothèque de l'Institut historique belge de Rome 24–26; Rome, 1977–83).

47. M. Andrieu, "L'ordinaire de la chapelle papale et le cardinal Jacques Gaetani Stefaneschi," *EL* 49 (1935) 230–60.

48. *De sacro altaris mysterio libri sex* (PL 217:774–914).

49. A Lateran *Ordo* of the mid-twelfth century allows no room for private prayers of the celebrant: L. Fischer, *Bernhardi cardinalis et Lateranensis ecclesiae prioris ordo officiorum ecclesiae Lateranensis* (Historische Forschungen und Quellen 2–3; Munich: Datterer, 1916). See A. Ebner, *Quellen und Forschungen zur Geschichte und Kunstgeschichte des Missale Romanum im Mittelalter. Iter italicum* (Freiburg: Herder, 1898; repr., 1950), 307.

Chapter III

The Celebration of the Eucharist in the West from the Council of Trent to Vatican Council II

BIBLIOGRAPHY

P. Le Brun, *Explication littérale, historique et dogmatique des prières et des céré-monies de la messe* (4 vols.; Paris, 1716–26; many reprintings, especially of volume I).

[J. B. Lebrun-Desmarettes], *Voyages liturgiques en France ou recherches faites en diverses villes du royaume, contenant plusieurs particularités touchant les rits & les usages des Eglises . . .par le Sieur de Moléon* (Paris, 1718; another printing, 1757).

J. De Viguerie, "La dévotion populaire à la messe dans la France des XVIIe et XVIIIe siècles," in *Histoire de la messe XVIIe-XIXe siècles* (Actes de la IIIe Rencontre d'histoire religieuse, Fontevraud, 1979; Paris: Librairie D.U.C., 1980), 7–25.

G. Oury, "Les explications de la messe en France du XVIe au XVIIIe siècle," *ibid.*, 81–93.

§1. The Council of Trent and the Missal of St. Pius V

BIBLIOGRAPHY

H. Jedin, "Das Konzil von Trient und die Reform der liturgischen Bücher," *EL* 59 (1945) 5–38.

At the beginning of the sixteenth century many pastors felt that renewal in the Eucharistic practices of the faithful was a pressing necessity. The Church had to react against popular customs that were often infected by superstition or, in any case, so focused on superficial and secondary aspects of the Eucharist as to make impossible any real participation in the Mass.

I. THE COUNCIL

This concern was in the minds of many bishops as they went to the council that Paul III had convoked at Trent in 1514. The preoccupation undoubtedly left its mark on the debates in which they engaged during the sessions that followed until 1563. At the same time, however, the historical context—the Protestant Reformation—in which this assembly met forced the bishops to fight on two fronts at once. They had to make a clear statement of Catholic doctrine in face of the excesses of those who had departed from it; at the same time, they had to oppose the abuses that they themselves had denounced. A striking example is the decision regarding the language of the liturgy and, even more perhaps, the terms in which the decision was expressed.

> Although the Mass contains much instruction for the faithful, the Fathers did not think that it should be celebrated in the vernacular indiscriminately. Therefore, the ancient rite of each Church, approved by the holy Roman Church, the mother and teacher of all the Churches, being everywhere maintained, the holy Council, in order that the sheep of Christ may not go unfed, lest "the children beg for food but no one gives it to them" (Lam 4:4), orders that pastors and all who have the care of souls must frequently, either by themselves or through others, explain during the celebration of Masses some of the readings of the Mass and among other things give some instruction about the mystery of the most holy sacrifice, especially on Sundays and feastdays.[1]

The use of the vernacular was rejected solely in order that the Council might not seem to be crediting the reasons put forward by the Reformers to justify the vernacular. At the same time, however, the pastoral solicitude of the bishops finds clear expression in this declaration, as it does in many other instances.

Unfortunately, the very bitter controversies that raged during the years after the Council caused Catholic polemicists to lay a disproportionate emphasis on the one of the two aspects the Fathers had kept in balance, namely, the assertion of dogma. As a result, the second, or pastoral, aspect did not bear the fruit for which the Fathers had hoped. Thus, for example, the recommendation given in the passage just cited was for practical purposes forgotten.

---

1. Session 22, ch. 8 (September 17, 1562) (DS 1749), trans. in *The Christian Faith in the Doctrinal Documents of the Catholic Church*, ed. J. Neuner and J. Dupuis (Staten Island: Alba House, 1982), no. 1554 (p. 427). A comparison with the first draft as emended by the Fathers shows the latter's pastoral concern. In any case, the use of Latin is presented as a disciplinary matter, and no theological arguments are invoked; see H. Schmidt, *Liturgie et langue vulgaire. Le problème de la langue liturgique chez les premiers Réformateurs et au Concile de Trente* (Analecta Gregoriana 53; Rome: Gregorian University, 1950).

The doctrinal decisions of Trent were accompanied by decrees concerned with reform: the Mass was to be celebrated "with interior cleanness and purity of heart and with a devotion that finds outward expression"; superstition was to be eliminated, as were undue monetary exactions, secular music, etc.[2] But the Council left it to the pope to publish a new missal.

II. THE MISSAL OF 1570

Pius IV († 1565) began the work by appointing a commission, which, unfortunately, has not left us the minutes of its activities. In a Bull of July 14, 1570, Pius IV's successor promulgated *The Roman Missal as revised by decree of the Council of Trent and published by order of Pope Pius V*, along with *Rubricae generales* and a *Ritus servandus in celebratione missae.* The whole plan of the book was evidently drawn up in a reforming spirit. Thus the liturgical cycle was relieved of a multitude of saints' feasts with which the Middle Ages had overburdened it, causing the Sundays to disappear; only those saints' feasts were to be celebrated that Rome had accepted before the eleventh century. The result was a hundred and fifty days set free, without counting octaves. In like manner, the celebration of votive Masses was regulated in such a way as to prevent their multiplication.

In the Ordinary of the Mass most of the sequences were eliminated; order was introduced into the private prayers and gestures of the celebrant by excluding the undisciplined expressions too often resulting from unschooled devotion. So, too, limits were imposed on the songs that had taken over even during the recital of the Canon; the only songs henceforth permitted were those that belonged to the Mass liturgy itself.

Though it might not seem so, the same thinking lay behind the preference given to a "conventual" celebration with canons or religious men in attendance, over a "private" celebration without any singing. The preference did indeed reflect the situation of the time, when secular and regular clergy were sufficiently numerous that all churches of any size could normally provide itself with the ministers required for a solemn celebration, even on weekdays. Even more than that, however, the preference was a statement that the solemn celebration represents the normative Eucharistic liturgy; the prayers that the priest recited in a low voice had only the secondary importance proper to them.

---

2. Decree *De observandis et evitandis in celebratione missarum* (same session). Also to be taken into account are the points made about reservation of the Eucharist and communion of the sick (Session 13), the canons on communion under both kinds and the canon on communion for little children (Session 21), etc.

The Bull of promulgation made clear the reforming spirit that had guided the project: "to revise the Missal in accordance with the ancient rite and the norms of the holy Fathers." Pius V was a courageous innovator, and it is an almost unbelievable paradox that some should today be invoking his patronage to oppose a reform inspired by the same spirit as continued and brought to bear at the Second Vatican Council.

The pope's ambitious program could not be fully realized at the time. The commission that had been charged with implementing it had to work very quickly. As a result, many of the elements added in the Carolingian period were kept in the new Order of Mass; they were kept, moreover, in the form that they had taken at Rome and in Italy where, in particular, the private prayers of the priest at the offertory and communion had become more extensive than in other regions. I pointed out earlier the greater simplicity maintained by the Dominicans and especially the Carthusians in this aspect of the ceremonial.

In addition, the document promulgating the reform made the new book the prototype to be followed by all the Churches, with the notable exceptions mentioned earlier.[3] Thanks to printing, which was rapidly developing at this period, the desired unification could be effected; in order to handle difficulties raised by local circumstances Sixtus V established the Congregation of Rites in 1588. The Bull of Pius V had stipulated that nothing should henceforth be changed in the Missal that he was making obligatory for the entire West. The context provides the reason for such a clause: the pope wanted to prevent a return to the countless adaptations characteristic of the medieval period, and to this end he sought stability. But the document was never understood as claiming to prevent any and every future revision by papal authority; the two new editions of the Tridentine book that appeared in the seventeenth century—in 1604 under Clement VIII and in 1634 under Urban VIII—did not hesitate to introduce changes, to say nothing of the revision by St. Pius X in 1914.

§2. Eucharistic Practices from the Seventeenth to the Nineteenth Century

The Council of Trent intended to rid the Church of all practices that were superstitious or even ambiguous; by that very fact it distanced itself from the popular religion of the Middle Ages. This religion revived under new forms during the Romantic period. Meanwhile, however, the move-

---

3. See p. 149. The exceptions make it clear that there was no intention of making the Missal of Pius V the sole legitimate liturgical expression, as some persons today wish to regard it.

ment of reform that became widespread at the end of the sixteenth and beginning of the seventeenth century, with Charles Borromeo as one of its outstanding representatives, was aware of the indifference of the masses. This indifference the reformers attributed primarily to ignorance, and, inspired by profound pastoral concern, they undertook to instruct the people. Seminaries for the formation of the clergy, educational institutions for the young, parish missions—all aimed at forming an elite that would be conscious of the demands of an authentic faith; it was thought that this was the best way of deepening and extending the influence of the Church. As a result, the liturgy, stripped now of all suspect attitudes and carefully regulated by a body of rubrics that the replies of the Congregation of Rites rendered increasingly detailed and minute, became the preserve of competent specialists; the needs of the people were not always kept in mind.

I. CULT OF THE BLESSED SACRAMENT

This situation led to the development of Eucharistic devotions (henceforth purified and carefully controlled) that escaped regulation by the rubricists. Benediction of the Blessed Sacrament[4] and prolonged adoration of it came to be regarded as very important, especially in the Jesuit churches, and were promoted by lay associations that became extremely popular. Here people could freely indulge in expressions of devotion that had been eliminated from liturgical celebrations: polyphony, suspect in the eyes of the Tridentine reformers, created a festive atmosphere; prayer took on accents more familiar to the people; the vernacular found its place; and the exhortations delivered by pastors established a vital bond between everyday life and the presence of the Redeemer under the sacred species.

Churches, whether soberly classical or exuberantly baroque in style, had features in common that made them suitable for these popular gatherings as well as for liturgical display in the Counter-Reformation mode. They were like great meeting halls, with their tribunes in the form of galleries and loges and with their decoration that led every eye to the imposing reredos that usually adorned the eastern end of the building. A large tabernacle often occupied the most conspicuous place, and it was frequently surmounted by columns of marble or gilded wood that supported capitals and carefully wrought pediments; between the columns were paintings or statues that lavishly exalted all the values rejected by the Protestant Reformers.

---

4. On Benediction of the Blessed Sacrament and Eucharistic devotions in which exposition and a Eucharistic blessing played a part see P. Browe, *Die Verehrung der Eucharistie im Mittelalter* (Rome: Herder, 1967²), 141–85; E. Dumoutet, *Le désir de voir l'hostie et les origines de la dévotion au Saint-Sacrement* (Paris: Beauchesne, 1926), 91–98.

The altar was no longer the center of attention; it was now shaped like a tomb, while its horizontal part was simply a long narrow surface; it bore little likeness any longer to a table. Room was always provided above the tabernacle to put an "exposition" receptacle of gilded wood in which the monstrance could be placed, unless an immovable central niche for the monstrance was already part of the structure.

Everything was arranged for a court ceremonial, but we may not overlook the pastoral intention behind it all. At Versailles and the Escorial, at Schönbrunn or at Potsdam, sumptuous feasts were given solely for the aristocrats and dignitaries of this world. In the church, however, the least yokel had a place before the throne of the King of heaven and could share joys that surpassed those that are the boast of earthly sovereigns. These festivities inspired the joy and hope of the entire people, who found therein the strength to live in union with God in the midst of daily trials.

II. THE PARISH MASS

What has been said does not mean that Sunday Mass lost all of its significance. On the contrary, it was an important moment in Christian life, and the other Eucharistic celebrations only made its function all the more intelligible. In not a few instances, and despite protests from ecclesiastical authorities, Sunday Mass was celebrated in the presence of the exposed Blessed Sacrament.

In the seventeenth century there was still only one parish Mass in each church, at least in the towns and villages. The hour for it was determined in the synodal statutes of the diocese, and it could be quite a long ceremony. It began with the blessing of water[5] and the Asperges (an adaptation of ancient monastic custom), prone[6] with its prayers, announcements and instruction, and the ceremony of blessed bread, usually at the offertory. In some localities there was also an offertory procession in which the congregation advanced to the edge of the sanctuary and venerated the paten with a kiss, while each person placed his or her mite on a tray.

Abstention from Communion was so much a part of local mores that those who wished to communicate would do so after the crowd had gone, lest they appear to be "flaunting themselves." In time, the practice arose of celebrating a "communion Mass" for such people at an early hour, though attendance at it usually did not dispense them from also attending the main Mass later on.

---

5. Provision is made in the Missal of Pius V for the blessing of water, but it is done in the sacristy. In France it was usually done at the altar, "to please the people," as P. Lebrun puts it in his *Explication littérale . . .*, 69, n. 1.

6. See p. 155.

This main Mass was sung. The prescriptions in the Missal of Pius V for "conventual" celebrations were adapted to local need. Thus laymen were allowed to make up for the shortage of clerics: appointed singers, often robed in soutane and surplice, sang the melodies of the Proper and Ordinary, or read the epistle. The congregation was not invited to join in with them.

For many Christians the custom of attending Sunday Mass was one of the obligations imposed by life in society. This is not to say that their intention was not a pure one. On the other hand, there was little that could help them enter into the mystery; the essential thing in their eyes was still the simple presence of Christ on the altar (the veneration of the Blessed Sacrament, described in the previous section, was still central for them). There was still, of course, the element of propitiation, which led them to make offerings (especially in their wills) in order to have the sacrifice celebrated for themselves and their families. This, however, seems to have been unconnected in their minds with their veneration of Christ in the Blessed Sacrament; it was not easy for them to see a connection between the various aspects of the Eucharist.

§3. Catechesis of the Mass and Participation of the Faithful

Such was the practical situation of the Christian body as a whole: they attended Mass only on Sundays, even at the time of a parish mission (surely a significant pointer), while a good number of priests did not celebrate every day.[7] Progress seems to have been made in this respect during the eighteenth century, for daily Mass was now a requirement in all educational institutions; this presumably formed new habits among the classes of society that attended these institutions.[8] Daily Mass was also in the schedule at the royal court of France in the time of Louis XV and Louis XVI.

A large-scale pastoral effort was made to educate the most fervent of the faithful to a true understanding of the Eucharist. The means used was a series of liturgical commentaries based especially on the researches of scholars like the Benedictines of the Saint-Maur Congregation.

---

7. See Madame de Sévigné's letter to her daughter, July 8, 1671: "I am here with three priests, each of whom plays his role, except for saying Mass; that is the only thing I lack despite their company."

8. Note that daily Mass was also provided in the schools established for the people by St. John Baptist de la Salle; see his *Conduite des écoles chrétiennes* (Avignon: J. C. Chastenier, 1720), 84.

I. COMMENTARIES ON THE LITURGY OF THE MASS

These publications ranged from instructional books meant primarily for the clergy, like those of the Oratorian Pierre Le Brun,[9] to the work of Sulpician Jean-Jacques Olier,[10] and on to the many "Explanations of the Mass" for the use of the laity. This literature spoke consistently of the participation of the faithful. Thus a Montpellier catechism said that "the Mass is the sacrifice of the people as much as of the priest."[11] St. Francis de Sales urged Philothea to "offer together with the priest and the rest of the people,"[12] and an archbishop of Rouen wrote to his people that "the entire action of the Church is shared by the priests and those present; you offer sacrifice along with the priest, and the sacrifice is for you no less than for him."[13] Many expressions of this kind could be cited.

The conclusion drawn from this teaching, however, was that those "attending" should pray in a manner inspired by a fuller doctrine of the Eucharist.[14] There was, in general, no question of liturgical participation as we understand it today.[15] In quite a few instances the faithful were allowed to join in the *Confiteor* and *Suscipiat*—a choice which indicated a poor understanding of the authentic role of a celebrating assembly, but which also inculcated habits that would be lasting.[16]

II. "EXERCISES" AND TRANSLATIONS

In 1661 Pope Alexander VII condemned a French translation of the Ordinary of the Mass and threatened excommunication for any further

---

9. See the bibliography for this chapter. See also L. A. Bocquillot, *Traité historique de la liturgie sacrée ou de la messe* (Paris: Anisson, 1701), and C. de Vert, *Explication simple, littérale et historique des cérémonies de l'Eglise* (Paris, 1706–13).

10. *Explication des cérémonies de la grand'messe de paroisse selon l'usage romain*, published under the author's name (Langlois, 1656).

11. *Instructions générales en forme de catéchisme . . . imprimées par ordre de Messire Charles Joachim Colbert, évêque de Montpellier* (Paris, 1702), 3:143.

12. St. Francis de Sales, *Introduction to the Devout Life*, Part II, ch. 13, ed. and trans. A. Ross (Westminster, Md.: Newman, 1948): ". . . so that, together with the priest, you may offer the sacrifice of your Redeemer to God his father, for yourself and for the whole Church" (96); "this holy Sacrifice, which, together with the priest and the rest of the people, you will offer to God the Father, for his honour and for your salvation" (97).

13. F. de Harlay, *La manière de bien entendre la messe de paroisse* (Paris: chez F. Muguet, 1685), 108.

14. See, *e.g.*, St. Francis de Sales, *ibid.*, 95–97.

15. Some priests, however, especially in Jansenist circles, said the Canon aloud or had the congregation respond to certain prayers; but these practices occurred only sporadically and were usually rejected by the bishops. See J. de Viguerie, "La dévotion populaire à la messe dans la France des XVIIe et XVIIIe siècles" (in the bibliography), 17.

16. The post-Vatican II reform of the Order of Mass would transform these private prayers of the ministers into prayers of the congregation.

attempt to make these texts accessible to the faithful.[17] This decision, encouraged by Mazarin, whose political plans it promoted, weighed heavily on pastoral activity in the ensuing years; it did not, however, dry up the stream of which it disapproved. Parts of the Missal were published in a number of languages in the seventeenth and eighteenth centuries, especially for the use of converts from Protestantism, whose number increased in France after the revocation of the Edict of Nantes in 1685.

Another type of work exerted an even greater influence. This was the "Exercises for Holy Mass," which proposed "considerations" or "elevations" (of mind and heart) for use during the celebration. These considerations ranged from allegorizing meditations to paraphrases of the liturgical formulas that the faithful could recite in a low voice as a way of uniting themselves with the priest. The authors of such paraphrases showed great ingenuity in transposing without actually translating.[18]

§4. "Neo-Gallican" Missals

BIBLIOGRAPHY

G. Oury, "Contribution à l'étude des liturgies néo-gallicanes du XVIIIe siècle: Les messes de saint Martin," *Etudes grégoriennes* 6 (1963) 165–83.

P. Jounel, "Les sources françaises du Missel de Paul VI," *QL* 52 (1971) 305–15.

————, "Les sources liturgiques anciennes et les missels français du XVIIIe siècle: Le missel monastique de Saint-Vanne (1781)," in *Histoire de la messe XVIIe-XVIIIe siècles* (Actes de la IIIe Rencontre d'histoire religieuse . . . Fontevraud . . . 1979; Paris: Librairie D.U.C., 1980), 67–80.

————, "Les missels diocésains français du XVIIIe siècle," *LMD* no. 141 (1980) 91–96.

G. Fontaine, "Présentation des missels diocésains français du XVIIe au XIXe siècle," *ibid.*, 97–166.

F. Brovelli, "Per uno studio dei messali francesi del secolo XVIII. Saggi d'analisi," *EL* 96 (1982) 279–406.

For over a hundred years, from the second quarter of the eighteenth century to the middle of the nineteenth, many French dioceses abandoned the Tridentine book and adopted missals of their own. These are usually called "neo-Gallican," but the term is inaccurate, since they had nothing to do with the ancient tradition of Gaul but remained faithful to the Roman Order of Mass. These books obviously copied from one another, and the one that Archbishop Charles de Vintimille published for Paris in 1738

---

17. The translation was that of Joseph de Voisin, which had already been condemned by the Clergy Assembly in 1660. It was preceded, however, by others published between 1597 and 1660. See de Viguerie, *ibid.*, 19–20.

18. The Jesuits—Nepveu, Gonnelieu, and others—were particularly interested in providing "Exercises."

quickly became a document on which more than half the bishops of the country based their missals.

The chief characteristic of this reform was a greater abundance of formularies. Weekday celebrations on Wednesdays and Fridays throughout the entire year had readings drawn from the medieval lectionaries, while the euchology was enriched with prayers that were either taken from the ancient sacramentaries (brought to light through recent research) or composed in accordance with the spirituality and theology of the French School (especially the secret and the postcommunion prayers).

The Sanctoral, in which a concern for historical truth was evident, the Commons, and the Masses for Various Intentions all acquired a new appearance and a greater diversity as compared with the Missal of Pius V. The song texts were revised in the interests of a greater fidelity to Scripture, but in the process the gradual often ceased to be taken from the psalms; the antiphonary was doubtless the least successful of these liturgical adaptations. In addition, many old sequences were kept and some new ones were written in a move that was hardly in accordance with a return to the sources.

The movement, especially in the area of the production inaugurated by the 1736 Missal of Troyes, was marked by an attention to themes, usually inspired by the gospel, which determined the makeup of entire formularies and gave these a somewhat moralizing cast. This was true in particular of the 1767 Missal of Poitiers, which, for example, had a Mass of fraternal charity and almsgiving on the eighth Sunday after Pentecost. This tendency became more widespread in the final decades of the century.

The "neo-Gallican" liturgy certainly contained great riches on which more recent reforms were able to draw; on the other hand, they were the creation of intellectuals, which explains why they produced scarcely any improvement in participation by the faithful.[19] They did not, however, merit the biased reproaches that Dom Guéranger heaped upon them in his *Institutions liturgiques*, with a view to having them abolished.[20]

§5. The Last Reforms before the Missal of Paul VI

Despite what was questionable in his work, Dom Guéranger did succeed in presenting the liturgy as the principal source of the spiritual life.

---

19. There were no comparable experiments outside of France, but in Germany proposals for liturgical reform were made that did contain similar ideas. This was especially true of the proposals of J. M. Sailer (1751–1832), Bishop of Regensburg; see M. Probst, *Gottesdienst in Geist und Wahrheit. Die liturgischen Ansichten und Bestrebungen Johann Michael Sailers* (Studien zur Pastoralliturgie 2; Regensburg: Pustet, 1976).

20. P. Guéranger, *Institutions liturgiques* (Le Mans: Fleuriot, 1878²) 1:388–407; 2:204–6.

This conviction was communicated to many through their reading of *The Liturgical Year* (*L'Année liturgique*) and through the restoration of Gregorian chant that Guéranger undertook.

I. SAINT PIUS X

St. Pius X threw his authority behind the new movement. In 1907 he promulgated a new edition of the *Graduale Romanum*. Two years later he published the well-known decree on frequent and even daily communion. By means of various documents that restored the proper celebration of Sunday (which had once again been invaded by the Sanctoral) and simplified certain rites, he achieved in fact a reform of the Missal. The reform was codified in 1914 in the *Additiones et variationes in Rubricis Missalis*, which until 1960, took their place in the liturgical books after the *Rubricae generales*.

This pope also envisaged more radical changes, which might well have come about if he had lived longer or if his successors had been able to continue his work. In fact, however, the time for such changes was not yet at hand; first, a new spirit had to be inculcated. This was the work of the liturgical movement that Dom Lambert Beauduin inaugurated during the same period.[21]

II. PIUS XII

The liturgical movement, which spread from the Benedictine abbeys of Belgium and Germany, was to create a new outlook in many priests and laypeople. Missals for the use of the faithful multiplied, and Christians could now "follow" the Mass and take an active part in it by sharing in the singing and in the responses of "dialogue Masses." The final step to the maturity that would make possible an authentic renewal was the rediscovery of that sense of the "assembly" that the vicissitudes of history had so thoroughly eliminated. The rediscovery came about through the joint and providentially harmonized efforts of two groups. On the one hand, there were pastors and a laity inspired by the new missionary impulse that Catholic Action, so strongly encouraged by Pius XI, was creating. On the other, there were the liturgical scholars, whose historical researches were bringing to light the fundamental dimensions of the Church's tradition. After World War II the movement became interna-

---

21. See *The Church at Prayer* I. I shall speak here only of what concerns the Order of Mass and the participation of the faithful in the Mass.

tional and prepared the minds and hearts of Christians for the work of the Second Vatican Council.

In his Encyclical Letter *Mediator Dei* (November 20, 1947) Pius XII put his seal of approval on the results of all this work and thereby on the desire of an increasing number of Christians for a reform of the liturgy of the Mass. Such a reform could now be regarded as truly possible.[22]

III. JOHN XXIII

The Council had already been announced when the *Codex rubrica-rum* of 1960 was published. It gathered together in a unified way the modifications already made in the rules for celebration, and added some further developments: the celebrant was henceforth to listen to the readings (and not read them to himself) when another minister proclaimed them; the *Confiteor* before communion was suppressed; the *Ite missa est* was to be replaced by *Benedicamus Domino* only if the congregation was not being dismissed but was staying for a further liturgical action (in this case the blessing was likewise omitted).[23]

John XXIII also made an alteration in the Canon—his boldest move, since the popes had left the Canon untouched for many centuries. A decree of the Congregation of Rites on November 13, 1962, added the name of St. Joseph to the *Communicantes*.

IV. PAUL VI

The Constitution *Sacrosanctum Concilium* on the Sacred Liturgy was promulgated at the Second Vatican Council on December 4, 1963. In anticipation of the new Missal that the Constitution called for, a series of changes was made in the Order of Mass. On January 25, 1964, the Motu Proprio *Sacram Liturgiam* made it a duty for all pastors to deliver a homily on Sundays and holy days of obligation.[24] On September 26 of that same year the Instruction *Inter oecumenici* introduced the use of the vernacu-

---

22. The decree of the Congregation of Rites, March 23, 1955, only simplified the rubrics for the presidential prayers, the Creed, the prefaces, and the last gospel: *De rubricis ad simpliciorem formam redigendis* (*AAS* 47 [1955] 218–24).

23. *Codex rubricarum*, promulgated by a Motu Proprio of July 25, 1960 (*AAS* 52 [1960] 596–740). This gave rise to a new *Ritus servandus* that became part of the final typical edition of the Missal of Pius V, in 1962.

24. *Sacram liturgiam* (*AAS* 56 (1964) 139–44 (= *EDIL* 178–90). English translation in *DOL* 20 nos. 276–89.

lar for certain parts of Masses celebrated with a congregation.[25] In addition, the Instruction called attention to the distinct character of the Liturgy of the Word, recommended the introduction of the General Intercessions or prayer of the faithful, ordered the priest to sing or say aloud the prayer over the gifts, the *Per ipsum*, and the embolism of the Our Father, ordered the entire congregation to say the Our Father, restored the formula "Body of Christ. — Amen" for the communion of the faithful,[26] and eliminated the last gospel.[27]

---

25. *Inter oecumenici* (*AAS* 56 [1964] 877–900 (= *EDIL* 199–297). English translation in *DOL* 23 nos. 293–300. According to this Instruction the ecclesiastical authority of a territory could allow the vernacular for the readings, all the songs, the General Intercessions, the greetings and dialogues, the Our Father with its introduction and embolism, and the communion formulas.

26. This point had already been the object of a decree of the Congregation of Rites on April 25 of the same year; see *AAS* 56 (1964) (= *EDIL* 197).

27. All this led to the *Ordo missae* and *Ritus servandus* of January 27, 1965: Decree of the SCR and the *Consilium*, *AAS* 57 (1965) 408–9 (=*EDIL* 380 = *DOL* 196).

THE CELEBRATION OF THE EUCHARIST AFTER VATICAN II

The Order of Mass of Paul VI

BIBLIOGRAPHY

> *Missale Romanum ex decreto sacrosancti oecumenici concilii Vaticani II instauratum auctoritate Pauli pp. VI promulgatum* (Vatican City, 1970; second typical edition, 1975). English translation by the International Committee on English in the Liturgy: *The Roman Missal. The Sacramentary* (Collegeville: The Liturgical Press, 1974; revised edition, 1985).
>
> R. Cabié, "Le nouvel *Ordo missae*," *LMD* no. 100 (1969) 21–35.

On April 3, 1969, Pope Paul VI signed the Apostolic Constitution that promulgated the *Roman Missal Revised by Decree of the Second Vatican Ecumenical Council*.[1] The document introduced the new Order of Mass, which was accompanied by an important *General Instruction*. The Missal itself was published in 1970[2]; a second typical or normative edition was published in 1975 and contained a certain number of variants.[3]

Unlike its Tridentine predecessor the book did not contain the readings from sacred Scripture. An *Ordo lectionum* ("order of readings" or lectionary), which was published at the same time as the Missal, likewise appeared in two successive forms.[4] These works were translated into the

---

1. Apostolic Constitution *Missale Romanum: AAS* 61 (1969) 217–22 (= *EDIL* 1362–72 = *DOL* 202 nos. 1357–66). English translation in *The Sacramentary*. Three days later the new Order of Mass was published: Decree of April 6, 1969, in *Notitiae* 5 (1969) 158 (= *EDIL* 1373 = *DOL* 203).

2. Decree of March 26, 1970: *Notitiae* 6 (1970) 169–93 (= *EDIL* 2060 = *DOL* 213).

3. Decree of March 27, 1975 (*DOL* 207)—The *General Instruction* had meanwhile been modified on several occasions; details in *EDIL* 1373–76 and *DOL* 208, footnote at title.

4. Some days after the promulgation, on May 25, 1969, the Congregation for Divine Worship published a list of biblical readings, and the typical edition of the new lectionary appeared in three volumes on September 30, 1970 (= *EDIL* 2187 = *DOL* 231). A revised and enlarged second edition (including Masses for the various rites, Masses for Various Needs,

various languages in accordance with methods set down in the law. The English translation of the Missal for the dioceses of the United States of America received its final approval on February 4, 1974,[5] and was published in that year. The English translation of the lectionary had been approved earlier and was published in 1970.[6]

The plan set forth by Vatican II for the reform of the Eucharistic liturgy was thus brought to fulfillment:

> The Order of Mass is to be revised in a way that will bring out more clearly the intrinsic nature and purpose of its several parts, as also the connection between them, and will more readily achieve the devout, active participation of the faithful.
>
> For this purpose the rites are to be simplified, due care being taken to preserve their substance; elements that, with the passage of time, came to be duplicated or were added with but little advantage are now to be discarded; other elements that have suffered injury through accident of history are now, as may seem useful or necessary, to be restored to the vigor they had in the tradition of the Fathers.[7]

It took hardly more than five years for the project to be completed. The project was that which St. Pius V had adopted—a revision "in accordance with the . . . original standard of the holy Fathers"—but had been unable to do more than sketch out. To this plan the new Missal added the contribution made by the liturgical movement that came to fruition in the Constitution *Sacrosanctum concilium*. Thus the "conscious and active participation" of all the faithful is an essential objective; its attainment presupposes a clear grasp of the various components of the ritual as well as of the connection between them in the dynamics of the celebration.

§1. The Spirit Guiding the Reform

BIBLIOGRAPHY

A. M. Franquesa, "Presentación de la nueva ordenación general del Misal romano," *Phase* 9 (1969) 221–68.

---

etc.), which was also changed to conform to the Neo-Vulgate, was published on January 21, 1981, in the form of *Variationes: Notitiae* 18 (1981) 357–462.

5. The National Conference of Bishops approved it on November 13, 1973. Confirmation from the Congregation for Divine Worship was dated February 4, 1974.

6. The English translation of the Introduction, Titles, Rubrics and Antiphons was copyrighted in 1969 by the International Committee on English in the Liturgy. The readings from sacred Scripture may be taken from several translations.

7. VSC 50 (*DOL* 1 no. 50).

A. M. Roguet, "L'arrière-plan doctrinal de la nouvelle liturgie de la messe," *LMD* no. 100 (1969) 72–88.

P. Cneude, "L'assemblée," *ibid.*, 89–103.

J. Gelineau, "Les chants dans le nouvel *Ordo missae*," *ibid.*, 104–16.

P. Jounel, "Le missel de Paul VI," *LMD* no. 103 (1970) 16–45.

G. Oury, *La Messe de S. Pie V à Paul VI* (Solesmes, 1975).

J. M. Sustaeta, *Misal e eucaristia. Estudio teológico, estructural y pastoral del nuevo Misal Romano* (Series Valentina 3; Valencia: Facultad de teología S. Vicente Ferrer, 1979).

The *General Instruction* is entirely different in character from the *General Rubrics* of the Missal of Pius V. The aim is no longer a simple description of the rites but a presentation of the celebration in which doctrinal and pastoral considerations take first place and give meaning to rubrical instructions. According to the original meaning of the Latin title, *Institutio (generalis)*, we are being given an "instruction" inspired by an interpretative intention and a pedagogical purpose. To the extent that regulations are given, they are explained and related to a truly authentic tradition that has been purified of all dross; the regulations thus serve the pastoral aspirations of a Church that sees itself as being for humankind a "sacrament" of the salvation bestowed by Jesus Christ.

I. "UNCHANGING FAITH . . . UNBROKEN TRADITION"

The *General Instruction* begins with an Introduction that uses two phrases: "unchanging faith" and "unbroken tradition," to show the continuity of Catholic teaching on the Eucharist. It reminds the reader of the sacrificial nature of the Mass, the mystery of the Lord's real presence under the appearances of bread and wine, the nature of ministerial priesthood and the baptismal priesthood, as well as the authentic meaning of the Church's living tradition, which expresses this one faith with varying emphases as the centuries pass.

II. THE ASSEMBLY

The spirit of the new Missal manifests itself very specially in the constant and primordial preoccupation with the assembly as a whole, which it regards as the primary agent in the celebration. The normal or "typical" Mass is a Mass at which a congregation is present. With this norm as point of reference, adaptations are then made to particular situations, such as a Mass without a congregation, which, while legitimate, remains an extreme case.

Moreover, the time is now past when the rubrics in the liturgical books dealt solely with the priest and other ministers and went into finicky detail that took no account of the number of those "attending" or of the level of their faith or their educational background or their concrete situation. Henceforth, many options are offered that will make possible any necessary adaptations; the priest is insistently reminded that he must look to the spiritual good of the faithful rather than to his own desires and must even consult with the faithful themselves in matters that concern them more directly (see especially no. 313).

III. THE MINISTERS

Far from restricting the functions of the various ministers, the primacy given to the assembly requires them to be signs of the Mystical Body of the Lord. It is the duty of the celebrant, whether bishop or priest, to "serve God and the people with dignity and humility" (no. 60). But it is by reason of his ordination, which makes him the representative of Christ the Head, that he must provide this service: "He therefore presides over the assembly" "in the person of Christ" (no. 60). It is also as the result of an ordination that deacons exercise their functions in the service of the people (no. 61).

Provision is made for other ministers depending on the needs of the community. Three seem to have a privileged place inasmuch their presence is constitutive of the "typical form" of Mass (no. 78). First in rank, because the proclamation of God's word is so important, is the reader, who will ordinarily be a layperson (no. 66)[8]; next comes the cantor, who directs the vocal participation of the congregation; and finally at least one minister at the altar. Other agents will play a part in the celebration to the extent required by the form of the liturgical action and the number of participants (nos. 65, 68, 69).

The conception of ministries that is operative here is one based on function; the time is past when priests were vested as deacons and subdeacons and when the call went out to those who could "wear pontificals" for the simple purpose of "making the ceremony more splendid." This point is made with regard to a presiding bishop: "This is done not to add external solemnity, but to express in a clearer light the mystery of the Church, which is the sacrament of unity" (no. 59).

---

8. The lay reader is empowered for the function either by being "instituted" in a permanent way (*GIRM* 66; *DOL* 208 no. 1456) or being chosen at each celebration by the president of the assembly.

IV. A RETURN TO THE SOURCES

The new Missal often represents a return to older forms that existed before the alterations made from the eighth century on. In each part of the celebration we discern convergences with the ancient usages explained earlier in Section II of this book. The intention, however, is not archaeological reconstruction: there has been a return to older forms insofar as this seems "useful or necessary" so that the Church of today may celebrate the paschal mystery in an authentic manner. The positive contributions of later periods, far from being scorned, have been retained at several points.

§2. The Introductory Rites

BIBLIOGRAPHY

P. Dacquino, "I saluti liturgici nel nuovo rito della messa," *Notitiae* 6 (1970) 254–57.

J. Miazek, *La "collecta" del "proprium de tempore" nel "Missale Romanum" di Paolo VI. Avviamento ad uno studio criticoteologico* (Rome: Pontificio Istituto S. Anselmo, 1977).

"After the people have assembled" (*populo congregato*): these are the first words in the description of the Mass both in the *Order of Mass* (no. 1) and in the *General Instruction* (no. 25). It is the passage from the scatteredness of everyday life to an assembly now being formed that gives meaning to the opening rites.

I. THE ENTRANCE SONG

This song is the first action of the celebration and has a threefold function:

1. To *"intensify the unity of the gathered people"*: the song is therefore intended not primarily to add solemnity but to promote communication; the union of voices expresses a communion among the singers. Consequently, the song should therefore involve the active participation of the congregation, usually in the form of a refrain, the "entrance antiphon."

2. To *"lead their thoughts to the mystery of the season or feast"*: Song creates an atmosphere and can set a tone by placing on the lips of the participants words that help them enter into the spirit of the celebration. A large number of the formularies in the Roman Missal, especially for Lent and Ordinary Time, are taken from the psalter. Most of the others

are biblical, sometimes in adapted form, but there are also more than twenty other compositions, especially in the Sanctoral, the Commons, and the votive Masses, of which only some come from the Tridentine book. It is permitted, however, to choose another song, the text of which is "approved by the conference of bishops" (no. 26); it is important that these other songs be appropriate to the day or season.

This aspect of the entrance antiphon explains why, if it is not sung, it is to be read, after the greeting, by the congregation or a reader or, if necessary, the priest himself.

3. *To "accompany the procession"*: Depending on circumstances the celebrant's entrance will take a more or less solemn form, but it is always part of the act that establishes the assembly. The Book of the Gospels is normally carried in by the deacon or reader and placed on the altar. In the procession may also be included the crucifix and the candles that will surround the table of sacrifice, and, as the case may be, the censer, whose fragrance will waft over the altar. The priest, having bowed to it, venerates the altar with a kiss. The altar is, however, only one of the two focuses of the celebration. The other is the presidential chair to which the priest now goes.

II. THE GREETING

The celebrant's greeting and the congregation's response have their proper place at the very beginning of the liturgical action. Greeting and response show both the presence of the Lord as signified by the ordained minister and the grace that explains this gathering of the people; the gathering does not spring from a human initiative but from a call of God who thus turns a group of individuals into an ecclesial assembly.

1. *The Formulas for the Greeting*

In addition to the traditional greeting, "The Lord be with you," two others are offered as options. The first already existed in the Eastern liturgies at the beginning of the anaphora.[9] The second is, in substance, one often used by St. Paul at the beginning of his letters.[10] The wish that the other have peace is a characteristic trait of biblical greetings and is still found in Semitic civilizations down to our own time; on the lips of the risen Lord, however, it acquires a new meaning that the Antiochene tradition and the Roman pontifical Mass have perpetuated in the greeting

---

9. See p. 92.
10. Rom 1:7; Gal 1:3; 1 Cor 1:2; 2 Cor 1:2; Eph 1:2; Col 1:3; 1 Thess 1:2; 2 Thess 1:2.

"Peace be with you" (this *"Pax vobis"* has been retained in the reformed liturgy[11]).

The ancient response of the congregation "And with your spirit," which alludes to the Spirit received through the sacramental imposition of hands, can be replaced, when the third greeting is used, by a typical expression— now given a Christian meaning—from the prayer of Israel: "Blessed be God, the Father of our Lord Jesus Christ."[12]

2. *The Sign of the Cross*

In the Roman Missal the greeting is preceded by a sign of the cross: the priest says "In the name of the Father, and of the Son, and of the Holy Spirit," and the people answer, "Amen." This means that, contrary to the practice of the early Christians, the greeting and response are no longer the first words exchanged by president and congregation. This is a regrettable alteration.[13]

3. *Introduction to the Mass of the Day*

The greeting may be prolonged by brief remarks that the celebrant (or other minister) addresses to the people in order to "introduce the faithful to the Mass of the day" (no. 29). The reference is, it seems, less to the formularies of the Mass than to the act of celebrating, since Christians living scattered in the world must do a certain violence to themselves if they are to form an authentic assembly. In any case, there is no question here of a homily on the readings to be proclaimed later on or of a detailed presentation of the life of the saint being commemorated.

III. THE PENITENTIAL RITE

Once they form a congregation, the people of God turn to their Lord with a view to acknowledging their sinfulness and preparing themselves to receive the gift of God that will come through the celebration of the mysteries. In this penitential act the celebrant first urges the people to recall their sins; a moment of silence follows, then all recite the *Confiteor*. Here

---

11. John 20:19, 21, 26 — Order of Mass 2.

12. The French translation does not make the formula optional. The reason is a practical one: the congregation must know what response to give, and the response must be short. The Italian translation adopts the same approach. The German translation uniformly uses "And with your spirit."

13. To avoid this undesirable change, some episcopal conferences, including those of Germany and the French-speaking countries, have the celebrant himself say the "Amen" to his sign of the cross, so that the first response of the faithful is to the initial greeting. This decision has been approved by the Congregation for Divine Worship.

a formula that entered the ritual of Mass as a private prayer of the celebrant has acquired a new status. The text of the prayer has been simplified in accordance with ancient models,[14] and it is said simultaneously by celebrant and faithful as all publicly acknowledge their common sinfulness.

The *Confiteor* may be replaced by two psalmic verses[15], with celebrant and people saying half-verses alternately: "Lord, we have sinned against you: Lord have mercy. — Lord, have mercy." "Lord, show us your mercy and love. — And grant us your salvation." The *Confiteor* may also be replaced by three invocations to which the congregation responds with "Lord, have mercy," "Christ, have mercy," "Lord, have mercy." This response takes on here a penitential coloring that it did not have in its traditional usage, where it was a supplication.

If the *Confiteor* or the psalmic verses are used for the penitential rite, the rite is to be followed by two *Kyrie*(s), two *Christe*(s), and two *Kyrie*(s); but the number may be changed. The penitential rite itself concludes with the "May almighty God have mercy on us . . ." that has always followed the *Confiteor*. The *General Instruction* speaks of this as "the priest's absolution" (no. 29).

The Missal allows the penitential preparation to be replaced at Sunday Masses by a "Rite of Blessing and Sprinkling Holy Water."

IV. THE "GLORY TO GOD IN THE HIGHEST"

The *Gloria* is henceforth more clearly intended to create a festive spirit, since it is sung or said only "on Sundays outside Advent and Lent, on solemnities and feasts, and in special, more solemn celebrations" (no. 31).

V. THE COLLECT OR OPENING PRAYER

Whereas the Missal of Pius V called the first presidential prayer simply *Oratio* (Prayer, Oration), the Missal of Paul VI calls it a *Collecta* (Collect), in order to bring out its structure and function.[16] Henceforth there is but a single opening prayer in each Mass; it is also the formula that offers the greatest variety, since in many instances it alone gives expression to the special character of the celebration. It always has a Trinitarian conclusion, which is followed by the congregation's "Amen."

A good many of the collects are taken from the older Roman Missal, but the compilers have also drawn upon the treasures in the ancient books,

---

14. See p. 151.
15. The first verse is inspired by the psalter, the second is taken from it: Ps 85:8.
16. See p. 52 and *GIRM* 32 (*DOL* 208 no. 1422).

even those outside the Roman tradition: the sacramentaries and *Ordines,* first of all, but also Visigothic, Gallican, and neo-Gallican sources.[17] The ancient texts have at times been slightly altered in order either to restore their primitive form or to make them more relevant to us or, finally, to make prayers from other traditions conform to the principles at work in the Roman collect, where the Father is always addressed and all repetitions are avoided. These new creations are to be found in the Sanctoral and especially in the "Masses and Prayers for Various Needs and Occasions" where they give expression to the thematic unity of the formulary as a whole.

§3. The Liturgy of the Word

BIBLIOGRAPHY

Missale Romanum: Lectionarium (Vatican City, 1970–72). 3 volumes: I. *De Tempore: ab Adventu ad Pentecosten;* II. *Tempus per annum post Pentecosten;* III. *Pro missis de Sanctis, ritualibus, ad diversa, votivis et defunctorum.* English translation: *Lectionary for Mass* (Collegeville: The Liturgical Press, 1970).

Missale Romanum: Ordo lectionum missae. Editio typica altera (Vatican City, 1981).

C. Wiener, "Présentation du nouveau lectionnaire," *LMD* no. 99 (1969) 28–49.

G. Fontaine, *Paroles de Dieu pour le temps de l'Avent* (Paris: Mame, 1979).

J. Evenou, "Le psaume et les antiennes de la messe," *LMD* no. 151 (1982) 91–115.

The Liturgy of the Word is not a "Fore-Mass," as it has sometimes been called. It is not a simple preparation for the sacrament that follows. Rather, it is an integral part of the celebration and effects a presence of the Lord in the midst of his people, since "it is he himself who speaks when the holy Scriptures are read in the Church,"[18] and since the faithful are truly provided "a richer share in God's word."[19] It is therefore essential "that the intimate connection between words and rites may stand out clearly in the liturgy."[20]

I. THE READINGS, RESPONSORIAL PSALM, AND ALLELUIA

The Council had decided that the lectionary for Mass should be reformed: "The treasures of the Bible are to be opened up more lavishly

---

17. See A. Dumas, "Les sources du nouveau Missel romain," *Notitiae* 7 (1971) 37–42, 74–77, 94–95, 134–36, 276–80, 409–10. The author indicates the sources of the collects, prayers over the gifts, and postcommunion prayers, as well as the prefaces; — H. Ashworth, "Les sources patristiques du nouveau missel romain," *QL* 52 (1971) 295–304; — P. Jounel, "Les sources françaises du missel de Paul VI," *ibid.,* 305–16.

18. *VSC* 7 (*DOL* 1 no. 7).

19. *VSC* 51 (*DOL* 1 no. 51).

20. *VSC* 35 (*DOL* 1 no. 35).

so that a richer share in God's word may be provided for the faithful. In this way a more representative portion of the holy Scriptures will be read to the people in the course of a prescribed number of years."[21]

To this end the lectionary has become a book distinct from the Missal, and it is from the ambo or lectern, a place distinct both from the altar and the president's chair, that the Word is proclaimed.

1. *The Various Parts of the Reading from the Scriptures*[22]

a) On Sundays and solemnities there are two biblical readings before the gospel; other celebrations have but one such reading. The proclamation of this reading or readings is the function of a lector.

b) After the first reading, a responsorial psalm is sung by a cantor or read by a lector. The congregation participates by singing or saying a refrain.

c) The gospel is proclaimed by a deacon or, if there is no deacon, by a priest other than the celebrant or, if there is no other priest, by the president himself. The reading is done with solemnity and is preceded by the traditional greeting and announcement.

d) The alleluia is sung before the gospel, usually during the procession from altar to ambo or lectern. The alleluia frames a biblical verse, often from the psalms or the gospel. During Lent, it is omitted and there is simply the verse before the gospel. The alleluia is meant to be sung; if it cannot be sung, it may be omitted.

e) The sequences in the old Missal have been kept and placed before the alleluia. They are optional, however, except on Easter and Pentecost.

f) The formulas after the readings, which were private prayers of the ministers in the old Order of Mass, are now said by the entire congregation: "Thanks be to God" and (after the gospel) "Glory to you, Lord." The reader elicits these responses by saying "This is the Word (Gospel) of the Lord."

g) The ritual for the readings still has two private prayers: "Almighty God, cleanse my heart,"[23] which the priest says before reading the gospel but which is replaced, when a deacon reads it, by a blessing from the celebrant, and "May the words of the Gospel," which the minister who has proclaimed it says as he kisses the book.

2. *The Organization of the Sunday Lectionary*

a) *The gospel.* The vast majority of the passages in the Synoptic Gospels are proclaimed, in a three-year cycle, on the Sundays of Ordinary Time.

---

21. *VSC* 51 (*DOL* 1 no. 51).
22. *GIRM* 34–40 (*DOL* 208, nos. 1424–30).
23. The prayer is simplified by comparison with the formulary in the Missal of Pius V.

The order followed is that of the Bible, that is, Matthew in Year A, Mark in Year B, and Luke in Year C. In Year B the sixth chapter of John, which reports the multiplication of the loaves and the discourse on the bread of life, is read on Sundays 17 to 21 to supplement the Book of Mark, which is shorter than the others. It is, however, above all in the special seasons and, in particular, during Lent and the fifty-day period after Easter that the Fourth Gospel is proclaimed, in keeping with its character as a catechesis of the sacraments. The pericopes of the Samaritan Woman, the Man Born Blind, and the Raising of Lazarus have recovered (at least in Year A[24]) their ancient role as preparation for the celebration of baptism at Easter.

This semicontinuous reading enables the people of God to discover the riches of the Good News of Christ, which differs in aspect and emphasis depending on the gospel author and the community for which he wrote.

b) *The Old Testament.* There can be no question of a continuous reading of the Old Testament; instead, an attempt has been made to find a passage that will correspond to each gospel pericope. Sometimes the passage reports a word or event in the history of Israel to which the Lord himself refers more or less explicitly; sometimes it offers a meditation on human sin and wretchedness, by way of introduction to the messianic hope; sometimes it describes the journey of the human beings in the Bible toward discovery of the mystery that will be made manifest in Christ.

Paired in this way are, for example, the calls of Samuel and of the first apostles (2nd Sunday, B); the evocation of the night of Passover in the Book of Wisdom and the exhortations to watchfulness in expectation of the Master's return (19th Sunday, C); the prophecy of Zechariah concerning the Messiah who triumphs through humility, and the thanksgiving of Jesus for the revelation to the lowly (14th Sunday, A). These random examples suggest the wide range of biblical books used. There is no guiding thread to link the first readings from Sunday to Sunday; this drawback has been accepted for the sake of a much more basic value: the idea that the gospel is the fulfillment of the prophecies as well as of the promises and hopes of Israel.

The same impression of disorder is not given in the lectionary for the special seasons. In the Advent and Christmas seasons Isaiah dominates the scene; his writings are complemented by other passages that have eschatological resonances. In Lent we are given the history of salvation in outline; the story culminates on the fifth Sunday in the prophecies of a new covenant.

24. Years B and C have other readings, but with the rubric: "The readings given for Year A . . . may be used in place of these."

In the Easter season, passages from the Old Testament are replaced by the Acts of the Apostles, as in the ancient tradition. The proclamation of the Lord's resurrection as given in the memoirs of the first witnesses contains the entire law and the prophets, as most of the sermons in this book make clear.

Note that the responsorial psalm is usually chosen to complement the reading that precedes it.

c) *The "Apostle."* While there is a harmony between the first and third readings, the same is not true of the second, which follows its own order: passages from the Apocalypse and from the Letters of Peter and John during the Easter season, and passages from the Letters of James and Paul during the remainder of the year.[25] During Advent, Christmastide, and Lent, this semicontinuous reading yields place to passages from the various New Testament books; these are chosen for their harmony with the other readings.

3. The Organization of the Weekday Lectionary

a) *The special seasons.* The readings for these seasons are chosen in accordance with a kind of compromise between an adaptation to the mysteries being celebrated and a semicontinuous reading, especially of the gospels.

During Advent, until December 16, the joyous and hope-filled oracles of Isaiah are read in a semicontinuous form. As the Nativity draws near, the readings tell us of the human roots of Jesus and of the expectation of the Old Testament "poor." The gospels for the first days of Advent are chosen for their connection with the passages from the prophet; beginning on the second Thursday they recall the mission of John the Baptist.

On the weekdays after Christmas the First Letter of John is read, its first verses being appointed for December 27, the feast day of the evangelist; his testimony sheds an especially important light on the mystery of the incarnation. In the gospel the story of the presentation of Jesus in the temple is read from St. Luke; after that and until Epiphany the gospel reading is from the first chapter of John. After Epiphany the gospel passages tell of the various manifestations of the Lord at the beginning of his ministry; they are taken from the Four Gospels.

During Lent the first reading is from the Old Testament and, like the gospel reading, is chosen in function of the basic themes in the catechesis

---

25. 1 Corinthians, which is long and deals with various questions, has been distributed throughout the three years, at the beginning of Ordinary Time. Hebrews is also divided into two parts, which are read from the 27th to the last Sunday of Year B and the 19th to the 23rd of Year C. Year A also includes Romans, Philippians, and 1 Thessalonians; Year B includes 2 Corinthians, Ephesians, and James; Year C includes Galatians, Colossians, Philemon, 1 Timothy, 2 Timothy, and 2 Thessalonians.

and spirituality of the season: call to conversion and repentance; the essential requirements of a baptismal life; participation in the redemptive sufferings of the Savior. The gospel pericopes are from the Synoptics until the end of the third week; a semicontinuous reading of John begins at that point.

During the fifty days after Easter the Acts of the Apostles naturally provide the pericopes for the first reading. During the Easter octave the gospel readings tell of the appearances of the risen Lord. After the octave the semicontinuous reading of John begins again, using passages, different from those of Lent, that focus on the proclamation of Easter joy in the gift of the sacraments, especially as found in chapter 6, in the discourse after the Supper, and in the priestly prayer.

b) *Ordinary Time.* The compilers then had to distribute the other essential passages of Scripture over the remainder of the year, in such a way as to provide coherent sequences.

The gospels are the same every year: Mark (weeks 1–9), Matthew (10–21), Luke (22–34).[26]

In the first reading the organization differs depending on whether the year is even or uneven. Each year the Old Testament and New Testament are read alternately in approximately the same proportion. All the New Testament letters, except for those of James and John, furnish numerous pericopes, as does the Apocalypse. The choice of Old Testament readings is guided by a desire to give an overview of the history of salvation prior to the incarnation of the Lord. The religious meaning of events is sometimes brought out in passages from the sapiential books, which serve as prologue or epilogue to a series of historical readings. Almost all the Old Testament books are used in the weekday lectionary.[27]

4. *The Organization of the Other Lectionaries*

A choice of appropriate readings "that will bring out a particular aspect of the spiritual life or activity of the saint"[28] being celebrated has always characterized the commemorations in the Sanctoral. The Lectionary of Paul VI has three pericopes for solemnities and two for feasts. Simple memorials likewise have their own readings, but their use is optional, ex-

---

26. Everything in Matthew and Luke is included that has no parallel in Mark. But several times passages are included that have a really different coloration in the various gospels and are needed in order to follow the thread of the narrative. The eschatological discourse in Luke is read in its entirety at the end of the liturgical year.

27. The only prophetic writings omitted are those that are too short, like Obadiah, or that are hardly suited for public reading, like the Canticle of Canticles, as well as Judith and Esther, some passages of which are read on Sundays, feast days, or weekdays of other liturgical seasons.

28. *Lectionarium Romanum* III, Praenotanda, 1b.

cept in cases of biblical personages who are mentioned in the readings. The celebrant is in fact encouraged not to interrupt the weekday cycle unless pastoral reasons require him to do so.[29] A wide choice of passages is given for the Commons.

There is also a set of readings for votive Masses, Masses for the dead, Masses for Various Needs, and Masses connected with various rites, that is, Masses in the course of which other sacraments or the various monastic institutions are celebrated.

5. *Options Available*

If a continuous reading has been interrupted by a solemnity, feast, or special celebration, the pericopes omitted can be read on another day if they are preferred to those assigned to that day (the two sets of readings can also be combined). So, too, in a community that does not attend Mass every day and therefore cannot profit from the continuous reading of Scripture, the most suitable readings may be chosen from among those of that week. In addition, at celebrations for special groups, passages best adapted to the situation may be read, provided they are from an approved lectionary.[30] If intelligent use is made of the options offered, the Scripture readings chosen can be made to form a coherent pattern, without omitting, for example, the passages of the Bible that are the most difficult to understand.

II. THE HOMILY

The *General Instruction* reminds us that the homily is an "integral part" of the liturgy and should ordinarily be given by the celebrant. It should develop some aspect of the readings or of "another text from the Ordinary or from the Proper of the Mass of the day" and form a bridge between the mystery being celebrated and the lives of the faithful who hear it. It is to be given on Sundays and feast days of obligation, and it is strongly recommended on other days as well, especially those "when the people come to church in large numbers."[31]

III. THE PROFESSION OF FAITH

This is the name by which the Creed is referred to in the new Missal.[32]

---

29. *Ibid.*

30. *GIRM* 319 (*DOL* 208 no. 1709).

31. *Ibid.*, 41–42 (*DOL* 208 nos. 1431–32).

32. *Ibid.*, 43–44 (*DOL* 208 nos. 1433–34) and Order of Mass 15.

It calls to mind our baptism and the acceptance of God's Word as a condition for receiving the sacrament. The Creed, which expresses a personal adherence (even though the English version uses "we") to the Church's rule of faith,[33] is said or sung only on Sundays throughout the year, on solemnities, and in special celebrations, the importance of which the celebrant wishes to emphasize. The profession of faith at the Easter Vigil and at celebrations of baptism evidently replaces the Creed.

IV. THE GENERAL INTERCESSIONS
OR PRAYER OF THE FAITHFUL

In the General Intercessions the people, ". . . exercising their priestly function, intercede for all humanity."[34] These intercessions have now recovered their place in the Roman liturgy after fourteen centuries of neglect. They are introduced by an exhortation and concluded by a prayer of the president; they take the form of a litany said or sung by a deacon or, if there is no deacon, by laypeople, and they call to mind the various needs of humankind. On the other hand, the intercession being expressed is that of the entire assembly: this finds expression after each intention either in a common invocation, which should be in the form of a supplication, usually addressed to Christ, or in a moment of silence. In order that the intercessions may be truly universal, a four-part scheme is proposed by way of example: for the Church, for the earthly city and those who hold responsible positions in it, for those afflicted in any way, and for the local community.

§4. The Eucharistic Liturgy

I. THE PREPARATION OF THE GIFTS

BIBLIOGRAPHY

J. B. Molin, "Depuis quand le mot 'offertoire' sert-il à désigner une partie de la messe?" *EL* 77 (1963) 357–80.
N. K. Rasmussen, "Les rites de la préparation du pain et du vin," *LMD* no. 100 (1969) 44–58.

---

33. The Creed is the Nicene-Constantinopolitan Creed; in Masses for children it may be replaced by the Apostles' Creed, because this was part of the catechetical initiation. See *Directorium de missis cum pueris*, November 1, 1973, no. 49 (= *EDIL* 3163); English translation, "Directory for Masses with Children" in *DOL* 276 nos. 2134–88.
34. *GIRM* 45 (*DOL* 208 no. 1435).

V. Raffa, "Le orazioni sulle offerte del Proprio del Tempo nel nuovo Messale," *EL* 84 (1970) 299–322.

J. Janicki, *Le orazioni "super oblata" del ciclo "de tempore" secondo il "Missale Romanum" di Paolo VI. Avviamento ad uno studio critico-teologico* (Rome: Pontificio Istituto S. Anselmo, 1977).

The purpose in this part of the liturgy is to do again what Christ did at the Supper: "He took bread . . . the cup." The bringing of the material of sacrifice to the altar has always been the most meaningful way of expressing this intention. The new Missal has restored this rite to its proper place.

1. *The Bread and Wine*

In order to avoid the ambiguities that had in practice crept in, the name of this set of ceremonies has been changed. It is to be known henceforth not as the "offertory" but, according to the *General Instruction*, as the "preparation of the gifts." The *Instruction* considers it "desirable" that the faithful bring the offerings to the altar: "The rite of carrying up the gifts continues the same spiritual value and meaning" as when in the past the people brought "bread and wine for the liturgy from their homes."[35]

Consequently, the essential act of the priest who receives the offerings no longer consists in his elevating the paten and chalice in a gesture of offering, as the medieval ritualists imagined, but rather in placing them on the corporal and then holding them a little above the table as he says a prayer. The prayer is no longer the one found in the Tridentine Order of Mass but is modeled on the "blessings" in the Jewish liturgy. It speaks of the bread and wine as being fruits of the earth and therefore both gifts of God and products of human work:

> Blessed are you, Lord, God of all creation.
> Through your goodness we have this bread (wine) to offer,
>   which earth has given and human hands have made (fruit of the vine and work of human hands).
> It will become for us the bread of life (our spiritual drink).[36]

Many of the Missals in other languages avoid translating the Latin word *offerimus* literally,[37] in order to preclude the undesirable inferences already

35. *Ibid.*, 49–53 (*DOL* 208 nos 1439–43).

36. Latin: "Benedictus es, Domine, Deus universi, quia de tua largitate accepimus panem (vinum) quem (quod) tibi offerimus, fructum terrae (vitis) et operis manuum hominum, ex quo nobis fit panis vitae (potus spiritalis)."

37. French: "Nous te presentons"; Italian: "ti presentiamo"; Spanish: "te presentamos"; German: "wir bringen vor dein Angesicht." — The Order of Mass is not in full agreement with the thrust of the whole reform; thus it speaks of the "offertory song" (for which there are no longer any set texts in the Mass formularies). See G. Fontaine, "Institutionis generalis Missalis Romani concordia verborum," *Notitiae* 5 (1969) 304–22.

mentioned. The translators regarded it as all the more necessary to avoid ambiguities, because the ancient formulary, understood apart from its historical context, had led to a suspect interpretation of the offertory. Back in the thirties, Catholic Action, in a legitimate desire to link Mass and life, had turned this part of the celebration into an offering of the efforts of human beings to achieve conversion, transform the world, and proclaim Christ. The danger here was to see in the offertory a sacrifice before the Sacrifice. In fact, the sacrifice of the faithful cannot be distinct from that of the Lord. Moreover, it is the Eucharist in its entirety, and especially in the essential act expressed by the prayer of anamnesis, that shows the relation between the Eucharist and the lives and self-giving of the faithful.[38]

The new "blessings" can be said aloud, and the faithful can respond with "Blessed be God for ever." This procedure is optional, however, and one may prefer to have a bit of organ music or a song from the choir or a period of silence during this ceremony.

The *General Instruction* expressly provides that the preparation of the chalice may be done at the credence table[39] before it is brought to the altar. The sign of the cross is no longer made over the water. On the other hand, there is a private prayer to be said by the deacon (or by the priest, if there is no deacon) as he pours some water into the wine. The presence of this prayer has unfortunately given the action an importance in practice that has no historical basis.[40]

The *General Instruction* adds that the gifts may be incensed once they are laid on the altar: "This is a symbol of the Church's offering and prayer going up to God." The deacon or other minister may then incense the priest and the people.[41]

2. The Private Prayers

The new Order of Mass still has three private prayers, which are to be said in a low voice.

I have already mentioned the first of these prayers; it accompanies the mixing of water with the wine. It is a shortened form of an ancient Roman prayer, the theological import of which is not very clear; the prayer still refers to "the mystery of this water and wine," as though to a sacrament that gives us a share in the divinity of Christ. Some translations therefore

---

38. This relation used to emerge in the act of bringing symbols of human toil to the altar or in the words of offertory songs: "Let us offer the Master our hearts on the paten with the host"; "The priest has put drops of water in his chalice with the wine; let us all bring our sacrifices." See B. Capelle, "Nos sacrifices et le sacrifice du Christ a la messe," in *La messe et sa catechese* (Lex orandi 7; Paris: Cerf, 1947), 154–79.

39. *GIRM* 133 (*DOL* 208 no. 1523).

40. See pp. 16, 78, and 157.

41. *GIRM* 51 (*DOL* 2108 no. 1441).

exercise freedom in handling this phrase; the French Missal, for example, says: "As this water is mixed with the wine for use in the sacrament of the covenant, so may we be united to the divinity of him who has taken our humanity."[42]

The second prayer is from the old offertory: "Lord God, we ask you to receive . . ." (*"In spiritu humilitatis . . ."*).[43]

The third accompanies the *Lavabo*, a rite that serves "as an expression of his [the priest's] desire to be cleansed within."[44] A verse from Psalm 51 replaces those from Psalm 26.[45]

While the element of *apologia* has become less obtrusive, it continues to play an important part in these private prayers of the celebrant.

3. The Orate, fratres *("Pray, brethren")*

This exhortation is now addressed to the entire congregation and not simply, as in the past, to the ministers at the altar. On the other hand, the request for prayers for the priest has become an invitation to enter into the Eucharistic action. Some expressions in the Latin text nonetheless betray the original intention of the prayer and are no longer well placed: *meum ac vestrum sacrificium* ("my sacrifice and yours" in the former English version of the prayer) and *de manibus tuis* ("at your hands," which is still found in the English). To the problems raised by these expressions we add the difficulty a congregation has in saying correctly a formula several lines in length.[46]

4. The Prayer over the Gifts

The prayer *Super oblata*, which concludes the preparation of the gifts, is no longer said in a low voice; in addition, it now has the short ending. The formularies for the prayer are generally taken from the treasures of antiquity.[47] In the Sanctoral this prayer does not refer, as the collect does, to the intercession of the saints; the saints are mentioned only to the extent that this makes it possible to enter more fully into the Eucharistic mystery. In the celebration of memorials that lack a proper of their own,

42. See the German Missal: "As water is united to wine to form a holy sign, so may this cup give us a share in the divinity of Christ who took our humanity."

43. Dan 3:16-17 (39-40): "With a contrite heart and a humble spirit may we be accepted . . . such may our sacrifice be in thy sight this day."

44. *GIRM* 52 (*DOL* 208 no. 1442).

45. Ps 51:2: "Wash me thoroughly from my iniquity, and cleanse me from my sin."

46. We can understand why the episcopal conferences of the French-speaking countries adapted the prayer rather than translated it: "Let us pray together, at the moment of offering the sacrifice of the entire Church — For the glory of God and the salvation of the world."

47. See n. 17, p. 197.

this prayer is taken either from the Common or from the weekday formulary.[48]

II. THE EUCHARISTIC PRAYER

BIBLIOGRAPHY

P. Jounel, "La composition des nouvelles prières eucharistiques," *LMD* no. 94 (1968) 38–76.
M. Thurian, "La théologie des nouvelles prières eucharistiques," *ibid.*, 77–102.

In its chapter on the Mass, the Constitution on the Liturgy did not order a revision of the Eucharistic Prayer. In the years after the Council, however, important decisions on this point were taken in the spirit that the Constitution had fostered. In 1967 it was decreed that the Canon might be said "audibly"[49] and that in Masses celebrated with a congregation it might be translated into the vernacular.[50] In 1968 three new formularies were provided, thus ending the Roman tradition that the anaphora should always be one and the same.[51] The publication of the new Missal in 1969 completed this work of renewal.

1. *Changes Affecting All the Eucharistic Prayers*

a) *The account of institution and the anamnetic acclamation.* The decision to use the same version of Christ's words at the Supper in all four texts entailed some changes in the Roman Canon or Eucharistic Prayer I. To the words *"Hoc est enim corpus meum"* ("This is my body") are now added *"quod pro vobis tradetur"* ("which will be given up for you"). This addition, which is in the New Testament accounts of Paul and Luke and has been taken over into almost all the Christian anaphoras, beginning with that of Hippolytus, expresses the reference to the paschal mystery; most of the Eastern anaphoras complete the reference by adding "for the forgiveness of sins."

The fact that the Eucharistic Prayer was now to be said aloud meant that the question of participation by the congregation was raised in new terms. As the reader knows, the Eastern liturgies customarily introduce Amens or other interventions by the people into the account of institu-

---

48. *GIRM* 323 (*DOL* 208 no. 1713).

49. Second Instruction *Tres abhinc annos* of the Consilium (May 4, 1967), no. 10 (= *EDIL* 819 = *DOL* 39 no. 456). This document also did away with all but the first of the signs of the cross in the Roman Canon.

50. *Ibid.*, no. 28a (= *EDIL* 837 = *DOL* 39 no. 474a). The decision depended on the episcopal conference.

51. Decree of the Congregation of Rites, May 23, 1968 (= *EDIL* 1032–43 = *DOL* 241 and 242).

tion or after the anamnesis or epiclesis. It is in this same spirit that the Eucharistic Prayers now include an acclamation addressed to Christ: it proclaims that he is alive even though he died and that we await his return. The Roman Missal provides three formulations of this idea; these have been freely translated in the various languages, as, for example, the first of them, which becomes in English: "Christ has died, Christ is risen, Christ will come again."[52]

On the other hand, it was thought that the words *mysterium fidei* ("the mystery of faith"), which used to be part of the consecration of the chalice,[53] should be omitted, since they gave the impression of being a foreign body in this context. However, the revisers did not want to omit them entirely and therefore placed them at the end of the account of institution, where they serve to introduce the acclamation of the faithful.

Finally, the Lord's command regarding repetition has been simplified and brought closer to the gospels. "Do this in memory of me" (*"Hoc facite in meam memoriam"*) replaces the more solemn "As often as you shall do these things, you shall do them in memory of me" (*"Haec quotiescumque feceritis, in mei memoriam facietis"*), which was closer to St. Paul.

b) *Increase in the number of prefaces.* The beginning of the Eucharistic Prayer is still called the "preface," because the term is a handy one. In the Roman tradition this part of the prayer has also been variable, but in the past the choices available were quite limited; at any given time there were usually about ten prefaces, though the number varied according to period and place. The new Missal has more than eighty, thus making it possible to express thanksgiving in ways more in harmony with the theology of the seasons and feasts; the prefaces endeavor to give a clear exposition of this theology. The authors of the prefaces have in large measure drawn their inspiration from ancient texts, but they have also freely altered these and made them integral parts of new compositions.[54]

2. *The New Eucharistic Prayers*

In addition to traits that they share with the Roman Canon, the three new prayers display common characteristics. First of all, the Holy Spirit

---

52. Latin: "Mortem tuam annuntiamus, Domine, et tuam resurrectionem confitemur, donec venias." French: "We proclaim your death, Lord Jesus, we celebrate your resurrection; we await your coming in glory." German: "We proclaim your death, Lord, and we extol your resurrection, until you come in glory."

53. The origin and meaning of the words are disputed. See B. Botte, *Le canon de la messe romaine. Edition critique, introduction et notes* (Textes et études liturgiques 2; Louvain: Mont César, 1935), 62. — J. Brinktrine, "Mysterium fidei," *EL* 44 (1930) 493–500. — B. Botte, "Mysterium fidei," *Bible et vie chrétienne* no. 80 (1968) 29–34.

54. The source studies listed in n. 17 of this chapter show only partial borrowings or implicit citations.

is explicitly invoked upon the bread and wine in order that he may change them into the Body and Blood of Christ. In order, however, to avoid rekindling old controversies about the moment of consecration, this epiclesis is placed just before the account of institution, so that it appears to be one with it. Justification for this decision can be found in the Alexandrian tradition.[55] After the anamnesis the Spirit is once again asked to come in order that he may sanctify the communicants. Here, for example, is the passage in Eucharistic Prayer (EP) IV:

> Father, may this Holy Spirit sanctify these offerings. Let them become the body and blood of Jesus Christ our Lord as we celebrate the great mystery which he left us as an everlasting covenant. . . .
>
> . . . and by your Holy Spirit gather all who share this one bread and one cup into the one body of Christ, a living sacrifice of praise.[56]

The intercessions, which form a single unbroken series, come after this last formula and therefore at the end of the anaphora, as in Antiochene practice.[57] Finally, the conclusion is always the same: "Through him, with him, in him . . .," as in the Roman Canon.

These similarities do not, however, exclude important differences between the various new Eucharistic Prayers.

The first of them (EP II) is an adaptation of the anaphora of Hippolytus of Rome[58]; the main change is the addition of the *Sanctus*[59] and the intercessions. The second of the new prayers (EP III) is a revised version of an anaphora that had been composed during the work of the Consilium as an alternative to the Roman Canon.[60] The last prayer (EP IV) is based on the structure found in such Eastern anaphoras as that of St. Basil. These differences in origin and style lead to divergent emphases in each part of the formulary.

a) *The expression of thanksgiving.* In keeping with Roman tradition, EP III allows no text a privileged place in the section preceding the *Sanc-*

---

55. See p. 101.

56. Latin: "Quaesumus igitur, Domine, ut idem Spiritus Sanctus haec munera sanctificare dignetur ut corpus et sanguis fiant Domini nostri Iesu Christi ad hoc magnum mysterium celebrandum, quod ipse nobis reliquit in foedus aeternum. . . . Concede benignus omnibus qui ex hoc uno pane participabunt et calice, ut, in unum corpus a Sancto Spiritu congregati, in Christo hostia viva perficiantur ad laudem gloriae tuae."

57. See p. 103.

58. See p. 26.

59. The Ethiopians, who use the prayer of Hippolytus, place the *Sanctus* between the evocation of the incarnation and that of the paschal mystery; the introduction in EP II of a preconsecratory epiclesis prevented this solution, and the hymn of the Seraphim has therefore been placed after the mention of the passion and resurrection.

60. See C. Vagaggini, *The Canon of the Mass and Liturgical Reform,* trans. P. Coughlin (Staten Island, N.Y.: Alba House, 1967). — P. Rouillard, *Le canon de la messe et la réforme liturgique* (Lex orandi 41; Paris: Cerf, 1967).

tus; instead there is a series of prefaces, as in EP I. It is also permitted to draw on this series of prefaces when using EP II, although the latter normally has its own proper preface. Hippolytus' prayer has been simplified in order to make it clearer; the presentation is distinctly christological: Jesus is the creative Word who became incarnate, and the image of the arms extended on the cross ("For our sake he opened his arms on the cross") dominates the evocation of the paschal mystery, which is seen as a manifestation of the resurrection ("he put an end to death and revealed the resurrection").

EP IV allows for no substitution, since what precedes and follows the hymn of the Seraphim forms a single whole. Contemplation of God as light and source of life ("you live in unapproachable light. Source of life . . ."), whose praises are sung by the angels that serve him day and night, leads, in the second part, to consideration of his human creatures to whom the world has been entrusted ("You . . . set him over the whole world") and whose glory it is, despite sin, to seek him ("You . . . helped all men to seek and find you"). This search, the landmarks of which are the biblical covenants ("Again and again you offered a covenant to man"), was brought to fruition by the love of Christ, whose teaching in the synagogue at Nazareth ("To the poor he proclaimed the good news of salvation, to prisoners, freedom, and to those in sorrow, joy") defined his mission. The culmination of this fulfillment came with Christ's sending of the Spirit "to complete his work on earth and bring us the fullness of grace."

b) *The words of consecration.* The old formula of transition, *Vere sanctus,* is used in EP II and III ("you are holy indeed"). It leads to the epiclesis ("Let your Spirit come upon these gifts . . ."; "We bring you these gifts. We ask you to make them holy . . ."), which in EP IV is attached to the preceding mention of the Holy Spirit ("Father, may this Holy Spirit . . ."). The epiclesis is followed by the account of institution, in which the words of Christ himself are the only thing the various formularies have in common. EP IV uses citations from John,[61] while EP II echoes the *Apostolic Tradition* ("Before he was given up to death, a death he freely accepted") and EP III makes use, in another form, of the Pauline inspiration at work in the Roman Canon ("On the night he was betrayed").[62]

c) *The anamnesis and the invocation of the fruits of sacrifice upon the communicants.* "Do this in memory of me." The commemoration of the Lord's death and resurrection in EP II ("in memory of his death and resurrection") is prolonged in EP III by expectation of his return ("and ready

---

61. John 17:1 and especially 13:1. The symbolism of the vine is also present in the expression *genimen vitis* ("fruit of the vine"), which is taken from Matt 26:29 or Mark 14:25.
62. 1 Cor 11:23.

to greet him when he comes again") and is enriched in EP IV by commemoration of the descent among the dead, the ascension, and the sitting
at the right hand of the Father.[63]

The commemoration is completed in the offering of the sacrifice by
those who, as EP II says, have been accounted "worthy to stand in your
presence and serve you." What is offered is, according to EP II, the bread
and chalice ("this life-giving bread, this saving cup") or, according to EP
III and IV, the "sacrifice" ("this holy and living sacrifice"; "the acceptable
sacrifice which brings salvation to the whole world"). This sacramental
language is, in the Roman tradition, always explained by naming the reality
that is hidden beneath the signs: "the sacred body and blood" (EP I). It
is by participating in the Body and Blood of the Lord (EP II: "May all
of us who share in the body and blood of Christ"; EP III: "we, who are
nourished by his body and blood"[64]), that the faithful receive, in the Spirit,
the grace of unity (EP II: "May all of us . . . be brought together in unity
by the Holy Spirit") and of themselves becoming a living sacrifice (EP IV).

d) *The intercessions.* In EP II the intercessions in a sense prolong the
second epiclesis: the unity that is the fruit of Eucharistic communion is
asked for the people of God in union with their pastors. In EP IV those
for whom the offering is made ("those for whom we offer this sacrifice")
form, as it were, concentric circles around the altar: first the ministers
("N. our Pope, N. our bishop, and bishops and clergy everywhere"), then
those who make the offering (we might say: those who have given a Mass
stipend—"those who take part in this offering"), then the congregation
("those here present") and all Christians ("and all your people"), and finally those who honestly seek God ("and all who seek you with a sincere
heart").

Thus, in accordance with the theology of Vatican II, prayer for the
living and dead members of the Church extends to those whose connection with the Body of Christ is invisible (EP III: "all your children wherever they may be"; EP IV: "those . . . whose faith is known to you alone")
and to those who have died in the love of the Lord (EP II: "bring them
and all the departed into the light of your presence"; EP III: "all who have
left this world in your friendship"). These invisible members are always
named after the "brethren" (EP II: "our brothers and sisters"; EP III: "the
entire people your Son has gained for you"; EP IV: "those who have died
in the peace of Christ").

The Church prays that all these individuals and groups may obtain

---

63. Latin: "Unde et nos, Domine, redemptionis nostrae memoriale nunc celebrantes,
mortem Christi eiusque descensum ad inferos recolimus, eius resurrectionem et ascensio-
nem ad tuam dexteram profitemur, et, exspectantes ipsius adventum in gloria. . . ."

64. See EP I: "as we receive from this altar the sacred body and blood of your Son. . . ."

the kingdom as their inheritance (EP II: "make us worthy to share eternal life"; EP III: "enable us to share in the inheritance of your saints"; EP IV: ". . . to enter into our heavenly inheritance"), together with the Mother of God, the apostles, and all the saints. EP III adds the martyrs and Saint N., that is, the saint being commemorated or one considered to be the special protector of the local community. In keeping with tradition, expression is thus given to our communion with the heavenly Church.

3. *The Embolisms in the Eucharistic Prayer*

Despite its unchanging character the Roman Canon was always characterized not only by variable prefaces but also by insertions that varied according to circumstances.[65] There are a good number of these insertions, or embolisms, in the Missal of Paul VI:

a) EP I. (1) In the account of institution on Holy Thursday; (2) in the *Communicantes* ("In union with the whole Church") on Christmas, Epiphany, Holy Thursday, Easter, Ascension, and Pentecost; (3) in the *Hanc igitur* ("Father, accept this offering") on Holy Thursday, Easter, and in Masses for baptism, confirmation, ordination, marriage, the consecration of virgins, and religious profession; (4) in the commemoration of the living at the celebration of adult baptism and in scrutiny Masses (prayer for the godparents).

b) EP II, III, and IV. In the intercessions in Masses for the dead (except in EP IV) and in Masses for adult baptism, the consecration of virgins, and religious profession.[66]

4. *The Choice of a Eucharistic Prayer*

In the Eastern liturgies the choice of anaphora is generally determined by the calendar. For the Roman Mass the *General Instruction* sets down some norms governing the use of each formulary, but, except for those determined by the very structure of EP IV, these norms speak only of appropriateness.[67] The essential criterion is pastoral; the spiritual good of the faithful must be the primary concern.[68]

---

65. See pp. 89 and 104.

66. The formulas given in the Missal for the new Eucharistic Prayers are thus less numerous than for EP I. Therefore the episcopal conferences of the French-speaking countries, following the lead of Germany, obtained permission on November 5, 1977, for embolisms in EP II and III wherever they are found in the Roman Canon and, in addition, one embolism for Sundays, corresponding to the one in the *Communicantes* of the Roman Canon.

67. According to *GIRM* 322 (*DOL* 208 no. 1712), EP I is preferable for days that have a special embolism, for feasts of the apostles and other saints mentioned in EP I, and for Sundays, unless some pastoral reason makes another EP preferable. EP II is better suited to weekdays and special circumstances, and EP III to Sundays and feastdays. EP IV is excluded on days that have a proper preface of their own.

68. It is also for pastoral reasons that permission was given, "as long as the Apostolic

III. THE COMMUNION

BIBLIOGRAPHY

R. Béraudy, "Les rites de préparation à la communion," *LMD* no. 100 (1969) 59–71.

S. Bianchi, "Offerte vobis pacem," *Notitiae* 65 (1971) 273–75.

A. Verheul, "L'ordonnance de la communion selon le nouvel *Ordo missae*," *QL* 53 (1972) 119–33.

H. Bohl, *Kommunionempfang der Gläubigen: Probleme seiner Integration in der Eucharistiefeier. Eine liturgiewissenschaftliche Untersuchung* (Disputationes theologicae 9; Frankfurt: P. D. Lang, 1980).

T. A. Krosnicki, *Ancient Patterns in Modern Prayer* (Studies in Christian Antiquity 19; Washington, D.C.: The Catholic University of America Press, 1973).

In the Order of Mass the communion is seen as the organic culmination of the entire celebration and the high point of the participation of the faithful. Preparation for it takes the form of rites that no longer overlap one another but form a series of ordered unities: the Our Father, the fraction or breaking of the bread, and the peace.

1. *The Our Father*

The entire congregation says or sings the Our Father. In the English Missal four versions of the introductory exhortation are given.[69] The embolism that follows upon the Our Father asks for deliverance from evil[70] and for peace in our day; it no longer includes mention of the saints as it did in the past, and it ends on an eschatological note with a citation of Titus 2:13: "as we wait in joyful hope for the coming of our Savior, Jesus Christ."[71]

The most important novelty here is that the people in their response use the doxology from the *Didache*. This is also found in some manuscripts of the Gospel of Matthew and traditionally follows the Lord's Prayer in

---

See does not judge otherwise," for three Eucharistic Prayers reserved "to Masses celebrated solely for children or for congregations made up primarily of children," and for two Eucharistic Prayers of Reconciliation which "may be used for special celebrations on the theme of reconciliation and repentance, especially during Lent, on the occasion of pilgrimages, and at spiritual gatherings" (Circular Letter of the Congregation for the Sacraments and Divine Worship, December 15, 1980). In addition the "Prayer for Large Gatherings" (granted to the Swiss dioceses on the occasion of their synod) can be celebrated in France (Decree of the same Congregation, February 2, 1978), as in some other countries.

69. The priest may also use a formula more adapted to the congregation: SCDW, Letter *Eucharistiae participationem* to the Presidents of the Episcopal Conferences, April 27, 1973, no. 14 (= *EDIL* 3050 = *DOL* 248 no. 1988).

70. The adjectives "past, present, and future" in the Missal of Pius V have been omitted.

71. Full text of Titus 2:13: "awaiting our blessed hope, the appearing of the glory of our great God and Savior, Jesus Christ."

most Eastern Churches and among the Protestants: "For the kingdom, the power, and the glory are yours, now and for ever."[72]

2. *The Peace*

The Order of Mass has once again turned this into a rite with meaning for the congregation as a whole. After the people have replied to the celebrant's wish ("The peace of the Lord be with you always. — And also with you"), the deacon or, if there is no deacon, the priest himself exhorts them: "Let us offer each other the sign of peace." The members of the congregation then exchange some sign of brotherhood and sisterhood with their neighbors. The form this takes is to be adapted to the sensibilities of various cultures ("according to local custom"[73]).

This sequence of actions is preceded by a prayer of the celebrant: "Lord Jesus Christ, you said to your apostles . . . ." This is another formula originating in the private devotions of the priest before communion,[74] but it has now acquired a different function: it is said aloud; it speaks of "our sins," not "my sins"; it has taken on the meaning of the ancient prayers "At the rite of peace" (*ad pacem*) in the Hispano-Gallican liturgy,[75] with this important difference that the text of it does not change.

3. *The Fraction or Breaking of the Bread*

The *General Instruction* seeks to restore the original meaning of this action: It is ". . . a sign that in sharing in the one bread of life which is Christ we who are many are made one body."[76] The passage also refers to a "practical aspect," which we can discover, I think, in the recommendation given by Vatican II: "The more complete form of participation in the Mass by which the faithful, after the priest's communion, receive the Lord's Body from the same sacrifice, is strongly endorsed."[77]

And in fact, even if for convenience' sake small hosts are used, it is still possible to use a few larger hosts that can be broken at Mass and shared with at least some of the communicants. The symbolism of the fraction is important enough in the ecclesial tradition to keep a celebrant from being deterred by a little inconvenience.

---

72. Latin: "Quia tuum est regnum, et potestas, et gloria in saecula." In the Eastern liturgies this doxology is an ecphonesis (prayer said aloud); it is reserved to the priest (so much so that in his absence it is omitted from the Office). The Roman liturgy has adopted a contrary usage by making it an acclamation of the congregation.

73. Order of Mass (no. 129). The exchange of a gesture of peace is not made obligatory.

74. See pp. 166–167.

75. See p. 114.

76. *GIRM* 56c (*DOL* 208 no. 1446c).

77. *VSC* 55 (*DOL* 1 no. 55).

The *Agnus Dei*, in keeping with its original intention, accompanies the rite of breaking the bread. The *General Instruction* remarks that "this invocation may be repeated as often as necessary" to allow time for breaking all the larger hosts.[78] It must be admitted, however, that this practice is not facilitated by the divergent text of the final formula in the series: "grant us peace" no longer has any meaning, now that the rite of peace has already been accomplished.

The priest still puts a particle in the chalice,[79] but the action passes almost unnoticed; the prayer accompanying the action no longer includes the word "consecration," which used to cause difficulty.[80]

4. The Immediate Preparation for Communion

It is appropriate that the actual communion be preceded by a moment of recollection. Meanwhile the priest chooses one of two prayers; he is to say it in a low voice,[81] since he must respect the other members of the assembly who are praying in silence[82] as they engage in intense spiritual preparation.

The celebrant then displays the Eucharistic bread to the faithful. To the words "This is the Lamb of God . . ." he adds a verse from the Apocalypse.[83] The response of the congregation is a single "Lord, I am not worthy . . .," and not a triple one as in the past. The verse from the Apocalypse, *"Beati qui ad cenam Agni vocati sunt,"* is difficult to translate in an unambiguous way, since it supposes a better than average biblical formation. For this reason our Missal has: "Happy are those who are invited to his supper."[84] The penitential tone that historical circumstances[85] had attached to this moment of the celebration needed

---

78. *GIRM* 56e (*DOL* 208 no. 1446e).

79. For the meaning of this rite see p. 111.

80. "May this mingling [and consecration] of the body and blood of our Lord Jesus Christ bring eternal life to us who receive it."

81. These are the second and third prayers of the Tridentine Order of Mass, *Domine Iesu Christe, Fili Dei vivi* and *Perceptio*. As we just saw, the first of the three has been made part of the rite of peace.

82. *GIRM* 56f (*DOL* 208 no. 1446f).

83. The verse is from Rev 19:9, omitting the word "marriage": "Blessed are those who are invited to the marriage supper of the Lamb."

84. Other Missals, the Italian and the French, for example, adopt the same solution and put this verse before the words, "Behold the Lamb of God . . .," and not after them as in the Latin. This was done for practical reasons: the people were accustomed to saying "Lord, I am not worthy" as soon as they heard the words "sins of the world"; in addition, the new order makes better sense. The German Missal takes a different line: The priest says, at first, only "This is the Lamb of God . . . sins of the world"; then, after the response, "Lord, I am not worthy . . .," he can add, "Happy they who are called to the marriage supper of the Lamb."

85. See p. 167.

this addition, which makes it somewhat like the "Holy things to the holy!" of the Eastern Christians.[86]

5. *Communion in the Body and Blood of Christ*

Here, more than elsewhere, there is a concern to get back to the sources[87]; this concern is evidenced, for example, by the restoration of the dialogue between the minister and the communicant who professes his or her faith in Christ: "The body of Christ. — Amen." Nor is this the only important alteration in the rite.

a) *Permission to receive Communion in the hand.* A number of episcopal conferences have expressed a desire for authority to permit those of the faithful who wish it to receive Communion in the hand. This faculty was given to the episcopal conference if they asked it (Congregation for Divine Worship, in a notification of April 3, 1985).

The original custom (Communion in the hand) was abandoned in the Middle Ages; the motive, which the medieval mind found congenial, was respect for the Eucharist. But the very same argument is invoked by many laypeople today for restoring the original practice: to open the mouth and stick out the tongue (they say) is not a gesture of respect; they find it difficult to do in a dignified way, because it is not a way in which they would spontaneously express veneration. They think it a much more "human" gesture to extend the hand, inasmuch as this action expresses a self-commitment. Evidently, different sensibilities are at work in the two practices.[88] For this reason the Church leaves it to each communicant to decide how he or she will express the common faith. It is not for the minister who distributes Communion to make this decision for them.

The ritual proposed for Communion in the hand is inspired by the description given in ancient texts, especially in the Jerusalem Catecheses from around the year 400.

b) *Communion in the chalice.* The Constitution on the Liturgy determined that in certain circumstances the faithful might have access to the chalice; the change implied no derogation from "the dogmatic principles laid down by the Council of Trent."[89] The number of cases in which the new rite might be practiced was extended in 1970.[90]

---

86. See p. 117.

87. See pp. 117–21.

88. Reactions sometimes take the form of an appeal to prescriptions dating from the Middle Ages and forbidding laypersons to touch the host or even the empty paten and chalice. The much older outlook, which the Church is asking us to rediscover, saw the matter in a different light: respect and adoration are to be found primarily in the human and spiritual intensity with which the gesture of receiving Christ's Body is made.

89. *VSC* 55 (*DOL* 1 no. 55).

90. SCDW, Instruction *Sacramentali communione* (June 29, 1970) (= *EDIL* 2144–53

It is true that the reality received is the same whether a person receives under one or both species. On the other hand, the sacrament's full wealth of meaning is brought out by the combined signs of bread and cup. In keeping with biblical symbolism, reception of the bread suggests above all a vital assimilation, a nourishment for a journey, and fellowship at the same table. Reception of the cup conjures up a feast that gives a foretaste of the banquet in the kingdom.

> Holy Communion has a more complete form as a sign when it is received under both kinds. For in this matter of reception . . . a fuller light shines on the sign of the eucharistic banquet. Moreover there is a clearer expression of that will by which the new and everlasting covenant is ratified in the blood of the Lord and of the relationship of the eucharistic banquet to the eschatological banquet in the Father's kingdom.[91]

c) *The ministers of Communion.* The rite of communion traditionally requires the mediation of a minister, thus making it clear that a gift is being received. Under normal conditions only bishops and priests take the sacrament for themselves directly from the table of sacrifice, since they are, in a way, one with the altar. The profession of faith made by the communicant who says "Amen" is in the form of a response to a dialogue involving another. All of the Christian liturgies bear witness, in their age-old practices, to these two modes of receiving Communion. These considerations make it clear that the "ordinary ministers" of the Eucharist are those who have received an ordination. Deacons can assist bishops and priests in distributing the Body of Christ, while by law it is their function to present the Precious Blood for reception; according to the *General Instruction* the deacon "gives communion to the people (in particular, ministering the chalice)."[92]

There may in fact not be enough "ordinary ministers" for the task. Then, rather than do without ministers and allow the faithful to take the bread or cup for themselves, the Church prefers to fall back on the service of the laity. This makes it possible for the brethren to receive Holy Communion from one of themselves and to say their "Amen" in response to a human voice that tells them that the bread and the cup are the Body and Blood of Christ. Evidently, the Church attaches great importance to this human mediation that is an integral part of the sacramental signs. In 1973 the Church specified the conditions in which "extraordinary

---

= *DOL* 270 nos. 2109–15). In France, the second edition of the *Missel Romain* (1975) adds some details on communion under both species.

91. SCR, Instruction *Eucharisticum mysterium* (May 25, 1967) no. 32 (= *EDIL* 930 = *DOL* 179 no. 1261).

92. *GIRM* 61 (*DOL* 208 no. 1451).

ministers" may exercise their function.[93] The bishops then further determined how the decree was to be applied: if there are among the laity any
who have been appointed acolytes, the ministry is to be entrusted to them;
the minister receives Communion from the priest whom he is to assist,
and the ciborium is then given to him.[94]

d) *Communion procession and communion song.* There is a "communion antiphon" that is symmetrical in structure with the entrance antiphon; it is always from the Bible or, in a few rare cases, heavily inspired
by the Bible, and is often from the gospels. Many Sunday Mass formularies provide a choice of two, one of which is from the psalter. This is
the song that should normally accompany the procession of the faithful
as they come up in an orderly manner to receive the Lord. This song, says
the *General Instruction,* ". . . is to express outwardly the communicants'
union in spirit by means of the unity of their voices, to give evidence of
joy of heart, and to make the procession to receive Christ's body more
fully an act of community."[95] When the antiphon is not sung, it is read
by one or more members of the congregation or, if this is not possible,
by the priest, in order to provide food for prayer during the ensuing silence.

6. After Communion

a) The deacon or priest purifies the paten and chalice at the side of
the altar or at the credence table; this can also be done after Mass.[96] To
this action of purification the Order of Mass attaches the last of the private prayers of the priest: "Lord, may I receive" (*"Quod ore sumpsimus"*).[97]

b) Then "the priest and people may spend some time in silent prayer.
If desired, a hymn, psalm, or other song of praise may be sung by the
entire congregation."[98] Recollection after reception of the Body of Christ
is so legitimate that it has quite frequently had a place in Christian devotion at the end of Mass. The name "thanksgiving" that has been given
to these moments of prayer is somewhat ambiguous, and it would be
preferable to reserve the name to the Eucharistic action. Fortunately, this
time of prayer can now be incorporated, to some extent at least, into the
celebration itself. This is one of those periods of silence, meant (as the

---

93. Sacred Congregation for the Discipline of the Sacraments, Instruction *Immensae caritatis* (January 29, 1973), section 1 (= *EDIL* 2969–76 = *DOL* 264 nos. 2074–81).

94. A ritual has been proposed for the installation of extraordinary ministers: "This is the bread of life. Go and serve your brothers and sisters at the table of the Lord."

95. *GIRM* 56i (*DOL* 208 no. 1446i).

96. *GIRM* 120 (*DOL* 208 no. 1510). The English Order of Mass even says "if possible at the side table." According to *GIRM* 147 (*DOL* 208 no. 1537), an acolyte may also purify the vessels.

97. See also *GIRM* 120 (*DOL* 208 no. 1510).

98. *GIRM* 56j (*DOL* 208 no. 1446j).

rubric makes clear) both for the celebrant and the entire assembly, that are a novelty in the Missal of Paul VI. This time of prayer may end with a hymn, especially if there has been no communion song; we should not forget, however, that preference is to be given to the communion song, whenever possible.

c) The "prayer after communion" or "postcommunion prayer" follows the same rules as the prayer over the gifts; the formularies of both have been constructed from other prayers in the euchology.[99]

IV. THE CONCLUDING RITES

BIBLIOGRAPHY

E. Moeller, "Les Bénédictions solennelles du nouveau missel romain," *QL* 52 (1971) 317–25.

P. Borella, "La benedizione della messa," *Ambrosius* 43 (1967) 7–36.

If announcements are to be made about coming assemblies or the life of the Christian community, they are normally made before the concluding rites. The latter are simply omitted if another liturgical action immediately follows, as it does on Holy Thursday, at funeral Masses, etc. The concluding rites include:

1. The celebrant's greeting.

2. The blessing which, if the celebrant chooses, can in certain circumstances take a more solemn form: After a diaconal exhortation, "Bow your heads and pray for God's blessing" (or some similar formula), the celebrant uses either a tripartite formula that is inspired by the ancient Gallican episcopal blessings, has three Amens from the congregation, and is followed by the usual Trinitarian blessing, or a "prayer over the people" (*oratio super populum*) that is again followed by the usual blessing.[100] The Missal provides the needed formularies in an appendix.

3. The dismissal, *"Ite missa est,"* which is usually translated by one or more other obviously Christian formula, according to the pattern of Eastern practice; for example, "Go in the peace of Christ."[101]

---

99. See the studies listed in n. 17 of this chapter and especially R. Falsini, *Commento alle orazioni dopo la comunione delle dominiche e delle feste* (Sussidi liturgico-pastorali 17; Milan: Opera della Regalità, 1967).

100. The Latin typical edition has a different form for solemn blessings, one that used to be in the Roman Ritual and the Dominican Missal: "May the blessing of almighty God, the Father, the Son, and the Holy Spirit, descend upon you and remain for ever." The English Missal gives the ordinary blessing.

101. The *Ite missa est* (or its adaptation in the vernaculars) is now never replaced by a different formula.

§5. Conclusion

Could the new Order of Mass have done a better job in implementing the program established by the Council? As it stands, it certainly provides ways for the faithful to participate and thus fulfills the primary aim set for it. It also brings into proper harmony the various functions exercised in the Eucharistic celebration: each minister and the congregation do what is proper to them, without the priest repeating it. For example, the priest listens to the readings, which relate to him as they do to all the baptized; he prays silently with the people instead of doing something else during these intervals; and so on. For these reasons, provided that the Eucharist is celebrated in accordance with the provisions and spirit of the Missal, we shall henceforth see realized one of the essential aims of the Constitution on the Liturgy:

> The Church, therefore, earnestly desires that Christ's faithful, when present at this mystery of faith, should not be there as strangers or silent spectators; on the contrary, through a good understanding of the rites and prayers they should take part in the sacred service conscious of what they are doing, with devotion and full involvement. They should be instructed by God's word and be nourished at the table of the Lord's body; they should give thanks to God; by offering the immaculate Victim, not only through the hands of the priest, but also with him, they should learn to offer themselves as well; through Christ the Mediator, they should be formed day by day into an ever more perfect unity with God and with each other, so that finally God may be all in all.[102]

---

102. *VSC* 48 (*DOL* 1 no. 48).

Chapter II

Eucharistic Concelebration

BIBLIOGRAPHY

P. De Puniet, "Concélébration liturgique," *DACL* 3 (1914) 2470-88.

L. Beauduin, "Concélébration eucharistique," *QL* 7 (1922) 275-85; 8 (1923) 23-34.

J. M. Hanssens, "De concelebratione eucharistica," *Periodica* 16 (1927) 143*-54*, 181*-210*; 17 (1928) 93*-127*; 21 (1932) 193*-219*.

B. Botte, "Note historique sur la concélébration dans l'Eglise ancienne," *LMD* no. 35 (1953) 9-23.

A. Raes, "La concélébration eucharistique des les rites orientales," *ibid.*, 24-47.

F. Vandenbroucke, "La concélébration, acte liturgique communautaire," *ibid.*, 48-55.

B. Schultze, "Das theologische Problem der Konzelebration," *Gregorianum* 36 (1955) 212-70.

A. G. Martimort, "Le rituel de la concélébration eucharistique," *EL* 77 (1963) 147-68.

P. Thion, "De la concélébration eucharistique," *Nouvelle revue théologique* 86 (1964) 579-607.

A. G. Martimort, "La concelebrazione eucaristica," in *Costituzione conciliare sulla sacra liturgia*, ed. F. Antonelli and R. Falsini (Sussidi liturgico-pastorali 7; Milan: Opera della Regalità, 1964), 237-40; 2nd rev. ed., *ibid.*; 3rd ed. (1965), 281-85.

P. Jounel, "La concélébration de la messe," *LMD* no. 83 (1965) 175-79.

A. King, *Concelebration in the Christian Church* (London: Mowbray, 1966).

B. Neunheuser, L. Della Torre, R. Falsini, E. Lanne, V. Joannes, A. Franquesa, and F. Dell'oro, *Théologie et pratique de la concélébration* (Paris: Mame, 1967).

S. Madeja, "Analisi del concetto di concelebrazione eucaristica nel Concilio Vaticano II e nella riforma liturgica postconciliare," *EL* 96 (1982) 3-56.

A. G. Martimort, "Le geste des concélébrants lors des paroles de la consécration: indicatif ou épiclétique?" *Notitiae* 18 (1982) 408-12.

The Constitution on the Liturgy speaks as follows: "Concelebration, which aptly expresses the unity of the priesthood has continued to this day as a practice in the Church of both East and West. For this reason

221

it has seemed good to the Council to extend permission for concelebration. . . ."[1]

The Council's words are an invitation to us to ask how the "unity of
the priesthood" was manifested at the altar in the early Church and then
how it has remained in use in the East and the West. After that we may
go on to see how the practice is understood in the current liturgical books.

§1. The "Unity of the Priesthood" at the Altar in the Early Church

Without asking whether ancient practices fit the definition we may give
of concelebration today,[2] it will be worth our while to ask how the "unity
of the priesthood," which, according to the Council, concelebration "aptly
expresses," was implemented at that time. The Council's view is doubtless based on the strong convictions expressed by St. Ignatius of Antioch
as far back as the first years of the second century. "Be careful to take
part in but a single Eucharist; for there is but a single flesh of our Lord
Jesus Christ, a single chalice in which we are united with his blood, and
a single altar, just as there is a single bishop with his presbyterium and
deacons, who are my companions in service."[3]

This passage doubtless envisages more than concelebration, since the
unity in question includes the deacons and is an ideal set before the people
as a whole. At the same time, however, it does affirm the principle of
a single altar, which most of the Eastern Churches have respected down
to our own time. Not until the *Apostolic Tradition* of Hippolytus of Rome
(*ca.* 225), however, are we given more specific information on the participation of priests in the bishop's Mass. Here the text of the Eucharistic
Prayer, which we read early in this book,[4] is preceded by a rubric: "The
deacons are then to present him [the newly consecrated bishop] with the
oblation. Laying hands upon it, together with the entire presbytery, he
is to say the thanksgiving."[5] The gesture is made by all, but the bishop
alone pronounces the words.

The *Teaching of the Apostles*, which is almost as early but comes from
a quite different milieu, shows a bishop welcoming a traveling colleague
and having him say the thanksgiving or, if he refuses this honor, inviting

1. VSC 57 (DOL 1 no. 57).

2. The verb *concelebrare* made its appearance only in the Middle Ages; the Greek equivalent, *sylleitourgein*, is found in the ninth century in Photius.

3. St. Ignatius of Antioch, *Ad Philad.* 4, ed. and French trans. P. T. Camelot (SC
10; Paris: Cerf, 1951), 142–45.

4. See pp. 26–27.

5. *Traditio apostolica* 4 (Botte 10–11); trans. in L. Deiss, *Springtime of the Liturgy*, 129.

him at least to pronounce the words over the chalice.[6] We have no other witness to such a practice, nor are we even sure that it does not spring from the compiler's imagination.[7] At least, however, it shows a conviction that could hardly have surprised anyone: the two celebrants offer a single sacrifice and act as men exercising a single priestly ministry.

The passage calls to mind a story told by St. Irenaeus: the bishops of Rome and Smyrna in the second century were in disagreement on the question of the date of Easter. Nonetheless "they remained in communion with each other, and in church Anicetus made way for Polycarp to celebrate the Eucharist—out of respect, obviously."[8] Not only did they admit one another to communion with them (the word *koinōnein* does not necessarily mean communion in the sense of participation in the Body and Blood of Christ), but the pope allowed his guest to act as president at the Eucharist, a prerogative of the leader of the local community. It is clear, of course, that we cannot think of them reciting the sacramental formulas together; these formulas were not yet fixed, any more than they were in the time of Hippolytus and the *Teaching of the Apostles*.

Nor did the manner of concelebration change once the sacramental formulas became fixed. The Jerusalem Catecheses show the deacon washing the hands of the bishop and priests around the altar, and Pseudo-Dionysius not only mentions the same rite but explains its meaning: "Those about to enter upon the sacred action must be purified."[9] It was not necessary, therefore, for a man to pronounce the formulas in order to be regarded as an agent of the *hierurgia* or sacred action.

At the Council of Constantinople in 680, a Latin bishop, Fortunius of Carthage, celebrated with the Greeks, although he certainly did not know their language well enough to be able to read the anaphora. The only question that arose as he was about to celebrate (*"mellontos autou leitourgein"*) was whether his place should be in front of or behind the metropolitans present.[10] A comparable case comes to light later on in a letter that Pope John VIII wrote in answer to a complaint of Photius: two Roman priests sent as legates were unwilling to celebrate with the patriarch: *"sylleitourgēsai soi"* or, as the original Latin has it, *"tecum . . . consecrare."*[11]

---

6. *Didascalia Apostolorum* II, 58, 3 (Funk 1:168).

7. The *Constitutiones Apostolorum* (Funk 1:169) replace the thanksgiving over the chalice with a blessing of the people.

8. According to a fragment preserved in Eusebius of Caesarea, *Historia ecclesiastica* V, 24, 17, trans. by G. A. Williamson, *The History of the Church* (Baltimore: Penguin Books, 1965), 233.

9. St. Cyril of Jerusalem, *Catecheses mystagogicae* V, 2 (SC 126: 146–49). — Pseudo-Dionysius, *De ecclesiastica hierarchia* III, 10 (PG 3:437 and 440).

10. Mansi 11:593.

11. Mansi 17:413 (Greek text) and PL 126:871 (Latin text).

Rome thus regarded this manner of "concelebrating" as legitimate, since the refusal of the pope's representatives was not based on a discrepancy in rites. Nonetheless, the West was already familiar with a quite different practice. *Ordo Romanus* (*OR*) III, which seems to date from the eighth century, describes the ceremonial of the stational Masses on the major feasts of the year: the cardinal priests stand around their bishop at the altar and say the Canon with him while holding three loaves; they were thus unable to make any gestures but were united to the president through their words.[12] This text has come down as a codicil to *OR* I and is almost contemporary with it; the latter, however, specifies that the pope alone straightens up after the *Sanctus*; the other bishops and priests remain bowed, which would seem to exclude their vocal participation in the prayer.[13] Did the change in ritual take place between the dates when these two texts were redacted, or may we think that despite the divergence in texts the change occurred earlier? In any case, the spoken form of concelebration was not primitive.

§2. The Continuance of "Concelebration"

1. *In the East*

Practices vary widely among the Churches. Among the Eastern Syrians, Copts, and Ethiopians, the presiding bishop appoints one of the priests to say the anaphora and carry out all the functions of the "celebrant." Other priests may be at the altar with him; they will have actions to perform, but none that seems closely connected with the consecration.[14]

In the Byzantine rite the bishop is the principal celebrant. Except in the Russian Church, the present-day practice is to distribute the ecphoneses among the various officiants; the latter also say certain formulas in a low voice, but not during the anaphora. They can also add to the commemorative particles of the proscomide, since, as Symeon of Thessalonica (fifteenth century) says, they are capable of offering sacrifice (*prospherein*), whereas deacons are not.[15] But these practices are latecomers on the scene; the fur-

---

12. *OR* III, 1 (Andrieu, *OR* 2:131): "They say the canon together with him . . . so that the voice of the pope is louder, and together they consecrate the body and blood of the Lord." What precisely did they say together? Only the Eucharistic Prayer, probably to the exclusion of the introductory dialogue and the singing of the preface.

13. *OR* I, 88 (Andrieu, *OR* 2:95–96). The codicil deals with Easter day, that is, one of the feasts with which *OR* III is concerned.

14. In certain circumstances the Western Syrians and Ethiopians celebrate "synchronized Masses": several priests celebrate at separate altars or the same altar, each having his own gifts that he consecrates. This is the only departure from the principle of a single altar.

15. Symeon of Thessalonica, *De sacra liturgia* (PG 155:289).

ther back we go in time, the more limited and unobtrusive becomes the role of those gathered around the table of the Divine Liturgy.

Among the Slavs, on the other hand, the concelebrants join in saying the most important parts of the Eucharistic Prayer, and especially the words "Take, eat . . ." and "Drink, all of you . . . ." The rubrics require that no one either get ahead of the president or lag behind him. The concelebrants also say the formulas of the epiclesis in a low voice. These practices, however, do not go back beyond the seventeenth century; in them is doubtless to be seen the influence of the school of Kiev and Patriarch Peter Moghila (1633–46), who were in turn influenced by Western theology. Similar practices are found among the Greek Catholics, the Maronites, and the Copts who are in union with Rome.

The rites that have recently adopted the practice of vocal participation by all the concelebrants claim justification in the ancient tradition of their Churches. They do not think, therefore, that the introduction of vocal participation (due probably to theological tutiorism) means a profound departure from what had been done previously.

2. *In the West*

In Gaul "concelebration" seems to have fallen into disuse by the time the Roman liturgy was introduced there. The ultimate explanation of this phenomenon must have been the fact that rural communities were so widely scattered. The dispersion created a situation that, in many other parts of the Church as well, led to abandonment of the primitive rule of the single Mass. Thus St. Leo advised the Patriarch of Alexandria to repeat the Eucharist on major feast days, lest a part of the population be deprived of it, since even the largest churches could not hold all the people.[16] Another factor was the devotion of Christians who wanted Mass celebrated for special intentions.

Traces of the ancient practice nonetheless survived in the Middle Ages on major solemnities and especially on Holy Thursday, when the collegial blessing of the oil of the sick led to a collegial celebration of the Canon, into which the rite of blessing was inserted. This Holy Thursday practice is still attested in some cathedrals of eighteenth-century France, and has continued in Lyons down to our own day. Rome perhaps continued to have newly consecrated bishops and newly ordained priests concelebrate the Mass at which they received the sacrament; alternatively, the practice reappeared and spread, due to the pontificals of the twelfth and thirteenth centuries.

According to the rubrics, all the concelebrants were to say, half-aloud, all the prayers from the offertory on; in some places there was even a

---

16. St. Leo the Great, *Ep. ad Dioscurum Alexandrinum* (PL 54:626).

tendency to extend this practice to the entire celebration, including the sung parts, which the concelebrants executed as a choir. The ceremonial underwent all kinds of alteration, even to the point of having the priests receive Communion while kneeling, and in the form of bread only.

St. Thomas mentions only the concelebration of the newly ordained, and this only "in certain Churches." On the other hand, he gives an important theological explanation when he calls attention to the fact that "the priest consecrates in the person of Christ" and that "many are but one in Christ"; consequently "it does not matter whether one or many consecrate, provided the rite of the Church is followed." He goes on to say that the Eucharist "is the sacrament of ecclesial unity, which comes from the fact that many are one in Christ."[17]

In the pontificate of Pius XII the liturgical movement was creating a desire for the extension of concelebration, while at the same time historical research and the science of comparative liturgy were raising the problem of the forms concelebration might take. In 1956 the pope gave the following definition:

> In the case of a concelebration in the proper sense of the term Christ acts not through one minister but through several. It is not enough for the concelebrants to have and manifest the intention of making their own the words and actions of the celebrant; they must themselves say the words "This is my body," "This is my blood," over the bread and wine, or their concelebration will be limited to the realm of external ceremonial.[18]

It is clear that this declaration was not a basis for passing judgment on earlier practices. The issue was one of positive law: it is for the Church, to which the administration of the sacraments has been entrusted, to decide on the words and actions of the concelebrants. The decision of Pius XII nonetheless provided the framework within which Vatican Council II approached the subject.

§3. The Present Ritual of Concelebration

The Constitution on the Liturgy ordered that a new rite of concelebration be composed and introduced into the Pontifical and the Roman Missal.[19] The new rite was in fact published as early as 1965[20] and is

---

17. St. Thomas Aquinas, *Summa theologiae* III, 82, 2, ad 2 et 3; see his *In IV Sent.*, d. 13, q. 1, a. 2, qc. 2.

18. Address to the Assisi Congress (September 22, 1956): *AAS* 48 (1956) 718.

19. *VSC* 58 (*DOL* 1 no. 58).

20. SCR, Introduction, *Ritus servandus in concelebratione missae* (March 7, 1965) General Decree (= *EDIL* 387–92 = *DOL* 223).

remarkable for the harmony it establishes between precise rubrics and a wide freedom of choice. It describes the course of the action in an episcopal Mass, a Mass with a deacon, a Mass sung or read. Concelebration introduces desirable modifications into the rites of episcopal and presbyteral ordination as well as the blessing of an abbot. It also provides a solution for cases of sick or blind priests who can now participate in the sacrifice along with a healthy principal celebrant.

The prescriptions of the 1965 document have been made part of the *General Instruction of the Roman Missal*, where account is also taken of the new Eucharistic Prayers that were introduced in 1968.[21] Everything is organized in such a manner as to emphasize the unity both of the ministerial priesthood and of the sacrifice of the Lord. We may note, for example, that during a concelebration no private Mass may be celebrated at the same time in the same church.[22]

1. *The Principal Celebrant*

This function is normally a prerogative of the local bishop or, in his absence, another bishop. He is then the real president of the concelebration, and the college of priests around him is one with him. When he is not there, the presidency may be said to be collective, since the principal celebrant in this case is only a first among equals; any priest may fill the role and, if there were no practical difficulties involved, he could even be appointed at the last moment, as is done in some Eastern Churches. In any case, it is important that this collegial ministry be symbolized by a person who alone greets the congregation, dialogues with them, pronounces the exhortations and presidential prayers (except for the few that are said by all the concelebrants), shows the consecrated bread and wine to the people, and blesses the congregation.

2. *The Other Concelebrants*

All the concelebrants share in the common action but in ways which it is for the Church to determine. The Church could have done otherwise, but the following are in fact the decisions it has legitimately made in determining the conditions for concelebration.

a) *The words.* Some are said by all together; specifically, these are the words that are the very heart of the Eucharistic Prayer: the first epicle-

---

21. *GIRM* 153–208 (*DOL* 208 nos. 1543–98).
22. See *VSC* 57, 2 (*DOL* 1 nos. 57, 2).

sis,[23] the account of institution, the anamnesis and second epiclesis,[24] as well as the concluding doxology. It is also decreed that "the parts said by the concelebrants together are to be recited in such a way that the concelebrants say them in a softer voice and the principal celebrant's voice stands out clearly . . . the congregation should be able to hear the text without difficulty."[25] Other prayers are distributed among the various concelebrants: specifically, the intercessions of the anaphora.

b) *The gestures.* The concelebrants take their places around the altar after the preparation of the gifts. This does not mean that they stand close up to it; on the other hand, the other ministers, even the deacons (except at moments when their functions require them to stand next to the principal celebrant), are to avoid positioning themselves between the concelebrants and the table of sacrifice.

Two gestures give expression to the participation of the concelebrants. The first prayer recited in common is said "with hands outstretched toward the offerings" (*"manibus ad oblata extensis"*).[26] This gesture is understood as an imposition of hands; it is the gesture which the old Order of Mass prescribed at the *Hanc igitur* of the Roman Canon and which has now been shifted to the following prayer in EP I. It calls to mind the rubric from the *Apostolic Tradition* of Hippolytus that was mentioned at the beginning of this chapter.

Secondly, "while saying the words of the Lord, each extends his right hand toward the bread and toward the chalice, if this seems appropriate" (*"manu dextra, si opportunum videtur, ad panem et calicem extensa"*).[27] Although the meaning of this gesture has been disputed, we should look for an explanation to the response given in 1965 to a question on the subject, since, despite its unofficial character, the response does bring out the meaning that the *Ritus* intended the gesture to have. The meaning is different from that of the preceding gesture: "The palm of the hand is to be turned to the side and not to the floor, in order that the act may be understood as a gesture of pointing, in keeping with the words, 'This is . . . .' "[28] We cannot but think of the attitude of the Byzantine priest who

---

23. In the Roman Canon this is the prayer *Quam oblationem* ("We pray you, O God"). The *Ritus servandus* of 1965 included the *Hanc igitur* ("We therefore beg you") as well, but this was subsequently withdrawn, since it is a prayer of intercession (see p. 104) that is said by the principal celebrant alone.

24. In the Roman Canon the anamnesis and second epiclesis are the three prayers that follow the account of institution.

25. *GIRM* 170 (*DOL* 208 no. 1560). Most of these formulas can also be sung.

26. *GIRM* 174a, 180a, 184a, 188a (*DOL* 208 nos. 1564a, 1570a, 1574a, 1578a).

27. *GIRM* 174c, 180c, 184c, 188c (*DOL* 208 nos. 1564c, 1570c, 1574c, 1578c).

28. *Notitiae* 1 (1965) 143.

at this point extends two fingers (the others being folded back) toward the offerings.

In addition to these two gestures there is a deep bow after each of the two elevations and during the *Supplices* ("Almighty God, we pray") of the Roman Canon (EP I).

c) *Communion and Substitutions*. The concelebrants receive Communion under both species; the ceremonial for communion allows wide freedom of choice. If a bishop presides, it is appropriate that the priests receive the consecrated bread from him; otherwise they take it themselves from the altar or from the paten as they pass it among themselves. Then all communicate themselves at the same time. The cup is presented to them by the deacon; it can also be left on the table of sacrifice, while the concelebrants approach it in order.

One or other concelebrant can also substitute in other functions: for example, preaching the homily or, if there is no deacon, reading the gospel or offering the chalice to the other priests and, if required, to the congregation.

d) *Vestments*. The concelebrants vest as if they were celebrating alone; however, for a good reason, they may simply wear a stole over an alb.[29]

3. *The Congregation*

The activity of the celebrants has its place within the activity of all present. They take part in the singing of the people, and especially the singing of the *Sanctus*, unless the response in question is being given to their own joint prayer (the anamnetic acclamation, the Amen at the end of the anaphora). In addition, the congregation should be helped by an appropriate catechesis to unite themselves to the celebration; the concelebrants, for their part, should form a half-circle that is open to the body of the church where the faithful are. For the unity that is expressed in the rite of concelebration embraces the entire priestly people as they gather around those who have received the grace of presiding at the rite.

§4. Conclusion

The Instruction *Eucharisticum mysterium* of 1967 speaks as follows of concelebration:

> Unless the needs of the faithful (which must always be regarded with a deep pastoral concern) rule it out, then, and without prejudice to the option of every priest to celebrate Mass individually, this excellent way for priests to celebrate Mass is preferable in the case of communities of priests, their

---

29. *GIRM* 161 (*DOL* 208 nos. 1551).

periodic meetings, or in other similar circumstances. Those who live in community or serve the same church should gladly welcome visiting priests to concelebrate with them.[30]

---

30. SCR, Instruction, *Eucharisticum mysterium* (May 25, 1967) no. 47 (= *EDIL* 945 = *DOL* 179 no. 1276).

WORSHIP OF THE EUCHARIST OUTSIDE MASS

Introduction

The Council of Trent not only inspired the publication of a new Missal, which appeared in 1570 under the name of Pius V; it was also the occasion for the publication of the *Roman Ritual* that was promulgated in 1614 by Pius' ninth successor, Paul V.[1] The Ritual was revised after Vatican Council II, but, unlike its predecessor, only part by part. The essential content of Section ("Title") V of the old Ritual appeared in revised form in 1973 as *Holy Communion and Worship of the Eucharist Outside Mass.* The document begins with a General Introduction, but each of its four chapters, except the last, also has introductory remarks.[2]

The Eucharist is, of course, first of all the celebration of the sacrifice of Christ, in which the faithful participate primarily by receiving Communion at it. Since early times, however, this liturgical action has been prolonged in various ways, inasmuch as when the action is completed, not all of the consecrated offerings have necessarily been consumed. I have already referred several times to such extensions in connection with the *Sancta*[3] and even the *fermentum*[4] as well as with adoration of the Blessed

---

1. Unlike the other Tridentine books the Ritual was not imposed on the various Churches, but simply proposed to them. This accounts for the continuance of divergent usages.

2. *De sacra communione et de cultu mysterii eucharistici extra missam*, published June 21, 1973 (Vatican City: Vatican City Press, 1973). English translation in: *The Rites of the Catholic Church*, trans. The International Commission on English in the Liturgy, I (New York: Pueblo, 1976), 449–512, but with a revised translation of chapter I (Holy Communion Outside Mass) in *DOL* 266 nos. 2091–2103. The document will henceforth be cited as *Holy Communion*. The four chapters are entitled: 1. Holy Communion Outside Mass; 2. Administration of Communion and Viaticum to the Sick by an Extraordinary Minister; 3. Forms of Worship of the Holy Eucharist; 4. Texts for Use in the Rite of Distributing Holy Communion Outside Mass and in the Worship and Procession of the Blessed Sacrament.

3. See p. 112.

4. See p. 111.

Sacrament.[5] Attitudes to these practices have not been the same, however, at all times and in all places. There was need, therefore, as we enter a new stage of liturgical history, of establishing some essential orientations:

> The primary and original reason for reservation of the Eucharist outside Mass is the administration of viaticum. The secondary reasons are the giving of communion and the adoration of our Lord Jesus Christ who is present in the sacrament. The reservation of the sacrament for the sick led to the praiseworthy practice of adoring this heavenly food in the Churches.[6]

In fact, Viaticum has been brought to the dying at all times and in all places. Communion outside Mass is also an ancient custom on days when Mass is not celebrated or when a person is prevented from attending Mass. On the other hand, adoration as we conceive it today derives from earlier practices and was introduced at a later time. Nor did adoration become widespread in all the Churches, though this fact does not make the practice any less legitimate or solidly based. First of all, therefore, I shall discuss the various forms of communion outside Mass; a second chapter will take up the question of adoration of the Blessed Sacrament.

---

5. See p. 177.
6. *Holy Communion* 5 (p. 456).

Communion Outside Mass

"Next, the gifts, which have been "eucharistified" are distributed, and everyone shares in them, while they are also sent via the deacons to the absent brethren." Such is the ending of the oldest description (second century) of the Mass that has come down to us.[1] It was thus possible to receive Communion without having been part of the assembly; at the same time, however, the organic link with the celebration of the Eucharist was evident to all.

§1. Viaticum and Communion of the Sick

BIBLIOGRAPHY

E. Martène, *De antiquis Ecclesiae ritibus*, Lib. I, c. 5, a. 5; M 583.

H. Leclercq, "Communion des absents," *DACL* 3 (1914) 2437-40.

_____, "Communion des mourants," *ibid.*, 2446-47.

L. Beauduin, "Le viatique," *LMD* no. 15 (1948) 117-29.

A. G. Martimort, "Comment meurt un chrétien," *LMD* no. 44 (1955) 5-28.

Viaticum and communion of the sick are not necessarily communions outside Mass, since the Eucharist can be celebrated in the place where the dying and the sick are; the rites for such celebrations are described in the *Rite of Anointing and Pastoral Care of the Sick*.[2] The usual practice,

---

1. St. Justin, *Apologia I* 67; see p. 16.

2. *Ordo unctionis infirmorum eorumque pastoralis cura*, published December 7, 1972 (Vatican City: Vatican City Press, 1972). English translation in: *The Rites of the Catholic Church* I, 573-642, but with a revised translation of the introduction in *DOL* 410, nos. 3321-61. Chapter I is on the visitation and communion of the sick; Chapter III is on Viaticum. The document will henceforth be cited as *Rite of Anointing.*

however, is to bring the sacred species from the church to the sick or dying; for this reason I discuss this matter here.

1. *Viaticum*

Viaticum is a solemn communion. Thus while the Tridentine Ritual dealt with it under the heading of *Communion of the Sick*, it nonetheless devoted a special chapter to it. The new *Rite of Anointing* says: "When in their passage from this life Christians are strengthened by the body and blood of Christ in viaticum, they have the pledge of the resurrection that the Lord promised: 'Those who eat my flesh and drink my blood have eternal life, and I will raise them up on the last day' (John 6:54)."[3]

The Church's concern to make this unparalleled source of strength available to the dying faithful goes back to the earliest times. Thus when the Council of Nicaea in 325 ordered that Viaticum not be refused to penitents, it spoke of it as a well established custom: "As to those who are departing from this life, the old canonical law is now to be kept. If anyone is about to die he should not be deprived of the ultimate and most necessary viaticum."[4]

The entire tradition shows the same emphasis on the necessity of this sacrament; it is a necessity that overrides all ecclesiastical laws, such as the Eucharistic fast in periods when this was quite rigorous, or the prohibition against receiving more than once on the same day, or even, for a priest, the law against celebrating more than once, if a second celebration should be required in order that a Christian not have to leave this life without having received the Body of the Lord. The lives of the saints, though sometimes full of legends, constantly mention the fact that these men and women received Viaticum before breathing their last.

This communion is solemn not only in its meaning but also in its ceremonial. In times when Christendom was still a reality, the solemnity was shown especially in the very visible procession of the priest with the Eucharist; his passage caught the attention and inspired the prayers of the faithful for the brother or sister who was preparing to fall asleep in Christ. This outward display is for the most part no longer possible today, but the special character of this liturgical act finds expression in ways that are even more essential and that distinguish it from the ordinary communion of the sick.

The first and foremost of these distinguishing marks is the profession of baptismal faith that is made whenever there is a "solemn communion,"

---

3. *Rite of Anointing* 26 (*DOL* 410 no. 3346).

4. Council of Nicaea, can. 13 (DS 129). Translated in J. Neuner and J. Dupuis, *The Christian Faith in the Doctrinal Documents of the Catholic Church* (Staten Island, N.Y.: Alba House, 1982), no. 1602 (p. 449).

especially at the Easter Vigil; this was an ancient practice that had fallen into disuse except among some religious and in the case of Viaticum given to bishops.[5] A further distinguishing mark is the formula spoken by the minister in giving the consecrated bread to the dying person: after "The body of Christ. — Amen," the minister adds: "May the Lord Jesus Christ protect you and lead you to eternal life."[6] Also to be noted is the instruction that begins the rite; here the priest urges those present to pray for the dying person, and describes this food for the last journey as a pledge of resurrection and a source of strength for the passage from this world to the Father's house.[7] Finally, there is the closing prayer:

> Father, your Son, Jesus Christ, is our way, our truth, and our life. Our brother (sister), N., entrusts himself (herself) to you with full confidence in all your promises. Refresh him (her) with the body and blood of your Son and lead him (her) to your kingdom of peace. We ask this through Christ our Lord. — Amen.[8]

2. *Communion of the Sick*

Except for the details just mentioned, the rite of viaticum is the same as for other communions of the sick. The latter ceremonial has taken various forms in the course of time: when possible, the suffering Christian used to be brought to the church; sometimes Mass was celebrated in his or her home, and the same possibility is expressly allowed in the new Ritual in case of a dying person.[9] The most convenient method, however, and therefore the one most favored, has been to bring the reserved Eucharist to the sick person.

Though communion under the species of bread alone was practiced from a very early date, communion in the chalice was also in use down to the twelfth century, as is attested by many hagiographical writings of the early Middle Ages and a number of *Ordines*.[10] In some cases, the Body

---

5. *Caeremoniale episcoporum*, published by Clement VIII in 1600, Liber 2, c. 38, n. 3.

6. *Rite of Anointing* 112 (p. 613).

7. *Ibid.*, 103 (p. 610).

8. *Ibid.*, 114 (p. 613). Note that the plenary indulgence for the dying may serve as a conclusion for the penitential rite.

9. *Ibid.*, 97–99 (pp. 608–9). The Mass is celebrated in white vestments; if the calendar allows, a special formulary can be used (*The Sacramentary*, Masses for Various Needs and Occasions, Section 4, Mass "for a happy death"); all present can receive under both species.

10. The expression *dominicum corpus* ("body of the Lord") is sometimes misleading, because it can in fact refer to both species. See *Vita sanctae Odilae* 22 (MGH, *Script. rer. merov.* 6:50): the saint's companions "said that they acted in this way lest they be accused of negligence if she should die without receiving the body of the Lord. She bade them bring the chalice in which the Lord's body and blood were contained, and took it into her hands; after receiving holy communion, she surrendered her soul in the sight of all."

and Blood of the Lord were received separately, with two different formulas.[11] But the bread could also be moistened in the chalice, so that the sick who had difficulty with solid food might swallow it more easily.[12] For this same reason, present law allows Communion to be received under the species of wine alone.[13]

In the new rite[14] the initial greeting ("Peace to this house and to all who live in it" or "The peace of the Lord be with you") and, if it be thought opportune, the sprinkling with holy water are followed by the *Confiteor* with its *Misereatur*, a short reading from Scripture, the Our Father, and the formulas used at Mass: "This is the Lamb of God. . . . Happy are those . . . . Lord, I am not worthy . . . . The Body of Christ. — Amen." (An abridged rite contains only these formulas from Mass.[15]) The celebration ends with a prayer.

3. The Minister

Starting in the Carolingian age the bringing of Communion to the sick and dying became the exclusive prerogative of priests, as we can see in, for example, the *Capitula* of Hincmar of Rheims (ninth century): "Does the priest visit the sick? Does he personally, and not through another, anoint the sick with holy oil and give them communion? Does he likewise give communion to the people and not entrust this ministry to a layperson, allowing the latter to take the Eucharist home because someone there is sick?"[16]

From that time on even deacons were excluded from this function under normal circumstances. The Ritual of Pius V subsequently designated them as "extraordinary ministers" in case of necessity but only with permission of the bishop or parish priest.[17] The other faithful were no longer permitted even to touch the host; the only exceptions were in cases of extreme urgency, as in times of persecution.

The situation had been quite different before the Carolingian period. While bishop and priests were evidently the only ones with power to con-

---

11. See the Ritual of Saint-Remi in Rheims (eleventh century) (PL 78:530).

12. See the Eleventh Council of Toledo (675), can. 11, ed. J. Vives, *Concilios visigóticos . . .*, 364–65. In other cases, the minister was content to dip the host in unconsecrated wine, and it was thought that the wine was then consecrated by contact. See the Pontifical of the thirteenth-century Roman Curia, 50 (Andrieu, *PR* 2:493): "Let the priest give him the Eucharist of the Lord's body dipped in wine as well as the wine that has been sanctified by this intinction."

13. *Rite of Anointing* 46 and 95 (pp. 594 and 608).

14. *Ibid.*, 49–58 (pp. 594–97).

15. *Ibid.*, 59–63 (p. 598).

16. Hincmar of Rheims, *Capitula* (PL 125:779).

17. *Rituale Romanum* of 1614, tit. 5, c. 1, n. 12.

secrate, and while it was for them and the deacons to distribute the Body and Blood of Christ at the celebration of the Eucharist, the laity not infrequently took Communion for themselves outside Mass or brought it to the sick. That is how many received Viaticum, as the hagiographical writings make clear.[18]

The new ritual explicitly provides that in the absence of ordained ministers or duly appointed acolytes, others of the faithful may carry out this ministry. It is enough that they have received delegation (which may be general) for the purpose. In fact, there is even a special ceremonial for acolytes or extraordinary ministers.[19]

§2. Communion in the Home in the Early Centuries

BIBLIOGRAPHY

M. Righetti, *Manuale di storia liturgica* 3 (Milan: Ancora, 1956²) 496–500.

The practice of daily communion was rather widespread in the early Church, even before the daily celebration of Mass made its appearance in some regions. We have witnesses to the practice in the third century. In Africa, Tertullian, in speaking of the disadvantages of marriages between Christians and unbelievers, stresses the point that the pagan husband may ask what it is that his wife eats before taking any other food and whether the appearances of bread do not conceal a magic spell or a poison.[20] At Rome, Novatian condemns the conduct of those who leave the liturgical assembly and go off to the theatre while carrying the Eucharist on their persons,[21] and Hippolytus seems to be alluding to the same practice when he urges that the consecrated bread be kept safe from those who would desecrate it and from mice or other animals.[22]

The practice of keeping the Eucharist in homes continued in the fourth and fifth century. Thus Paulinus the Deacon, in his account of the death of St. Ambrose, shows Bishop Honoratus, who lived in the same house, hurrying to the bedside with the Blessed Sacrament.[23] Many other examples

---

18. See Bede the Venerable, *Historia ecclesiastica* IV, 24 (PL 95:214): a young man who felt death approaching had one of his companions bring him the Eucharist.

19. *Holy Communion* 54–78 (pp. 475–83).

20. Tertullian, *Ad uxorem* II, 5, 2–3, ed. E. Dekkers (CCL I, 1954), 389–90.

21. Novatian, *De spectaculis*, ed. G. Hartel (CSEL 3/3; 1871), 8.

22. *Traditio apostolica* 37 (Botte 84). In the preceding section, 36 (Botte 82) there is the prescription that the Eucharist is to be taken before any other food.

23. Paulinus, *Vita Ambrosii* (PL 14:43).

might be cited of a practice that seems to have left traces in some areas as late as the seventh century.[24]

§3. The Liturgy of the "Presanctified"

BIBLIOGRAPHY

M. Andrieu, *Immixtio et consecratio. La consécration par contact dans les documents du moyen âge* (Paris: Picard, 1924). Previously published in *RevSR* 3 (1923) 433–71.

J. M. Hanssens, *Institutiones liturgicae de ritibus orientalibus* 2 (Rome: Gregorian University, 1930), 86–110; 3 (1932), 546–56.

B. Capelle, "Le vendredi saint et la communion des fidèles," *Nouvelle revue théologique* 76 (1954) 142–54.

The often-used term "Mass of the Presanctified" comes from the Greek *leitourgia tōn prohēgiasmenōn*. It is in fact not a Mass but a communion service on days when the Eucharist is not celebrated. At a liturgical gathering on such days, the faithful receive some of the bread consecrated at the preceding Mass. The practice seems to have appeared first in Churches of the Antiochene tradition; it has been maintained by the Byzantines, who celebrate such liturgies extensively during Lent, when the holy sacrifice is offered only on Sundays and Saturdays.[25] In the West, only the Roman rite seems to have adopted and maintained it, through many variations,[26] on the only aliturgical (Mass-less) day in its calendar: Good Friday.

In what does the liturgy of the "presanctified" consist? The following elements seem essential.

1. First of all, the Eucharist at which the bread is consecrated that will be received on a later day emphasizes this point in its ceremonial. Thus the Byzantine priest presents all the *prosphorai* to the faithful, saying "Holy things to the holy." Then, after pouring warm water into the chalice, he

---

24. We find in the *Ordines Romani* and then in the twelfth-century Pontificals that the Eucharist is given to new bishops and priests to be received during the days after their ordination and to consecrated virgins for their communion for a week after their consecration: Andrieu, *OR* 3:587–91. We may note too that in isolated monasteries of women, as in the Jacobite communities of the sixth century, the superiors "shared the mysteries with those under their authority": I. Rahmani, *Studia syriaca* 3 (Sharfé, 1908), 33.

25. In the East the practice of the presanctified is also found among the Maronites and the Catholic Syrians.

26. The rite is attested at Rome around the seventh century, but the papal chapel seems to have adopted it only later on, after the other churches of the city. The Missal of Pius V allowed only the celebrant to receive Communion, but this practice does not antecede the thirteenth century; there was also resistance to it, since as late as the seventeenth century the Roman Congregations were still urging its adoption.

makes a cross with the latter, before drinking from it, over the bread that he did not break at the time of the fraction; he then puts this bread in the place where it is to be reserved. At the Roman Mass on Holy Thursday the hosts to be reserved are placed in a ciborium at communion time and, after the celebration, are carried in solemn procession to the "repository."

2. Communion from the "presanctified" is received within the framework of a service. In the West this is the Office of the Lord's passion, with its Liturgy of the Word and its veneration of the cross. Among the Byzantines, it consists essentially of Vespers, with their "Little Entrance," psalms, readings, hymns, and prayers.

3. The reception of Communion has its own ritual that involves essentially:

a) The bringing of the sacred species either in a non-solemn procession from repository to altar (in the Roman liturgy) or in a "Great Entrance" (in the Byzantine liturgy). The consecrated bread is then placed on the Eucharistic table.

b) The Our Father (with its embolism, in the West).

c) The presentation of the Blessed Sacrament to the congregation; the accompanying Greek formula is "Presanctified holy things to the holy"; in the Roman rite, "This is the Lamb of God . . ." and "Happy are those . . . ." The congregation gives its respective customary responses: "One is holy . . ." or "Lord, I am not worthy. . . ."

d) Communion itself, given in the usual manner.

To these essential rites others have been added that are inspired by those of the Mass. Thus the Byzantine liturgy includes the placing of a particle of consecrated bread in a cup of unconsecrated wine. The Latin Middle Ages made many additions. The Roman Pontifical of the twelfth century had an incensation of the altar, the prayer *"In spiritu humilitatis,"* the breaking of the host, and the commingling[27]; the thirteenth-century Pontifical added even more ceremonies.[28] The *Order for Holy Week* of 1955 and then the new Missal have restored a primitive simplicity to the service of the "presanctified."

---

27. Roman Pontifical of the twelfth century 31, 11 (Andrieu *PR* 1:237). Of the commingling it says: "The unconsecrated wine is thus sanctified by the body of the Lord that is placed in it." The communion rite itself is not described.

28. Pontifical of the thirteenth-century Roman Curia, long recension, 43, 15–19 (Andrieu, *PR* 2:467–69). There was, however, an attempt in the time of Innocent III to return to primitive simplicity; see the short recension, 43, 14–15, *ibid.*

§4. The Ritual for Communion Outside Mass

The first chapter of *Holy Communion* contains a "Rite of Distributing Holy Communion Outside Mass." This rite takes into account the practices introduced into the Roman rite since the Carolingian period, but it also endeavors, through the elimination of abuses, to inflect these in the direction of a ritual that is fairly close to the liturgy of the presanctified.

1. *Lights and Shadows in the Latin Tradition*

I spoke earlier of currents of thought that led finally to the establishment of an Order of Mass in which no mention was made of a communion of the faithful. As early as the ninth century the tendency arose of postponing this communion until after the celebration; the excuse generally given was the large numbers of people wanting to receive on some feasts.[29] Paradoxically, however, the decreasing frequency of communions only caused this regrettable custom to become entrenched; the reception of the sacrament by the laity became a rite distinct from and independent of the holy sacrifice. As a result we find this odd rubric in the *Caeremoniale episcoporum* of 1600: on Easter the bishop should give Communion to his people at the solemn Mass; if he is absent, however, a priest other than the celebrant, and at a different altar or in a chapel, is to be ready at all times to distribute Communion before, during, and after the celebration of the Eucharist.[30]

The Council of Trent asserted, against the Reformers, the legitimacy of Masses at which the priest alone receives Communion. At the same time, however, it remarked: "The holy Council would wish that in every Mass the faithful who are present communicate not only in spiritual desire, but by a sacramental reception of the Eucharist, so that they may derive more abundant fruits from this most holy sacrifice."[31]

As a result, the pastoral decrees of reforming bishops contained both repeated exhortations that Communion be given during Mass and, at the same time, all sorts of derogations from this rule in more or less exceptional cases. But popular devotion overcame all the reluctances of bishops,

29. See P. Browe, "Wann fing man an die Kommunion ausserhalb der Messe auszuteilen," *Theologie und Glaube* 23 (1931) 755.

30. *Caeremoniale episcoporum* of 1600, Lib. 2, c. 29: "On Easter the bishop should celebrate solemn Mass and distribute communion"; c. 30, 5: "The other parishioners [those who are not the ministers of the celebration] of both sexes can receive communion, from the parish priest or the sacristan, at another altar or in a chapel prepared for the purpose, where it is continually distributed both before and after the principal Mass and even while the Mass is being sung."

31. Council of Trent, Session 22 (1562), can. 6 (DS 1747); trans. in Neuner-Dupuis, *The Christian Faith*, no. 1552 (pp. 426–27).

with the result that the Ritual of Paul V allowed priests to distribute the Body of Christ not only in the immediate context of the celebration (before or after it) but even apart from Mass.[32] This practice became quite common beginning in the eighteenth century; it used an abridged rite based on the one for communion of the sick. At the same time, however, many diocesan rituals continued to recall the rule of "during Mass" and to list the reasons that dispensed one from following that rule.

2. The Ritual of Paul VI

The General Introduction to *Holy Communion* recalls what is said in article 55 of the conciliar Constitution on the Liturgy: "The more complete form of participation in the Mass by which the faithful, after the priest's communion, receive the Lord's Body from the same sacrifice, is strongly endorsed."

The Introduction nonetheless envisages the possibility that those who have not been able to take part in the celebration may receive Communion at another time. They will thus realize "that they are united not only with the Lord's sacrifice but also with the community itself and are supported by the love of their brothers and sisters."[33] A suitable catechesis will help the faithful to bear in mind that even when they receive Communion outside Mass they are always participating in the paschal sacrifice.[34]

The ceremonial itself,[35] even in its short form,[36] always includes an introductory phase, with greeting and penitential rite; a Liturgy of the Word, which can be taken from the readings of the days or the readings of certain votive Masses; the Our Father and the kiss of peace, if the latter seems appropriate; and communion with its formulas. The liturgical act ends with a concluding prayer, a blessing, and the dismissal. The whole thus truly forms a brief synaxis that can be compared with the ritual of the "presanctified."

This rite, which includes adaptations for cases in which it is performed by a layperson,[37] can render important services in our time when the lack of ordained ministers makes it difficult for some Christians to share in the Eucharist. It can be used at times in Sunday gatherings for which there is no priest and, during the week, in monasteries of nuns when a chaplain

---

32. *Rituale Romanum* of 1814, tit. 5, c. 1, n. 13; if they were from elsewhere, they needed only the permission of the rector of the church.

33. *Holy Communion* 14 (*DOL* 266 no. 2092).

34. *Ibid.*, 15 (*DOL* 266 no. 2093).

35. *Ibid.*, 27–41 (pp. 465–69).

36. *Ibid.*, 42–53 (pp. 470–74). This ritual differs from the preceding in that it has only a short reading from Scripture instead of a full Liturgy of the Word.

37. *Ibid.*, 17 (*DOL* 266 no. 2095). The needed adaptations resemble those for the communion of the sick: *ibid.*, 54–67 (pp. 475–79).

is not available. If the participants enter into the true spirit of the rite as described in the General Introduction, it will not turn into a private devotion that detracts from the esteem due to the liturgical assembly and the paschal sacrifice that is its high point. This will not happen because the bread received in Communion will always be referred to the Mass at which it was consecrated.

Chapter II

Adoration of the Blessed Sacrament

BIBLIOGRAPHY

E. Martène, *De antiquis Ecclesiae ritibus*, Lib. I, c. 5, a. 3; M 594.

L. Beauduin, "La liturgie eucharistique au Concile de Trente," *QL* 1 (1911) 134-45, 199-213. = *Mélanges liturgiques* (Louvain: Mont César, 1954), 120-228.

W. Freestone, *The Sacrament Reserved* (Alcuin Club Collections 21; London: Longmans, 1917).

P. Browe, *Die Verehrung der Eucharistie im Mittelalter* (Rome: Herder, 1967[2]).

E. Maffei, *La réservation eucharistique jusqu'à la Renaissance* (Brussels, 1942).

H. Leclercq, "Réserve eucharistique," *DACL* 14 (1948) 2385-89.

M. Andrieu, "Aux origines du culte du saint Sacrement, reliquaires et monstrances eucharistiques," *Analecta Bollandiana* 68 (1950) 397-418.

A. G. Martimort, "La réserve eucharistique," *LMD* no. 51 (1957) 132-45.

M. Righetti, *Manuale di storia liturgica* 1 (Milan: Ancora, 1964[3]) 546-53; 3 (1956[2]), 529-50.

H. Caspary, "Kult und Aufbewahrung der Eucharistie in Italien vor dem Tridentinum," *ALW* 9 (1965) 102-30.

A. King, *Eucharistic Reservation in the Western Church* (London: Mowbray, 1965).

O. Nussbaum, *Die Aufbewahrung der Eucharistie* (Theophaneia 29; Bonn: Hanstein, 1979).

G. M. Oury and B. Andry, *Les Congrès eucharistiques* (Solesmes, 1980).

J. C. Didier, "L'évolution de la piété eucharistique au XXe siècle. Lumières et ombres," *Esprit et vie* no. 91 (1981) 193-206.

N. Mitchell, *Cult and Controversy. Worship of the Eucharistic Sacrament Outside Mass* (New York: Pueblo, 1982).

Although adoration of the Blessed Sacrament is not the primary purpose of the Eucharist or of reservation of the sacred species after Mass, it is nonetheless one of the great treasures of the Western liturgical tradition. Prior to the first years of the twelfth century there is no trace of this cult that subsequently developed in the West on an ever broader scale. The cult is, however, based on a datum of faith that is as old as the Christian Church: the abiding reality of the Lord's Body and Blood in the mystery of the Supper. Before the sixteenth century no ecclesial community interpreted the words of Jesus, "Take and eat: this is my body," "Take and drink: this is my blood," as referring to a presence solely in the moment when the bread and wine are consumed. The Middle Ages saw the appearance of something that the East did not experience: a set of new practices based on the ancient belief.

§1. Historical Perspectives

I. THE ANCIENT PRACTICE AND ITS CONTINUANCE
IN THE EAST

The Eucharist has always been the object of profound veneration and respect outside of Mass, on the occasions when it is received in Communion or carried to the sick. This is still true today in the East; we may think, for example, of the genuflections and even prostrations of the people during the office of the "presanctified" when the Byzantine priest appears with the consecrated bread at the door of the iconostasis.

On the other hand, in the early centuries there was no thought of putting the sacrament in a place where it might receive an ongoing homage of adoration. The reserved sacrament was kept in an annex to the sanctuary (a room known by various names: *pastophorion, sacrarium,* etc.), usually under the care of deacons; it remained there, hidden as it were from the sight of the faithful.

The church, which in the beginning was simply the place where the people gathered for the liturgy, became a house of prayer as well. But when Christians came there at various times during the day to converse with God, or when monks gathered for the same purpose in the chapel of their community, there was no tabernacle to which they could turn. Instead their gaze was directed to the table of sacrifice, which was for them a symbol of the Lord's presence. Thus in reproaching the Donatists for destroying altars, Optatus of Milevis could write: "In what way have you been harmed by Christ, whose body and blood rested on those altars at certain moments?"[1] Speaking of his sister who prayed for a cure in a serious illness, Gregory of Nazianzus says: "She prostrated herself in faith before the altar, calling upon him who is honored there."[2] Later on, the

---

1. Optatus of Milevis († 400), *Contra Parmenianum Donatistam* VI, 1 (PL 11:1066).
2. St. Gregory of Nazianzus († c. 390), *Oratio* VIII, 18 (PG 35:809).

monastic rule of Fructuosus of Braga prescribed a visit to the chapel after meals in order to offer "thanksgiving to Christ before the altar."[3]

II. THE APPEARANCE OF A EUCHARISTIC CULT IN THE WEST

There is a further point that is noteworthy in these testimonies: according to them prayer is addressed to Christ, whereas during Mass, or at least in its central and essential part, praise and petition are addressed to the Father through the mediation of the Son. In other words, alongside the great movement of "to the Father through the Son," evangelical spirituality gave rise in the hearts of Christians to a desire to converse with the Lord Jesus, a quest for deeper intimacy with him, a search for the humanity of the Lord in his nearness to us, which makes him the sacrament of the invisible God. If the East did not adopt the same religious expression of this desire and longing as the West did, we may believe that this was largely due to the fact that the cult of icons satisfied the same mystical need. The image of Christ became as it were the transparent face of the Redeemer, the manifestation in our world of the glory of the transfigured Jesus; representations of Mary and the saints accompanied the image of Christ like a triumphal procession that forms a bond between earth and heaven and brings heaven closer to us in our human condition.

The course followed in the West was doubtless influenced by an intuitive shrinking of Christians from the errors of Berengarius of Tours, which threatened faith in the real presence of the Lord in the Eucharist. The attention of believers was thus focused on the paschal sacrament. Before the end of the eleventh century the monks of Cluny had begun to bow before the reserved sacrament and, shortly after, to keep lamps burning near the place where it was reserved.[4] Everyone knows, of course, the influence Cluny had on the rest of Christendom. This influence added its weight to other currents of thoughts that were highlighting the value of looking at the host during the celebration of Mass.[5]

III. EUCHARISTIC RESERVATION

Because of their new interest in the reserved Eucharist, Christians were no longer satisfied to leave in the sacristy the box (*capsa*) in which the sacrament was kept for the sick between Masses. In some places—and

3. Fructuosus of Braga († c. 665), *Regula monachorum* V (PL 87:1102).

4. P. Browe, *Die Verehrung der Eucharistie im Mittelalter* (Rome: Herder, 1967²), 19.

5. See p. 137.

this as early as the ninth century—they preferred to set it on the altar. This led to a greater concern for the appearance of the box or casket; inspiration in this area came from other pieces of liturgical furniture that had been or still were in use, as, for example, the "towers" in which the gifts were brought to the altar at the beginning of Mass in the old Gallican liturgy,[6] or the "doves" which were used for the sacred chrism in some baptisteries and which in France and England began to serve this new purpose. Here, for example, is an account from the Abbey of Cluny: "Every Sunday the body of Christ is replaced, and the deacon puts the bread recently consecrated in a gilded pyx. At the beginning of Mass he removes the pyx from the dove suspended above the altar, and replaces it when Mass is finished."[7]

This new arrangement had the advantage of making it possible to lock the container and make its contents secure. For, once the sacrament became the object of a cult, there was a concern to prevent profanations of it. After the Lateran Council of 1215, which had ordered the reserved Eucharist to be kept under lock and key,[8] we see the multiplication of portable chests, often with the significant name "propitiatory" (the name given to the place of the Lord's presence in the Jerusalem temple). William Durandus, bishop of Mende in the final years of the thirteenth century, tells us of their existence.[9]

In other countries, especially in Italy, wall tabernacles were preferred; the one in St. Clement's in Rome (twelfth century) and the one at Spoleto (fifteenth century) are real masterpieces that still elicit admiration. In Germany, the desire to see the host led to the construction of monumental tabernacles in the form of towers that were placed in the choir of churches; the Blessed Sacrament was enclosed in a glass-windowed container so that it was visible through a wire-mesh door.[10]

From the mid-sixteenth century on, after the Council of Trent, it became customary to place the reserved sacrament at the middle of an al-

---

6. See p. 78.

7. Bernard, *Ordo Cluniacensis* I, 35, trans. from the text cited in F. X. Raible, *Der Tabernakel einst und jetzt* (Freiburg/Br., 1908), 164.

8. Fourth Lateran Council, in Mansi 22:1107. Eudes de Sully, Bishop of Paris, had already promulgated this rule: "The most holy body of Christ is to be kept with great care and decency in the finest part of the altar; it is to be kept under lock and key if possible." The text is from the *Statuts synodaux de Paris* 21, ed. O. Pontal, *Les statuts synodaux français du XIIIᵉ siècle* 1 (Collection de documents inedits sur l'histoire de France, ser. in-8°, 9; Paris: Bibliotheque Nationale, 1971), 60.

9. William Durandus, *Rationale divinorum officiorum* I, 2, 5; IV, 1, 15.

10. See H. Thurston, "Exposition of the Blessed Sacrament," *The Catholic Encyclopedia* 5:713. Diocesan synods issued restrictive rules regarding these *Sakramentshäuschen* ("Little houses for the Sacrament," i.e., tabernacles), but to no avail. Some of them are still to be seen today in Münster, Nürnberg, Konstanz, Baden-Baden, Weilderstadt.

tar. This innovation is attributed to two Italian reforming bishops, Matteo Giberti († 1543) and especially Charles Borromeo.[11] The Ritual of 1614 encouraged this practice, which spread rapidly. But, except in churches of some size, the altar was usually in a chapel of the apse or in a side chapel.[12] It was the Eucharistic devotion of the baroque period[13] that led to placing the tabernacle at the center of the main altar in order to facilitate the prolonged periods of adoration that characterized that age. The new practice did not become general, however, until toward the middle of the nineteenth century.

§2. Forms of Worship of the Holy Eucharist

This is the title of Chapter III of the ritual for *Holy Communion and Worship of the Eucharist Outside Mass*, which appeared in 1973.

It is unfortunate that adoration of the Eucharist, which represents a splendid enrichment of the Western liturgical tradition, should have developed at a time when the authentic understanding of the Mass was being obscured, as I have already pointed out. The meaning of the assembly was being lost, the faithful had ceased to receive Communion with any frequency, popular participation was reduced to marginal aspects, and so on. All this gave rise to ambiguities and led to abuses that were prejudicial to an authentic liturgical piety, since adoration of the Blessed Sacrament could now easily seem more important than the Mass itself. It was up to Vatican Council II and the liturgical books that sprang from it to restore a healthy balance by promoting duly approved Eucharistic practices, but only as organically connected with the celebration of Christ's sacrifice.

The Introduction to Chapter III of *Holy Communion* reminds us that "the eucharistic sacrifice is the source and culmination of the whole Christian life" and that the cult of the Blessed Sacrament is one of those devotions that "should be in harmony with the sacred liturgy in some sense, take their origin from the liturgy, and lead the people back to the liturgy."[14] When the faithful adore Christ present under the sacred species, "they should remember that this presence is derived from the sacrifice and is directed toward sacramental and spiritual communion" and that "prayer

---

11. See G. Musante, "De tabernaculo eiusque ornatu," *EL* 70 (1956) 256.

12. *Rituale Romanum* of 1614, tit. V, c. 1, n. 3: ". . . in an immovable tabernacle that is located at the center of the altar and kept locked." The *Caeremoniale episcoporum*, XII, 8, speaks of "an altar or other place where the Blessed Sacrament is kept; it should not be the main altar or an altar at which the bishop or anyone else will celebrate solemn Mass."

13. See p. 177.

14. See *VSC* 13 (*DOL* 1 no. 13).

before Christ the Lord sacramentally present extends the union with Christ which the faithful have reached in communion." Adoration prolongs the "commemoration" of the paschal mystery, in which the risen Jesus gives his life to the members of his Body so that they may have a deeper faith, hope, and love and may themselves become a sacrifice and in which he enables them to enter into his intercession for his Church and the world.[15]

A clear distinction is thus made between, on the one hand, the celebration of Mass, in which the focal points are the altar, the president's chair, and the place from which the Word is proclaimed, and, on the other, the various forms of Eucharistic devotion, in which the focal points are the tabernacle and the sacred vessel containing the reserved sacrament. The regulations given in the Missal for the place where the consecrated species are to be kept show clearly the spirit at work:

> Every encouragement should be given to the practice of eucharistic reservation in a chapel suited to the faithful's private adoration and prayer. If this is impossible because of the structure of the church, the sacrament should be reserved at an altar or elsewhere, in keeping with local custom, and in a part of the church that is worthy and properly adorned.[16]

Chapter III of *Holy Communion* discusses the various forms of Eucharistic devotion under three headings: Exposition of the Blessed Sacrament; Eucharistic Processions; and Eucharistic Congresses.

I. EXPOSITION OF THE BLESSED SACRAMENT

The desire of seeing the host, which led in the Middle Ages to the elevation after the consecration of the bread, also found expression in devotional practices outside the celebration. The first witness to these is from the year 1394, in the life of St. Dorothy, who went to church every morning in order to see the Eucharist exposed in a monstrance.[17] This practice became very widespread, as we have seen, in the Counter-Reformation Church.[18]

It is this custom that is discussed in *Holy Communion*: the Blessed Sacrament is removed from the tabernacle and presented to the faithful

---

15. *Holy Communion* 79–81 (pp. 484–85).

16. *GIRM* 276 (*DOL* 208 no. 1666).

17. See A. Boudinhon, "La bénédiction du Saint Sacrement," *Revue du clergé français* 22 (1902) 164.

18. Beginning in the fifteenth century there were prolonged expositions known as the "Forty Hours," which were regulated by an Instruction of Clement XI (SRC, *Decreta authentica* 4 [1900]). The same spirit led later on, in the dioceses of France and Belgium, to the practice of "perpetual adoration": each day of the year was assigned to a parochial or religious community, which was to practice this adoration in the name of all the other communities.

in the vessel in which it is regularly kept (in the ciborium: *in pyxide*) or in a vessel that enables the consecrated bread to be seen (in a monstrance or ostensorium). The Ritual observes: "This kind of exposition must clearly express the cult of the blessed sacrament in its relationship to the Mass. The plan of the exposition should carefully avoid anything which might somehow obscure the principal desire of Christ in instituting the eucharist, namely, to be with us as food, medicine, and comfort."[19]

The holy sacrifice is therefore not to be celebrated in the body of the church as long as exposition lasts.[20] A solemn exposition begins at the Mass in which the bread meant for adoration is consecrated and placed in the monstrance or ostensorium after communion. It can last as long as there are faithful who come to meditate in the church. It includes prayers, songs, readings, and periods of prolonged silence. It ends with a blessing that is given with the Blessed Sacrament; this blessing is always preceded by a suitable hymn or song and prayer; after it the consecrated bread is put back in the tabernacle.[21]

A shorter form of benediction is possible, provided it allows time for real prayer; it is not permissible to expose the Blessed Sacrament solely for the purpose of giving a blessing with it.[22]

II. EUCHARISTIC PROCESSIONS

In the early Middle Ages processions were very popular; relics of the saints (on the occasion of their translation or on their feast days) or images of the cross or other religious symbols were often carried in them. The bringing of Viaticum to the dying was also a solemn affair: the faithful were summoned to accompany it and those unable to come were reminded by a tinkling bell to recollect themselves as the procession passed on its way to the home of the sick person. On Holy Thursday a certain solemnity regularly marked the transfer of the Eucharist from the altar of sacrifice to the place where it was to be kept for the office of the "presanctified" on Good Friday; this liturgical act was marked by festive expressions that made it especially eyecatching. These Viaticum Holy Thursday processions may be regarded as the first processions of the Blessed Sacrament, and indeed as models for such processions, since they made clear the organic connection between the Mass just offered and the later communion that justified the procession and the reservation.

---

19. *Holy Communion* 82 (p. 486).

20. *Ibid.*, 83 (p. 486).

21. *Ibid.*, 94–100 (pp. 490–92).

22. In the absence of an ordained minister, a layman who has permission from the local Ordinary may expose the Blessed Sacrament and replace it without any benediction: see *Holy Communion* 91 (pp. 488–89).

A different spirit was doubtless at work when, in about the same period, the custom arose of carrying a consecrated host in the Palm Sunday procession in order to signify the Lord's presence.[23] In any case, the establishment of the feast of Corpus Christi certainly gave rise to a new and different kind of manifestation; there was indeed no question of this in the Bull *Transiturus* by which Pope Urban V extended the solemnity to the entire Church in 1264, but we already find it in place at Cologne by the end of the century. The innovation spread quickly, first in the towns, then in the villages and countryside. It was perhaps on this occasion that reliquaries were used to carry the sacred species and make them visible to the people, thus constituting the first monstrances. The success of these processions caused them to be extended to other circumstances: as early as the end of the fifteenth century they were a way of lending solemnity to the major feasts of the year in some parts of Germany.

In the new Ritual, Corpus Christi is an occasion for the Christian people to give public witness, in the streets of the cities and villages, to their faith in the Eucharist and their devotion to it. But in the contemporary situation (we no longer live in a Christendom in which society as a whole joined the Church in its devotions) the suitableness of such manifestations is left to the judgment of the local Ordinaries.[24] Moreover, "it is fitting that a eucharistic procession begin after the Mass in which the host to be carried in the procession has been consecrated" or at least after "a lengthy period of public adoration."[25] It is also desirable that like every procession this one travel from one place to another; only if circumstances do not permit this may it return to the church from which it started. The service ends with benediction of the Blessed Sacrament.[26]

III. EUCHARISTIC CONGRESSES

As the Ritual points out, Eucharistic congresses are a recent institution. The first one took place at Lille in 1873, and in a context marked by the piety of the age and the political circumstances of the time: the participants spoke of reparation to Jesus in the Blessed Sacrament and of the Lord's reign over society. This first congress was followed by a multitude of national or local gatherings that were immensely popular before World War II, and especially by a series of forty-three international congresses, the most recent of which was held in 1985.

---

23. See E. Bishop, "Holy Week Rites of Sarum, Hereford and Rouen Compared," in his *Liturgica historica* (Oxford: Clarendon Press, 1918), 286.
24. *Holy Communion* 101 (p. 493).
25. *Ibid.*, 103 (p. 493).
26. *Ibid.*, 107-8 (p. 494).

The series of international congresses has reflected the developments that have occurred in a century's time in the content and expression of Christian Eucharistic faith. Thus the congress movement came into life-giving contact with the liturgical movement at Munich in 1960; since then the Mass has been at the center of each congress. The new spirit that was initiated at Vatican II has gradually permeated Christian practice.

The 1973 Ritual provides guidelines. The aim is clear: "that together the members of the church join in the deepest profession of some aspect of the eucharistic mystery and express their worship publicly in the bond of charity and unity."[27] The celebration of the Eucharist should be the center and high point of all activities and be prolonged by celebrations of the word, catechetical meetings, communal prayer, and private adoration and by processions of the Blessed Sacrament if circumstances permit.[28]

Among the objectives to be sought in the preparation for a congress the following are listed: a more profound reflection, adapted to various groups of people, on the Eucharist as the mystery of Christ living and working in the Church; an active participation in the liturgy in order to encourage the acceptance of the gospel and a sense of brotherhood and community; finally, research into and promotion of human development and an equitable sharing of even material goods, after the example of the first Christian community, so that an evangelical ferment may be diffused at the Eucharistic table and be a force in the growth of contemporary society and a pledge of the life to come.[29]

§3. Private Adoration

To all these more or less solemn and communal forms of Eucharistic worship we must add private prayer before the tabernacle. The Ritual does not devote a special chapter to this devotion, but it does regard it as one of the riches of the Western tradition. For this reason, the place of reservation should be so laid out as to foster recollection[30] and make possible the silent prayer that at any hour of the day and even of the night continues the prayer that the celebration of Mass has stimulated in the heart and life of Christians. This prayer includes thanksgiving for God's gifts, spiritual self-offering, intercession for the world, and meditation on the mystery of Christ. This is an especially fruitful way of making one's own the attitude of Mary, sister of Lazarus, who "sat at the Lord's feet and listened to his words."

----

27. *Ibid.*, 109 (p. 495).
28. *Ibid.*, 112 (p. 496).
29. *Ibid.*, 111 (pp. 495–96).
30. *Ibid.*, 9 (p. 457).

Index

The following pages list the people, places, and events about which a pertinent statement is made in this book. By no means should this index be considered a complete listing of the scores of people, places, and events recorded in this book.